THE
Choral Singer's
Companion

THE
Choral Singer's
Companion

RONALD
CORP

B. T. BATSFORD LTD · LONDON

The translation of the *Dies Irae* by William Mann
is reprinted with his permission.

ISBN 0 7134 4597 1

Typeset by Latimer Trend & Company Ltd, Plymouth
and printed by
Butler and Tanner Ltd Frome, Somerset
for the publishers
B. T. Batsford Ltd
4 Fitzhardinge Street
London W1H 0AH

Contents

Foreword	*7*
Acknowledgements	*8*
Introduction	*9*

Practical — *13*
Singing (by Barbara Alden)
  (a) Improve your singing — *13*
  (b) Breathing — *14*
  (c) Articulation — *15*
  Conclusion — *17*
Singing in a choir — *18*
Being a good chorister — *18*
Sight-reading — *19*
Size and types of mixed voice choir — *21*
Running a choir — *22*
Conducting technique — *24*
Rehearsal technique — *25*
Planning a programme — *27*
Planning—step by step — *31*
Obtaining music — *33*
Wider repertory — *35*

Composers — *39*

Works — *82*

Terms — *124*

Texts — *153*
Mass — *153*
Mass for the dead (requiem mass) — *155*
Apostle's Creed — *158*
Te Deum Laudamus — *159*
Jubilate Deo (Psalm 100) — *160*

Magnificat 161
The Lord's Prayer 162
Stabat Mater 162
Ave Maria 164
Ave Verum 164

Lists 165
Twentieth-century choral works by British
  composers 165
Secular choral works 166
Choir and strings 167
Works without strings 168
Choir and organ 168
Choir and piano 169
Works with harp 169
Christmas music 169
Easter music 170
Stage works for concert performance 170
Works for female voices 171
Works for male voices 172
Children's voices 173
The Masses of Haydn 174
Concert programmes 175
Orchestration of various works 177
Addresses 179

Select bibliography 181

Copyright 182

Index 183

Foreword

My first rection to this book was to wonder why nobody had thought of writing it before; after all singing in choirs has been a social pastime for so long and is at a height of popularity just at the moment. For the singer, belonging to a choir is the perfect amalgam of individual expression and corporate responsibility, wearying rehearsals and thrillingly invigorating performances. However, every singer knows the moment when he or she would like to be just that bit better, and this is the book to guide and help. For the choral director this book will be the answer to many prayers: from helping to compile programmes for the next season through to exacting the last ounce of effort in the concert itself.

SIMON PRESTON
Organist and Master of the Choristers
Westminster Abbey

Acknowledgements

A number of people have offered valuable help in the writing of this book. In particular William Mann has made available his excellent translation of the *Dies irae* from the requiem mass, and Barbara Alden has written the section on singing (pages 13–18)—she has years of teaching experience behind her and I am pleased to be able to include her practical guide. I am grateful also to Sue Harris for the lists of addresses and the book list.

Jane Burwell gave immense help and support with typing—but more than that, she scrutinized and questioned, and forced me to make order out of untidy scribblings. I hope the book will prove a source of inspiration to all involved in choral music-making.

Introduction

In this one volume I have tried to collect together all the information sought by the many thousands of people who sing in choirs. The material has been collected with choristers in mind, and particularly those who are members of larger choirs. It is inevitable that the accent is on the larger choral works (Handel's oratorios, Haydn's masses, and many nineteenth and twentieth-century choral classics) but works for small choir and chamber choir are also included. It is also inevitable that very small works such as madrigals and anthems should be generally overlooked except in passing.

The book should provide a useful companion to singers, conductors, and to committee members who would like to have a say in programme building.

It is a book you could spend hours dipping into. But to make things easier I have divided it into sections, as listed below. Information is scattered over the various sections of the book, and it is worth looking from section to section. For example, a certain amount of information is given about Berlioz's *Requiem* under Berlioz in the composer section, but more information can be found under *Grande Messe des morts* under the works section, and you can also look up requiem under terms to find out exactly what a requiem is. Further to this, the text of the requiem mass, and its English translation, can be found on page 155.

The division of the book into sections is clear-cut, but the contents of each section needs some explanation. There is of course a slight personal bias in the selection of works and composers selected and the amount of space devoted to them. I make no apology for devoting as much space to Stanford as to Mozart. I do not suggest that they are of equal merit, but I do insist that Stanford, as a neglected British composer, demands full coverage and exposure in these pages, while Mozart does not.

I have chosen the titles of works which I feel are most acceptable and generally known. I assume the reader will look under *Les Noces* for Stravinsky's ballet *The Wedding* although it may be difficult to justify the persistent use of its French title outside France. I have not provided cross-references to these.

Cross-referencing has been kept to a bare minimum. I hope that the reader will automatically look from section to section. Works mentioned under *Composers* marked thus* are dealt with more fully in the *Works* section. Composers marked thus* in the *Works* section have their own entry under *Composers*. If you hear that you are going to perform Vaughan William's *Hodie* next Christmas, you will find it under the works section, and then can look up Vaughan Williams to put the work in a wider context. You will see then that two extracts from it appear in *Carols for Choirs* Book 1 – and you may have sung these already.

There is no attempt to describe the music itself, and I have not graded pieces according to their difficulty. What seems difficult to one choir will appear easy to another. I have, however, indicated if a work is suitable only for the larger and more proficient choirs.

Publishers of works have not been given, partly because this information goes out of date, and also because there are often different publications of the same work. Some vocal music is on sale from a publisher, but the orchestral parts may be on hire only – you must check. Unfortunately some works are available in vocal form from one publisher, while the orchestral parts may come from another. There was no way of dealing with all of these problems.

The book is divided broadly thus:

Practical
In this section there are guides to singing, sight reading, conducting, running a choir, planning programmes and obtaining music. Practical guides to singing and conducting are difficult to communicate through the written word and require demonstration and personal tuition. Guides to running a choir can only be non-specific – circumstances from one choral society to another will be so different as to make certain remarks irrelevant.

Composers
A basic selection of over one hundred and forty composers has been made. Of course some composers have been omitted, but I hope I have not left out any major composer of choral music. Some composers who wrote relatively little for choir are, however, included, because what they did write seemed to me to be significant. I have discussed only their choral output, making reference to their other music only where it is relevant.

Works
Works with titles such as *The Dream of Gerontius* suggested themselves for inclusion immediately, and there are over a hundred and forty titles listed, but there are countless other works known only as *x*'s requiem or *y*'s mass. I have created individual entries for the best known in this category – for example *Requiem* (Mozart) and *Mass in B minor* (Bach). Most dictionaries of music fail to include works of this type unless they have a nickname. Haydn's masses are included in musical dictionaries (they all

have titles of some sort) while Mozart's are not (only the '*Coronation*' mass or perhaps the '*Credo*' mass have nicknames). I have also indicated orchestration (see below).

Terms
I have tried to explain technical or musical terms which may pertain to choral music. I have not attempted to include everything that a general music dictionary would, but it seemed vital to elucidate on common terms such as oratorio, mass, requiem, cantata as well as explaining Tonic Sol-fa, and things connected with the liturgy – particularly as choirs spend so much time singing sacred texts.

Texts
It is not always easy to track down the text and a translation of the religious works most often performed by choirs, unless you know exactly where to look. I have provided the most obvious texts in this section. These should be consulted with care – there are many variations in composers' settings of these standard words.

Lists
The various lists of works will provide useful information as a starting point for programme building. These lists are in no way complete, and some works in one section have not been duplicated in another although they have a claim to be there (Christmas music with string accompaniment, for example, may be found under one category only). I have provided lists of works according to their orchestration and also a list of twentieth-century choral works by British composers in the hope of bringing to attention the vast amount of excellent music which is being composed for voices at the moment. There is also a short bibliography and a list of useful addresses.

Orchestration
The orchestral and choral requirements for each work discussed in the works section is indicated by a series of letters and numbers. The soloists are listed first; S (soprano) Ms (mezzo-soprano), A (alto) T (tenor), Bar (baritone) and B (bass), followed by the choral forces required. The orchestration follows a basic pattern – the woodwind are listed first – flutes, oboes, clarinets and bassoon, most often in pairs and represented by the figures 2.2.2.2. If an extra member of the woodwind family is required – usually piccolo, cor anglais, bass clarinet or double bassoon – the number of woodwind becomes 2.picc.2.corA.2.bcl.2.dbn. If the extra instrument merely doubles with one of its relatives the = sign shows the doubling. 3(111 = picc).3(111 = corA).3(111 = bcl).3(111 = dbn) means three flute players, the third doubling on piccolo, three oboes with the third doubling cor anglais, three clarinets with the third player doubling

bass clarinet, and three bassoons with the third doubling on double bassoon. If the orchestration requires 3 flutes *and* piccolo, that is expressed 3.picc.

After the woodwind come the brass – most often 4.2.3.1. – four horns, two trumpets, three trombones (two tenors and one bass) and tuba. Sometimes the scoring requires cornets as well as trumpets; where they are specified I have indicated them. Next come timpani (kettledrums) and percussion, harp, organ, piano, xylophone etc. The number of percussion players required will have to be sorted out by consulting the score – there is no hard and fast answer in this area. The strings follow, and I have indicated all cases where 'strings' does not mean the usual first and second violins, violas, cellos and double basses.

I have given the duration of the works where known. In the case of Handel oratorios these may prove false if certain cuts are, or are not observed.

Handel oratorios also highlight another problem. How many vocal soloists do you really need? If you want your soloists to sing more than one part you may reduce the number of soloists.

Always check the score. You may notice a number of discrepancies between my orchestrations and those in recent manuals (the NFMS *Catalogue of Choral Works* for example). I have checked and re-checked my orchestrations, but there will no doubt be mistakes and ambiguities still. Haydn's masses are available in various editions – playing havoc with my system.

Practical

Singing

'Since singing is so good a thing,
I wish all men would learn to sing.'
William Byrd (Introduction to *Psalmes, Sonets and Songs* (1588)).

Improve your singing

It is virtually impossible to teach such a sensitive activity as singing through the written word, and this section is only intended to be a simple introduction to vocal technique and can in no way replace a live teacher.

Singing, like speech, is a natural function. The voice is the only musical instrument that is not man-made, and it is possible for most people to enjoy making music with their voice and to sing with ease.

Common vocal problems, such as tight or sore throats, hoarseness, lack of breath, harsh, wobbly or breathy tone, are usually caused by tension, bad posture and trying to push the voice out. Therefore some loosening-up exercises before singing are advisable.

The following are simple preliminary exercises which can be used with any group and take up very little time at the start of a rehearsal.

1 Stand with feet slightly apart and think that the spine lengthens towards the head. Gently shrug the shoulders then roll them loosely in a circular movement, (up, back and down) without tightening the neck.

2 Roll the head round slowly a few times in each direction, without tightening the neck or shoulders.

3 To loosen the jaw, relax the mouth and, leaving it in a smiling position, slowly drop the lower jaw as if a weight has been put on the lower back teeth. Slowly lift the jaw and repeat the movement several times. Make sure the jaw only moves up and down, *not* from side to side.

4 Let the jaw 'hang' with the mouth in a relaxed smile, and flick the tongue out and back, and then wiggle it from side to side, without moving the jaw. Use a mirror to check this.

5 When sitting to sing, sit well forward on the chair and feel the spine lengthen and rib-cage widen and feel flexible. Hold your music up towards the head – don't slump down to the music. Keep the posture upright but relaxed – don't let the shoulders rise or tighten.

Breathing

Singing is essentially a physical activity, but do not make the mistake of trying to 'do' too much; this causes tension which interferes with the free flow of the voice. Easy, natural breathing is the first thing to be adversely affected, but since everyone breathed freely and easily as a baby, it is possible to rediscover this ease if you learn to 'let go' and 'do' less.

The following exercises develop an action from the lower abdominal muscles, which gives an upward thrust to the diaphragm. This is a large muscular membrane situated just below the ribs, separating the chest from the abdomen, which assists the lungs in inhaling and exhaling. In order for the diaphragm to rise to support and control the outgoing breath, it must drop as breath is taken in. Therefore the abdominal muscles should relax and the whole abdominal wall should gently expand when inhaling. Avoid the common mistake of trying to take too 'large' a breath, causing the shoulders to rise and forcing air only into the upper chest, thus drawing in the abdomen and inhibiting the natural movement of the diaphragm.

1 Lie on the floor with knees bent, feet flat on the floor, and head supported by a book or cushion. Rest the hands on the lower abdomen and cough lightly. Feel the abdominal muscles contract. Let them relax, then try pulling them in again, but this time catch a hiss on the teeth as you expel the air with a firm abdominal movement.

2 Vary the length and strength of the abdominal contraction and feel that this controls the sound of the hiss.

3 Repeat this movement, but instead of hissing, say an 'M', catching it on the lips, and feel them buzz.

4 Repeat this, but sing the 'M' gently on any notes around the lower-middle range of the voice. Feel that any variation in length and strength of notes comes from the pull of the abdominal muscles.

5 Take some easy, relaxed breaths by smiling, opening the mouth and letting the air gently flow over the tongue. These breaths should be silent and the cold air ought to strike the back of an open throat. Feel the rib-cage gently expand and let the abdominal muscles relax. Try not to 'take' air in, but let it flow by itself. Control the exhalation by a steady pull of the abdominal muscles, whilst slowly hissing out on the teeth.

6 Repeat the above exercises in a sitting and standing position, remembering to keep the neck, shoulders and rib-cage free. Regular practice will improve the strength and flexibility of the relevant muscles, enabling you to support the sound from underneath, rather like squeezing a tube of toothpaste from the bottom.

When singing, continue to take breaths in this way, thus relaxing the diaphragm, and then use the contraction of the abdominal muscles to support high notes and give control of dynamics. Strong, firm tone comes from well-supported breath, and not by pushing or straining from the throat.

If you can achieve a feeling of ease, freedom and relaxation on the intake of breath, followed by active control of the outgoing breath, there will be less risk of forcing the voice.

Articulation

A stiff, heavy tongue and tight jaw make it harder to sing words clearly and can strain the voice, causing it to crack or go husky. Opening the mouth too much, especially on low notes, and over-gesticulating the mouth, tends to produce a chopped-up, woolly sound.

To produce words clearly and distinctly, without 'chopping-up' the tone, the jaw and tongue need to be light and flexible. Following the loosening-up exercises already mentioned, some simple singing exercises can be done to limber-up the tongue. It should move lightly and crisply without disturbing the jaw. Practise with the help of a mirror.

1 Sing descending scales – singing 'LA-LA-LA' and 'LEE-LAY-LA', keeping the mouth in a relaxed smile and moving the tip of the tongue neatly. Support the breath from the start, and feel that the vowel-sounds have a continuous flow.

La la la   la la la   la la la   la la la   la la la   la la la   la la la   la.

Lee lay la   lee lay la   lee lay la   lee lay la   lee lay la   lee lay la   lee lay la   lee.

2 To practise vowel changes, sing on one note, repeating, 'Lee-lay-loo-lŏ' (pronounce as in 'hot') and do not over-exaggerate the forward mouth-shape for 'Oo-ŏ'.

3 Work through the following examples. Remember to leave the jaw steady and concentrate on working the tip of the tongue crisply and lightly.

La la la la lee lay loo lŏ la.

Da da da da dee day doo dŏ da.

Na na na na nee nay noo nŏ na.

Ta ta ta ta tee tay too tŏ ta.

4 Exercises using the consonant 'V' are useful for loosening the jaw. Sing descending arpeggios – singing 'Va-Vay' on each note. Keep the jaw light and bouncy and the vowels smooth and clear.

In a), incorporate use of the diaphragm by gently drawing in the abdominal muscles for the first note and don't release them until the end of the phrase.

In b), keep the jaw movement just as free for all vowel changes and finish with a 'vum' as an introduction to humming.

5 Gentle, sustained *humming*, on one note, helps to bring the voice forward. Start the sound by activating the diaphragm and catching the vibration of 'Mm' on the lips (as explained under 'Breathing'). Do this only in the lower and middle part of the voice without using any pressure or strain from the throat.

6 To brighten the voice, sing scales and exercises on 'Vee' and 'Zee' keeping the mouth and jaw relaxed. Feel that the sound travels by itself, forward and up into the 'mask' (i.e. the front of the face).

Start with a simple musical shape, which can be *gradually* extended and this will help to improve runs. Feel that the breath is steadily supported throughout, and use an extra abdominal pull for the highest note in the phrase, which also needs a more open mouth.

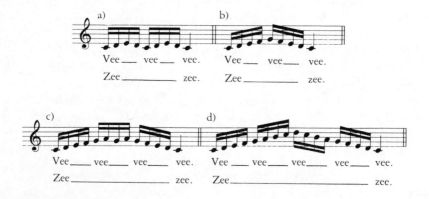

(N.B. All the musical examples in this section have, for convenience, been written in C major, but should be practised in different keys to gradually extend the range.)

7 To improve the clarity and interpretation of words, practise singing the words of entire phrases on one note. Gently support the breath from a controlled diaphragm and concentrate on crisp, clear articulation from the tip of the tongue, the teeth and the lips. Don't let the vowel changes pull the sound back, but keep the tone flowing forward, so that all the words feel on the same level.

8 Think about the *meaning* of the words, as well as their clear articulation. This also helps to improve the musical phrasing and develop a sense of 'line'.

9 Tongue-twisters are very useful exercises and can be good fun to sing in a group, especially in rounds, to enliven the warming-up session.

Practise thoroughly in unison before trying in parts, and aim for a brisk tempo.

Conclusion

The singing voice should always sound fresh and clear, with a natural ring or resonance. Voices will blend together more easily when the emphasis is on clarity, lightness and a free sound. Variation in dynamics can be achieved with control of the diaphragm, and not by tightening the throat muscles. Never push or strain the voice and avoid opening the mouth too much on low notes, as this also causes the throat muscles to tighten. Generally, sing with an easy relaxed smile – but not a tight, 'Cheshire-cat' grin! Feel that the voice flows freely from the supported breath, and, above all, enjoy making music through singing.

Singing in a choir

The experience of singing in a group, however large or small, is one of the most exhilarating of musical pleasures. It is for this reason, and for social ones too, that choral societies and small choirs flourish. In England there is a long tradition of choral performances, choral composition and organized amateur music-making, which pre-dates Handel. Inevitably the pleasure of performing Walton's *Belshazzar's Feast* with a massed choir is quite different from performing madrigals with a small group of more experienced singers, but the corporate effort of both extremes affords great enjoyment to all who take part.

Some singing teachers insist that their pupils do not sing with large choirs as it will impair their technique. This need not be the case: if you are producing your voice in the correct way, no damage can be done by joining with others. Damage is only done if you over-sing or sing incorrectly. One hazard, however, is singing in a choir while a new piece is being learned; if you are a good sight-reader you may be able to concentrate on your singing technique, but even so you may be tempted to 'lead' which may mean 'overblowing'. If sight-reading is a problem it is possible that by concentrating on the notes you will not give enough attention to your vocal production.

Amateur choral singers often complain of lack of breath while singing, and hoarseness after rehearsals or performance. All vocal problems are quite simply the result of faulty voice production. Hopefully your conductor will give you some warming-up exercises before a rehearsal, which will help you individually and corporately as a choir. If not (and there is not always time before a dress rehearsal or concert) try to find time to practise a few exercises yourself. (A number of the exercises given above can be performed quietly and unobtrusively.)

Being a good chorister

If you have joined a choir it is vital that you commit yourself to it. Do not join a choir and expect to miss rehearsals; you will suffer and so will your colleagues. Once you have joined, keep that evening free every week and turn up on time. All you need to bring is your music, a pencil and your wits.

From the very first rehearsal it is important to use your pencil to mark notes that you find difficult to sight-read, and you should certainly mark any note or passage that you just cannot seem to get right. Use your pencil as much as possible; it is too easy to sit in a choir and think you will remember what has been said the next time it comes round. For example, the conductor has just asked for no breath between two phrases of music and he has had to say so because the natural reaction of the entire choir was to breathe in the gap; if you do not mark this, you will make the same mistake next time. It is an odd fact that amateur choristers feel it is demeaning to use a pencil; professionals will instantly mark their scores so that they do not make mistakes more than once. All markings of tempo, dynamic, phrasing and mood should go into the score as soon as they have been given by the conductor.

Try to look at the score during the week, either playing over your part at the piano, or simply reading the printed score. Just looking through a score will make you familiar with a work, and if the work is in a foreign language, studying the pronunciation of the text is something everyone can do at odd moments. During rehearsals it is often necessary to rehearse single lines for certain voices; perhaps the altos are struggling with a difficult passage. Always follow what they are doing and learn from them how to sing the phrase because you are bound to have something similar to do. It is also important to be ready to come in again when the conductor asks for everyone to sing; in other words, don't 'doze off' when you are not singing!

Any section of the work which you have rehearsed one week should really be known for the next rehearsal. Make sure you know the passages you *should* know. By the time of the concert you should be so familiar with the work that you are not bound to your score but can watch the conductor. Nothing is worse for an audience than looking at a choir of people buried in their vocal scores. Hold the copy at a reasonable height so that you can see over it, and see the conductor. You should be able to glance at your score while giving the impression of watching the conductor the entire time.

Sight-reading

Most choirs will expect a certain proficiency in sight-reading from its members. More than likely you will have to pass an audition which will include sight-reading a passage of music.

Many people claim not to be able to read at sight. In some cases they really cannot, but in most cases an attempt to follow the line of music will be more successful than supposed. Everyone can see if a musical phrase goes up or down, and sight-reading is a refinement of this basic observation. Unfortunately the only way to improve sight-reading is to practise, and the best way to practise is to read works in a choir. The more singing and reading you do, the better you will become. You can help yourself by practising your part with or without a keyboard at home during the week between rehearsals.

Those who sight-read well normally have the ability to see not only the shape and pattern of their own line, but can relate the notes they sing to the chords and harmonies beneath, or to the other voice parts. This requires a degree of proficiency in musical theory; if you do not understand keys, chords, or harmony, it is going to be more difficult to grasp where the music is going. In some music (classical pieces by Haydn, for example) the chord progressions and the melodic lines present no problematic surprises to a modern performer; sight-reading the *Nelson Mass* may well prove fairly straightforward. But nineteenth and twentieth-century works are often very difficult, particularly for those who have no understanding of chords or harmony. Poulenc's *Gloria* may sound straightforward, but the notes written for the choir to sing often involve augmented intervals and leaps which are difficult to negotiate without a great deal of care and thought. However, all singers must try to relate their vocal line to the accompaniment, or to the other voice parts, particularly in choruses where entries pour in one on top of another (for example, in the final bars of the sixth movement of the Brahms *Requiem*).

Finding your note in a chord, or from the chord you have just heard, also requires a little knowledge of harmony. Common chords consist of the tonic, and notes a third and a fifth above that. Being able to sing the tonic, third or fifth of a chord should be a basic skill which you can learn easily. Some singers read their line by intervals, that is, by relating one note to the next. The 'Tonic Sol-fa' system was devised to aid this process, and hand signals were given to provide visual help. At their initial stages both devices are excellent, and learning to read tunes by means of tonic sol-fah should be encouraged. But music tends to be more complicated than basic doh, re, mi will accommodate; nothing beats reading intervals straight from the notes on the page.

An aid to reading intervals is to remember that certain intervals begin well known songs: a major sixth is represented by the first two notes of 'My bonny lies over the ocean', a fifth by 'Lavender's blue', a fourth by 'Some talk of Alexander' ('The British Grenadiers'), and so on. The interval of a major seventh can be learnt by thinking of the song 'Bali Ha'i' from 'South Pacific' where *Ba* and *Ha'i* represent the interval (the first two notes of the phrase are an octave apart). Memory of this sort is an aid only – you have no time to think of 'The British Grenadiers' in the middle of a performance of Fauré's *Requiem*!

You have probably noticed that you sight-read best when your neighbour is proficient and reliable. If you have the choice, always sit with the best members of your choir and 'read' as much music as possible.

Size and types of mixed voice choir

Choirs come in various shapes and sizes, but your musical director must have a clear idea of the aims of your particular body of singers and an awareness of your capabilities. First of all, are you a small choir trying to perfect an unaccompanied choral sound, or are you aiming to perform works with small orchestra, piano or organ? Obviously a mixture will prove aesthetically satisfying, but the degree of proficiency required for both is quite different. Many choirs who are successful when performing Haydn masses, Fauré's *Requiem* and other pieces (of similar difficulty) with orchestral accompaniment, can come seriously unstuck when tackling unaccompanied works such as Palestrina's *Stabat Mater* or Britten's *Hymn to St Cecilia*.

A choir of sixteen will need to be made up of very competent singers with good voices, probably of a soloistic standard. The repertory for this size choir includes all of the secular and sacred music written before 1600 (mainly unaccompanied) and may include the motets of Bach (with continuo accompaniment) and other baroque works with modest instrumental requirements. Various small romantic works with organ accompaniment may also be tackled, and a wide variety of contemporary works written for small (chamber) choir.

A chamber choir may consist of between sixteen and thirty singers. Obviously the available repertory is wider for this size choir. Music written before 1600 should be suitable although the choir may be too large for the more intimate motets. Baroque works with or without orchestra (but always with continuo) will be possible, including the oratorios of Handel and the passions and cantatas of Bach. Haydn and Mozart are also suitable for a choir of thirty with a small orchestra (but perhaps not *The Creation* or *The Seasons* unless the choir is strong). Some romantic works will be possible, such as the Fauré *Requiem*, but certainly not the larger works with extensive orchestral accompaniment. Music written this century, including Stravinsky's *Mass*, will work well with a choir of thirty, as will many other unaccompanied pieces.

Once a choir exceeds thirty singers (and approaches fifty, let us say) you will need to think carefully about repertory, because you will be too big for some works, and some works will be too big for you. You will not be singing unaccompanied except on rare occasions, such as Vaughan Williams's *Mass in G minor*, perhaps. A choir of fifty may be considered too large for baroque pieces, but Bach's *B Minor Mass*, Handel's oratorios and other baroque works are quite acceptable with a choir of this size as long as the singers are agile. Classical works such as Mozart's *Requiem* will also be quite satisfactory. Watch the orchestration of works from later periods: if there are too many woodwind or brass instruments you will have to employ a strong body of strings, and you will then run the risk of drowning your choir.

Choirs of sixty to one hundred voices should (with care) be able to tackle the larger pieces such as Haydn's *The Creation*, Beethoven's masses, Mendelssohn's *Elijah*, and Brahms's *Requiem*. Your conductor will know if you are strong enough to tackle the Verdi *Requiem*. Many twentieth-century works are available for choirs of this size, for example, Britten's *Cantata Misericordia* or *St Nicolas*.

Societies with over one hundred voices will want to tackle the largest scores which are out of the range of all other choirs mentioned so far: Walton's *Belshazzar's Feast*, Vaughan Williams's *A Sea Symphony*, Tippett's *A Child of our Time*, and Verdi's *Requiem*. Once again the volume generated by your choir will help you decide if these works are possible. Some works such as Delius's *A Mass of Life* and Mahler's *Symphony of a Thousand* are only to be performed with the largest forces – perhaps with two choral societies together!

The relevance of these comments relies on a number of factors. How good are your singers, and therefore, how much noise can they make? How large will your orchestra be? Will you be hiring a full symphony orchestra with the full complement of strings, or will you have a reduced string strength but full wind? Remember that one oboe can obliterate the entire soprano line of many amateur choirs, so do be careful to match the size of your choir and orchestra.

A great deal depends on the hall in which you perform, but as so many choirs have no choice in the matter (they are using the best available venue, be it church or concert hall, for many diverse and often unmusical reasons) it is irrelevant at this point to make any hard and fast rules. It is however worth investigating some sort of choir staging to ensure that the choral sound comes over the orchestra in front.

Choirs of various sizes inevitably tackle repertory outside the areas outlined here. There is nothing wrong with tackling anything you feel you are able to.

Running a choir

General

Each choir or choral society will have particular needs and problems, but by and large the running of a choir will depend on the working of a lively committee in co-operation with the conductor or musical director, who is usually *ex officio*. Every society will have its own individual way of:

(a) choosing the repertoire – you may be guided exclusively by your conductor, or you may have a committee meeting to discuss alternatives;

(b) booking artists – you may ask your conductor to approach artists first himself, because he already knows or works with them elsewhere, or you may choose your artists from agency lists;

(c) finding a venue – you may have a regular venue, or use a variety of venues;

(d) acquiring music – you may borrow, buy, or hire your vocal music and/or orchestral material;

(e) fixing an orchestra – you may hire the services of an existing orchestra, or you may book the individual players yourself in conjunction with your conductor;

(f) arranging financial assistance or raising money;

(g) arranging special publicity.

Committee

The committee must be active and everyone should do a specific job.

The *Chairman* is the figurehead, the decision maker and the person who delegates the work;

the *Treasurer* holds the purse strings, collecting subscriptions and ticket money, liaising with the NFMS (National Federation of Music Societies) or RAA (Regional Arts Association), and keeping control on the proposed budget and actual expenditure;

the *Secretary* deals with the paper work, writing the minutes and all correspondence;

the *conductor*, as an *ex officio* member recommends the works which will be performed and in this way moulds the artistic character of the choir. He or she should also provide facts and figures about the proposed works – how large is the orchestra? how many soloists are required? how expensive is the music to buy or hire?

Other members of the committee should each have a particular area of responsibility:

publicity co-ordination: posters, programmes (programme notes, biographies, etc.), tickets, advertising in the local press, and noticeboards;

hall bookings: rehearsal and concert venues, and the necessary equipment (i.e. chairs, staging, lighting, music stands);

membership secretary: keeping a register of rehearsal attendances, and chasing up absentees;

librarian: obtaining and distributing the vocal music, and perhaps the orchestral material as well;

entertainments officer: organizing entertainments in the broadest sense of the word – outings to concerts, social functions, parties, weekend courses or summer schools.

Concert organization – from beginning to end

It is vital at the outset to decide on works you are sure you can perform, that you can afford to perform, and that will sell. Your conductor must make a case for choosing a work, particularly if it will be expensive to mount. However, the more original a programme you put on, the more money you stand to receive in aid from organisations such as the RAA.

Having chosen the works, the next step is to engage the artists. These may well be chosen by your conductor, who will know which singers will be suitable for which parts, but do not let him use the same artists too often. The negotiation of a fee and all correspondence with the artist will then be carried out by the secretary. It is possible that you will be influenced in your choice of artist by the size of fee that you can afford; artists agencies will supply lists of singers together with lists of their fees. Try not to engage an artist whom no-one has heard; ideally one of the committee, preferably the conductor, should have heard the artist perform before a booking is made. The orchestra must then be engaged, and the committee booking officer must book the venue, and any necessary staging and lighting (he may well have the dates booked well in advance before the works are chosen). Publicity is in the hands of the publicity officer, who will have a schedule of dates by which posters, programmes and tickets should be available.

On the day of the concert an army of helpers is required who will arrange the staging, seating, lighting, and anything else that is necessary. The soloists and orchestra will need to be looked after; refreshments will be required for the break during the rehearsal and the soloists will need somewhere to rest and change between the rehearsal and concert – and perhaps during the interval. Your treasurer should be prompt in delivering the cheques at the end of the evening. After the concert helpers are required to put everything away – staging, chairs, lights, etc., and the librarian should collect up all the music (including the orchestral parts). The final job is for the secretary who should write 'thank you' letters to the artists involved in the concert.

Conducting technique

Conducting is communication. Watch any conductor and you will see that they all have a different style and more often than not, a different approach to their task. But they must be clear, and they must inspire (confidence at the very least!). The conductor of an amateur choral society has to do more than this – he has to coax his performers into giving their best, and that often means bullying, pleading, over-reacting and entreating. You have reached a great goal if your performers respond to you without a few histrionics at rehearsals.

The conductor's work begins before the first rehearsal. He must know the music thoroughly; it is not enough to be simply one step ahead of the choir. He must also know exactly what he wants at every point in the score; interpreting the music is as vital at rehearsals as teaching the notes. The conductor must also mark his score so that he is consistent in his requirements. At each rehearsal you expect to build upon what was achieved the previous week, thus moulding the piece into shape.

If the work is to be accompanied by orchestra the conductor must also know the orchestral score intimately. This way he will know if the voices are doubled by instruments, if the singers are unaccompanied, or accompanied by strings or brass; these points will give guidance as to the dynamics of the choral singing at certain moments in the score. The conductor should also supervise the orchestral parts, marking them ready for the performance if necessary, and certainly checking that helpful pencil marks which are already there are going to agree with his own thoughts. If you are going to beat a slow movement in quavers (let us say 'in 8') it will cause havoc if the players in a previous performance have pencilled in their parts 'in 4', meaning crotchets. It is not vital to use a baton for choral rehearsals, but do start using it some time before the dress rehearsal, so that the choir will become familiar with your modified gestures.

It is often said of a conductor who has made a name for himself as a choir trainer that 'he's a choral conductor', implying that he is not at home with purely orchestral conducting. In technical terms a choral conductor (with or without baton) is going to be more concerned with representing his ideas with his hands (and perhaps his fingers) than with keeping his beat strict and clear. An orchestral player needs to see a clear beat and is not happy if he looks up but cannot tell which beat of the bar is being given. An orchestral player needs to watch the point of the stick, whereas a singer is used to watching the conductor's hands. Conductors often put down their batons for unaccompanied choral passages in pieces with orchestral accompaniment (for example, during the last movement of the Verdi *Requiem*).

As a conductor you must rehearse alone, perhaps in front of a mirror. You need to think about and practise how you are going to deal with a particular passage. How are you going to negotiate a cadenza at the end of a baroque aria? How are you going to pick up a new tempo out of the old? How flexible can you be in recitative? How many leads can you give to the orchestra? You surely give some leads to the choir and you have had the benefit of a few weeks rehearsal with them, but you will not have much time with the orchestra to work this out.

The golden rule of conducting must be clarity. Always be definite in all of your gestures and in your physical and verbal direction. Never allow yourself to hesitate (you will not hesitate if you know the music intimately) and communicate with firmness.

Rehearsal technique

Always rehearse in a well-ventilated room, and devise a seating plan that will suit your choir. Some choirmasters place the women in front of the men; this may not be a good idea, and you may prefer blocks of voices: soprano, alto, tenor and bass, or other combinations, stretched in a phalanx in front of you. It may also be useful to alter the seating plan occasionally, even to the extreme of making everybody sit with someone singing a different part (but only do this at a stage when everyone should know the music!).

It is vital that the conductor knows what he is going to do at each rehearsal, so plan your rehearsals – in your head even – so that you have an overall schedule for the number of weeks at your disposal. If you rehearse the opening chorus at the start of each week's rehearsal you will find choruses at the end which you have hardly looked at. Before rehearsing it is important to warm up and to 'clear the cobwebs away'. Vocal exercises should be practised each week. Most members of choral societies have just rushed in from somewhere, so a warm-up will concentrate the mind and open the vocal mechanism, and will also help you to cultivate a particular and distinctive sound from your choir. It will enable your members to blend their voices, and the choir to give a uniform sound (see *Singing*).

At an early rehearsal – perhaps not at the beginning of the first – give an overall interpretation (as you see it) of the work, and explain what you want from it. Far too many choristers sing their lines without relating their contribution to the whole, or thinking about what happens in the rest of the work. Do not give a history lesson, but put the work in context, and always enthuse about it.

It is very tempting at the first rehearsal to sing straight through the work (or works) which you are preparing. Unless your choir is going to cope with this ordeal with flying colours, do not do it! If the choir manages to sing it all reasonably well they will go away with the impression that the music is easy, and your next rehearsals will suffer – people may actually stay away! Things are always more difficult than they appear. It is much better to sing certain portions several times, rehearsing them quite thoroughly. This will encourage the timid and provide something solid to sing at the next rehearsal, thus giving the foundation upon which you can build the rest of the work. For example, if your choir has never seen the work before, Haydn's *Nelson Mass* might be easily sight-read at the first rehearsal, as might the Fauré *Requiem*; but a first rehearsal run-through of Bach's *B Minor Mass* would surely prove totally impossible (and damaging) as would a run-through at sight of Walton's *Belshazzar's Feast* or Tippett's *A Child of our Time*.

Once the first rehearsal is over and a portion of the work has been rehearsed in depth, use that portion as a building block – revise it and add to it. Choirs need to go over sections a number of times before they will achieve the effect you require. Be careful to spot wrong notes and correct them at the outset – they will all too easily be 'learnt' if you let the choir sing them more than once. Stop and start as much as is necessary; do not accept the first shaky chord, but make the choir sing with attack (or at least with precision). Persuade your choir to use the words and to 'act'; you will find it necessary as a conductor to act yourself, and to demonstrate in an exaggerated way exactly what is wanted; most choirs will only respond in a small way to a call for exaggerated effects. Spot the sections which are difficult and rehearse them thoroughly, every week if necessary. Always rehearse the end of one movement into the next, particularly where a chorus comes straight after an aria, being sure to give a sufficient cue when rehearsing.

Towards the end of the series of rehearsals for the concert, it is often a good idea to run the whole work to give everyone an idea of how well they know the piece, and how much more has to be done. Plan this with care, because if you do it on the wrong week you may frighten everyone into a panic. You should always aim to arrive at the peak on the day of the performance – not the week before, nor at the dress rehearsal. Don't be disappointed if the dress rehearsal is something of a low point; all the things that were drilled into the choir can often be forgotten as the members struggle with their new surroundings, with the sound of an orchestral accompaniment (not the usual piano), and endeavour to see (and hear) you from the distance.

At the dress rehearsal you may prefer to rehearse the work in order, or to rehearse the choral sections first and send the chorus home. This will depend on the work (it is easy to isolate the chorus numbers in the Mozart *Requiem*, but not in *The Dream of Gerontius*) and the availability of chorus, soloists and orchestra. Always rehearse as if you are 'performing' – do not rehearse the choir as if they are still learning; they will respond more readily to a 'performance' style as they will see their own shortcomings and note them for the performance itself. Do not keep the chorus hanging around unnecessarily.

At all stages be as economical and efficient as is possible; the conductor of most choral societies has to appear to know the answers to everything; in any case everyone will come to you for your help and advice.

Planning a programme

The following paragraphs are concerned with choosing choral works to form artistically satisfying concerts. Obviously each individual choir will need to consider many other factors: the cost of soloists, and orchestra, the cost and availability of music, the size of the concert venue, and the number of performers in the orchestra and chorus.

1 When choosing a programme, look at a) the orchestration, b) the number of soloists required, and c) the timings of the works. These three factors will help dictate your programme. A concert consisting of one work only is relatively easy to mount, and will be artistically satisfying to performers and audience. But you may want to perform a work that will only take up half of a programme, or possibly even less than that. If you

want to perform Elgar's *The Music Makers* for example, you will see that it is only 40' long and you will then need to look at the orchestration. It is scored for full symphony orchestra (actually rather a large one) and requires one soloist, a mezzo-soprano (or alto). Now consider our three points in turn:

a. *Orchestration*: if you have chosen to perform *The Music Makers*, which is scored for full orchestra, it makes economic sense to choose a companion work with the same or similar scoring. Elgar's work is actually for triple wind (twelve players), full brass section, percussion and strings. A work such as Poulenc's *Gloria* may prove to be a good companion piece – the scoring is very similar indeed. Both works need a harp: one for the Poulenc, but according to the catalogues, two for the Elgar. It is always worth checking the score to see if a composer has asked for two harps merely to double the sound, and to see whether they in fact play the same music in unison. Looking at the Elgar score you will discover that the harps are in unison except for a passage one bar after figure 83, when for three bars of music they play separate lines.

Other points to notice about the orchestration specifications (and not only for the Elgar work you have chosen) include:

percussion: how many instruments do you need, and how many players? Most catalogues list the percussion as a number followed by the letter P. This simply means that five percussion instruments are used in the score – it does not mean five players; percussion players may double up on various instruments, unless of course all five are sounding together (and even then a certain amount of doubling may be possible).

strings: many works written during the baroque and classical periods do not include separate parts for violas. Some Haydn and Mozart works are scored for violins I and II and bass, usually played by cellos and basses in unison. Occasionally, though, a baroque work may require violins I, II and III (some works by Handel are scored in this way) and some divide the violas. Always look at the score.

continuo: all composers writing music before 1800 (and some beyond that date) expected the bass line to be supported by a keyboard instrument. It is usual to engage an organist for sacred works and a harpsichord for secular pieces, but they are interchangeable, and often both instruments would have been available with perhaps the harpsichord used for solos, and the organ to accompany the choruses. Handel's *Israel in Egypt* actually specifies both instruments. Bach's *Magnificat* could be performed using either. Late works such as Mozart's *Requiem* and Haydn's *Creation* all have continuo parts and the latter has secco recitative: an organ would be used for the Mozart, and an organ, or perhaps a fortepiano or harpsichord could be used for the Haydn. Brahms scores for an organ in his *German Requiem*, although it can be omitted.

organ: some later works (by Elgar for example) have sections for organ as an integral instrument of the full orchestra. Although the organ colouring is a feature of the score and should not be disregarded, it is often possible to omit the organ without spoiling the piece; often the organ part is marked 'ad lib' as in Vaughan Williams's *Dona nobis pacem*, for example. An organ is required in performances of Dvořák's *Stabat Mater* as it is the only instrument used to accompany the female chorus in the fourth movement. The organ is also a vital ingredient in a performance of Fauré's *Requiem*, where it again has a 'solo' spot.

b. *Soloists*: depending on how much solo work there is in your chosen piece, it makes good sense to use the same soloists in the other works in the programme. In many works the solo parts are comparatively modest – the masses of Mozart and Haydn, for example – so once you have employed four solo voices make sure that all four sing in the other works you have chosen. Nothing is worse for a soloist than to sing just one small item. The tenor soloist in Haydn's *Nelson Mass* has very little to do, the male soloists in Handel's *Dixit Dominus* sing just a few phrases, and the bass soloist in Mozart's *C Minor Mass* performs in one number only. The title role in Britten's *St Nicolas* is however a 'big sing', so it may be wise not to tax your tenor soloist in the other 'half' of the concert (already the *Nelson Mass* suggests itself as a companion piece). If we come back to our example of *The Music Makers* with its one soloist, perhaps a wise choice will be another work with the same soloist, such as Lambert's *Rio Grande*; or why not spread the soloist's load by programming Brahms's *Alto Rhapsody*, followed by his *Schicksalslied* in part one, with the Elgar in part two.

c. *Timings*: do not make your programme too long; a short concert in a church will be appreciated by those who have to sit on hard pews in the cold. Bear in mind that there will probably be an interval, so remember to add a timing for the interval in your calculations. *The Music Makers* lasts about forty minutes, so the other part of your concert could be about the same length if you are planning one work, or a little shorter if you decide on two (the two Brahms works mentioned above would amount to thirty minutes of actual music, which allowing for re-shuffling and applause would spread easily to thirty-five – arguably, quite long enough!). Remember too, that a programme consisting of predominantly choral music is inevitably tiring on the ear, no matter how much the choir may be enjoying itself. Choral works with extended solo sections are more satisfying for the audience.

2 That brings us neatly to a consideration of how much actual choral singing there will be in the proposed programme. Some works such as the Brahms *German Requiem* or Vaughan Williams's *Sea Symphony* involve the choir throughout (i.e. in every movement) while other works such as Elgar's *The Dream of Gerontius* or Haydn's *Creation* do not. Three of these four pieces constitute a whole programme in themselves, but the *Sea Symphony* needs a companion. If you decide to partner the *Sea Symphony* with Walton's *Belshazzar's Feast* (another piece which uses the choir

throughout) make sure your chorus will stand up to the strain! Orff's *Carmina Burana* may be a better choice as it is not so chorally demanding (although, incidentally, it is very tedious to rehearse because so much of the music is repetitious).

It is worth noting here that some 'choral' works have comparatively little choral music in them. The chorus work in Haydn's *Creation* amounts to just half-an-hour of music; the chorus sing for about 35 minutes in Elgar's *The Dream of Gerontius* (total duration 100'); while some baroque works, such as Purcell's *Come ye sons of art* and Charpentier's *Te Deum* have only the slightest choral writing. But, remember also that a number of minutes bears no relationship to the amount of rehearsal needed for a piece: all Haydn's *Creation* choruses are 'fast', as is 'Praise to the Holiest' (vs p. 113 onwards) in *The Dream of Gerontius*.

A number of full-scale pieces work better without an interval: there should be no interval in performances of the Verdi or Brahms Requiems, and arguably no interval in Elgar's *The Dream of Gerontius*. Haydn's *Creation* poses a problem because it is in three parts: an interval after Part One is unthinkable, and after Part Two, too late. Brahms's *Requiem* running just under 70' seems too short on paper, but is probably best performed alone; the *Tragic Overture* was not designed as a prelude to it.

3 It is vital that the programme as a whole should be appealing, as of course you want the public to buy tickets. A popular programme will always sell, but you will find it more rewarding to mix the familiar with the unfamiliar, the old with the new, the popular with the more modern. If you are performing the Fauré *Requiem*, be adventurous in your choice of companion piece, and remember to use the woodwind section in the second piece because they have so little to do in the Fauré.

4 Do not fill your programme with lots of small pieces. One work is best, two works can complement each other, but thereafter you will need to be careful in your choice. If you have chosen to perform *The Music Makers*, two pieces by another composer in part one will complement it, but two pieces by different composers would also have to complement each other.

5 Think of the music itself: how will the concert start? What will be the opening music? How will it end? Settings of the mass end with the words 'dona nobis pacem' (grant us thy peace), but whilst some composers have set those words quietly, others have turned this portion of the Agnus Dei into a jubilant cry for peace. Also consider how the first part of the concert will end: remember that quiet endings subdue the audience, whilst noisy finales encourage noisy applause. *The Music Makers* might make a good beginning to a concert: it ends very quietly indeed, but you may consider that a fitting end!

Planning – step by step

1 Vivaldi *Gloria*

Vivaldi's *Gloria* is scored for one oboe, one trumpet, strings (with violas) and continuo. The continuo should properly consist of a 'solo' cello and a keyboard instrument, either a harpsichord or organ. The soloists required are two sopranos and an alto, although the alto may agree to sing the second soprano part in addition, in which case only two women will be required. The work was intended for female voices, so a countertenor should perhaps not be considered. The *Gloria* lasts 30 minutes.

a. Other works by Vivaldi immediately suggest themselves as companions to the *Gloria*. A short *Beatus Vir* (8') is scored for two sopranos, alto chorus and strings with continuo, while his *Magnificat* (14'), also scored for strings, would require tenor and bass soloists in addition to the soprano and alto. That may suggest using the four soloists together in another work in the second half of the concert. Handel's *Dixit Dominus* (35') is also scored for strings and continuo, but requires two sopranos, alto, tenor and bass soloists. Thus you might engage two sopranos and one alto for the *Gloria*, soprano, alto, tenor and bass for the *Magnificat*, and employ all five in the Handel. The only disadvantage is that the oboe and trumpet are only used in the *Gloria*.

b. Alternatively, you could take the orchestra of the *Gloria* as a starting point and expand upon it in your other works. Keeping the companion pieces in the same era, and therefore in the same style, you could look to the works of Purcell, Charpentier or Bach. Purcell's *Come ye sons of art* is scored for two oboes, two trumpets, timpani, strings and continuo, but the soloists required are soprano, two altos, tenor and bass, and for this work the two altos must be countertenors. Charpentier's popular *Messe de minuit* (25') needs two sopranos, alto, tenor and bass soloists, but adds two flutes and two bassoons to the orchestra (no trumpets or timpani are required), while his *Te Deum*, for the same soloists, adds only a cor anglais (scoring 2.2.corA.0.1. – 0.2.0.0. – timp – keyboard – strings). It would be worth engaging a countertenor who will sing both the Vivaldi and Charpentier.

c. A baroque programme is always popular, but you may prefer to provide contrast. Vivaldi's *Gloria* would make a good partner to Britten's *St Nicolas* (50'), for example. You will need a good tenor for the title role, and will need to add to your string orchestra with organ, two pianists at one piano, and percussion. The chorus writing includes parts for a 'gallery choir' of sopranos and altos; you may either bring in a children's choir, or perform all of the gallery music from the main choir. One small boy sings the part of the young St Nicolas, and three small boys enter the church as the resurrected 'pickled' boys.

Another Britten work for chorus and string orchestra (this time adding harp and piano) is the *Cantata Misericordia* (20'), which is scored for tenor and baritone soloists. Whereas *St Nicolas* and Vivaldi's *Gloria* together may form a full evening's concert (but only just!), the *Cantata Misericordia* is not long enough, so you will need another work. Depending on your orchestra and rehearsal time you may choose a piece for string orchestra alone – it is not necessary for the choir to perform in every item in a concert.

d. Baroque pieces and works from the classical era (Mozart, Haydn, etc.) are not necessarily good musical companions, but both have a basic string orchestra with continuo, and many early Mozart masses only add two oboes, two trumpets and timpani to the string orchestra. It is likely, though, that there will be no viola part in the Mozart work, and you will need soprano, alto, tenor and bass soloists. Haydn's *Nelson Mass* would make a suitable pairing as it is scored for one bassoon, three trumpets. timpani, strings and continuo (in the Robbins Landon edition), but again requires four soloists (and remember that the tenor sings very little).

e. The Vivaldi *Gloria* is so popular that you could programme another work with it that is not well known, as a welcome change for audience and choir alike. *Pastoral* (32') by Bliss is scored for mezzo-soprano soloist, flute, timpani and strings, and is not at all difficult. Further suggestions can be found on page 165–6.

2 Fauré *Requiem*
The Fauré *Requiem* (40') is scored for 2.0.2.2. – 4.2.3.0. – timp – harp – organ – strings, with soprano (or treble) and baritone soloists. The woodwind play very little, and the violins perform in only some of the movements – the basic scoring is for divided violas, divided cellos and organ. The organ part is particularly important, and at various points is 'solo', so the work should be performed in a church, or with a proper pipe organ.

a. Works with the same soloists (soprano and baritone) include Dvořák's *Te Deum* (20') and Vaughan Williams's *Dona nobis pacem* (40'). Both of these would complement the Fauré, but although the Vaughan Williams is the right length for a complete concert, the Dvořák is not. Both are scored for a fuller orchestra; the Dvořák adds oboes, tuba and percussion (but without harp), and the Vaughan Williams is scored for 3.2.2.3. – 4.2.3.1. – timp – perc – harp – (organ) – strings.

b. To provide contrast you may consider programming a baroque work (or two) as companions to the Fauré, but you will disappoint your woodwind players who play only a few notes in the *Requiem*. Whilst your clarinets would not be needed in the baroque piece, you would probably have to bring in oboes (not required in the Fauré).[1]

c. It may be worthwhile to add two more soloists (an alto and tenor) and to perform another work scored for romantic orchestra. Perhaps the

---

[1] A recent edition of Fauré's Requiem by John Rutter purports to be an original version with greatly reduced orchestra.

Gounod *St Cecilia Mass* (41') (requiring additional flute/piccolo, two extra bassoons, two extra trumpets and percussion) or the third mass by Bruckner might be suitable.

    d. The Fauré is certainly a very popular work, but it is rather subdued. Why not consider something more lively and modern to complement it such as Brian Chapple's *Cantica* (20') scored for soprano and tenor soloists, 1.2.2.2. – 2.2.0.0. – timp and strings, or Stephen Dodgson's *Magnificat* (30') (scoring: soprano, alto, tenor and bass soloists, 2.2.0.1. – 0.3.0.0. – timp – perc – organ – strings) or *Te Deum* (35') (scoring: soprano, tenor and bass soloists, 1.3.0.2. – 0.3.0.0. – timp – organ – strings).

3 Mozart *Requiem*

Mozart's *Requiem* is scored for the unusual combination of two basset horns (clarinets may be used instead), two bassoons, two trumpets, three trombones, strings and organ continuo. The trombones (alto, tenor and bass) generally double the chorus (apart from solo in 'Tuba mirum') but are an essential feature of the scoring. The work lasts for 55', and requires soprano, alto, tenor and bass soloists.

    a. Very few works, even works written during Mozart's lifetime, are scored for exactly the same forces, so it will be necessary to add other instruments to the basic orchestra, and probably discard the clarinet/ basset horns. Only one of Haydn's masses, the *Harmoniemesse*, includes clarinets in the orchestra. The full scoring is 2.2.2.2. – 2.2.0.0. – timp – strings.

    b. Other works by Mozart make suitable programmes including the two Vespers settings or any of the four litanies. These will not require clarinets or basset horns, and watch to see whether they require a full complement of strings.

    c. Baroque works and classical works do not necessarily blend, but Purcell's *Funeral Sentences* (20') make a neat foil to the *Requiem*. The extended version of the *Funeral Sentences*, is scored for soprano, alto, tenor and bass soloists with continuo, with a march and canzona for brass (2.2.0.0.) alternating with the vocal sections. You may then consider other works for choir and brass, or brass and strings, by Gabrieli or Schütz, depending on the size of the choir.

    d. Another possibility is to perform something more modern (see p. 165–6).

Obtaining music

It is a sad fact of life that if you are adventurous and want to perform works that other choirs do not perform frequently, it is likely that you will have great trouble in getting hold of the music. Many nineteenth-century pieces are now out of print (for example, Sullivan's *The Golden Legend*), and even if you track down vocal scores, finding orchestral parts may be a problem. Some publishers have actually destroyed all their material and plates of works that have slipped from the repertory. When choosing your programme, work out straight away how you will get the music and find out how much it will cost the society or its members. Do not leave it until a month before the first rehearsal or until after you have given advance notice of your plans.

An obvious and cheap method of obtaining music is through the public library system, although you will generally only be able to borrow material of a more popular nature. Your library is more likely to have multiple copies of Joseph Haydn's *The Creation* than of Michael Haydn's *Requiem*; more likely to have Mozart's *'Coronation' Mass* than his *'Credo' Mass*; and very unlikely to have multiple copies of a new and expensive edition of a work that exists in an older but perfectly workable edition published many years ago.

Your local public library may not carry stocks of vocal material (it may not have music at all), but the inter-library loan system should enable you to obtain music from another library through your own branch. Unfortunately, not all libraries are part of the inter-library network, and not all will undertake to get items for you. However, your local library should be your starting point. The librarian should have access to the Laser catalogue (London and South East library region)[1] which will tell you which libraries hold copies of the music you wish to borrow.

The NFMS (National Federation of Music Societies) also has an index of music held by its member choirs who may be prepared to lend music at a modest rate. The BBC Music Library is not a public library (music held there is for broadcast purposes only), but it may be possible to hire material held by the BBC if it is otherwise unavailable.

Vocal material for the standard choral works can usually be purchased direct from the publisher. Many choir members like to have their own copies, but this can be an expensive hobby. Some works (such as the Poulenc Gloria) are also available in chorus scores (that is, without the accompaniment) but few singers will be prepared to buy these. Some works, even standard works which are available on sale, are available on hire from the publisher. Hiring is of course much cheaper than purchasing.

If a work is out of copyright in every respect (see Copyright) the material may be photocopied, but the quantity of copies required for a choral society makes this prohibitive. *Never* photocopy a copyright work (or part of it) for performance; it is illegal and the penalties are very high.

The choir now have their material, but the orchestra will of course require their parts too, although they will not need them until much nearer to the date of the concert. Always investigate the availability of the orchestral material at the same time you obtain the choral scores. The

[1] Or 'Vocal scores in the Northern Region' published by the Northern libraries.

methods of obtaining the orchestral material are the same as for choral scores, but it is more likely that it will be obtainable from libraries or on hire – you are unlikely to wish to purchase orchestral material for one performance. But do be careful – some orchestral material is only available from certain publishers on sale (Mozart's *Credo Mass*, for example, or Haydn's *Salve Regina*).

Make sure (particularly if you are dealing with different publishers for the orchestral and choral material of the same work) that the orchestral parts match those of the chorus. That is, not only making sure that bar numbers or figures in the score tally (it is infuriating to use scores and parts which have different systems of figuring) but also ensuring that the full score and vocal score agree in all details. Some works (such as the Bruckner *E Minor Mass* and Vivaldi *Gloria*[1]) have been published in versions with tiny discrepancies. In the case of the Bruckner, the composer made revisions, but in the case of the Vivaldi, two editors have made adjustments. In both cases the alterations are slight, but important. Your conductor may not be aware of all discrepancies; double check at each stage to make sure that the material you have is correct – it will be too late at the dress rehearsal.

Always order music in plenty of time – a few months in advance. Some music has to be shipped in from abroad.

Wider repertory

It is inevitable that the staple diet of a choral society will include the well-known choral works such as Bach's *B Minor Mass*, Mozart's *Requiem*, Handel's *Messiah*, Verdi's *Requiem* – and of course these will continue to satisfy choir and audience alike for generations to come. However, there are many works which are not as popular, but which deserve to be performed and would add variety to any concert season. There are lesser works by Bach, Handel, Mozart and Verdi themselves which are well worth investigating, as well as many more works by a variety of composers who are sometimes overshadowed and overlooked.

Baroque music
Bach wrote over two hundred church cantatas, and a number of these are quite well known. A major drawback in choosing a Bach cantata is that its

[1] The Vivaldi *Gloria* as published by Ricordi (edited by Casella) has bars missing in 'Et in terra pax', and variants in the soprano duet; the Walton edition of the vocal score and the Kalmus orchestral parts agree. The Walton vocal scores are available from Chappells. Ricordi publish a correct edition (edited by Malipiero). Bruckner's *E Minor Mass* has a number of small changes in the various versions – most obviously, one provides wind accompaniment for the Sanctus, while another does not. In one version there is an extra bar in the Agnus Dei.

number and title look daunting and uninviting on a programme: Cantata no. 75 *Die Elenden sollen essen* may be one of Bach's most impressive cantatas, but it is hardly likely to recommend itself to the average audience. But do not be put off – the very name of Bach will sell the work if it is judiciously programmed. Bach also wrote four other settings of the mass (settings of the Kyrie and Gloria only) which are very attractive.

The less well-known choral pieces by Bach's contemporary, Handel, include various anthems (see *Chandos Anthems*) which will fit well into part of a concert. His Italian works, of which *Dixit Dominus* is the most famous, also include the equally lively *Nisi Dominus*, and *Laudate Pueri* which are well worth considering.

Of the many other baroque composers writing choral music, Vivaldi is one of the most approachable. Why not bypass his *Gloria* and look instead at his other settings of latin texts for example, the *Credo*, the delightful *Magnificat*, or the *Dixit Dominus* for eight-part choir and double orchestra. Bach's great German contemporary, Telemann, wrote many thousands of choral works, and a few of them are available in good editions. His settings of the passions and his oratorios and cantatas would make a welcome change.

French baroque music includes the works of M.-A. Charpentier (there are other works apart from the famous *Te Deum*) and his contemporaries Lalande (1657–1726) (whose *De Profundis* is available) and Lully (1632–1687) (who wrote settings of the *Te Deum*). We should not forget English baroque music, such as the anthems and odes of Purcell, nor the baroque music of other countries: music by the Bohemian composer Zelenka (1679–1745) is becoming available and is very attractive and distinctive.

Other composers: Alessandro Scarlatti, Pergolesi, Rameau (1683–1764), Boyce (1710–1779), Cavalli (1602–1676), Monteverdi, Schütz, G. Gabrieli and Praetorius (1571–1621).

Classical music

The two towering masters of the classical period are Haydn and Mozart. Both wrote a wealth of choral music, much of which is not regularly performed and should be investigated, such as their mass settings, Te Deums and Litanies. Haydn's brother, Michael (1737–1806), has also left a number of excellent choral works – not least, a setting of the *Requiem* which was an obvious model for Mozart. Mozart's own father was also a composer, and there are various works by him which have been published.

Among their most interesting contemporaries are the sons of J. S. Bach. The music of C. P. E. Bach (1714–1788) bridges the gap between the baroque and classical periods, and his oratorios are superb examples of the so-called rococo style. His setting of the *Magnificat* should be better known. The 'London' Bach, Johann Christian, (1735–1782) also wrote music in a direct and tuneful idiom: his *Dies irae*, *Dixit Dominus*, and *Magnificat* are all available in modern editions.

The late music of Beethoven and Schubert reaches beyond the classical period in style, but their early works fall into this category for consideration. The earlier masses of Schubert are pleasant but uncommitted works (the *Mass in G* has always been the most loved), while his other religious works, including a *Stabat Mater*, are very melodious. Much more powerful are the two early cantatas by Beethoven (written on the death of Emperor Joseph II and the accession of Emperor Leopold II) which are arguably more impressive than his neglected oratorio *Christ on the Mount of Olives*.

Romantic music

Mendelssohn is best known for *Elijah*, Brahms for *A German Requiem*, and Dvořák for his *Stabat Mater*, or *Mass in D*, but each of these wrote other works no less satisfying. Mendelssohn's oratorio *St Paul* is a fine work, and probably more rewarding than the *Lobgesang* which is a symphony with a choral finale, or *Die erste Walpurgisnacht*, a secular cantata. Brahms wrote a number of choral works, mostly quite short, which should not be overlooked. Dvořák's large scale pieces, such as *The Spectre's Bride* and *Saint Ludmilla*, will sadly gather dust until someone offers a modern translation: it is unlikely that any choral society here will want to perform either work in the original Czech, although both are excellent scores. Dvořák's *Te Deum* and *The American Flag* are more obvious candidates for revival.

It is likely that a choir's committee will have the names of many romantic composers quite readily at their fingertips, but the following composers and works may provide ideas for discussion. Donizetti's *Requiem* was recently given its first London performances and is a strong candidate in a coupling with a more famous work. A *Requiem* by Suppé (1819–1895) was mounted by the BBC in 1984 and showed an aspect of this composer which one could not have expected. The *Mass* by Nicolai (1810–1849) has been commercially recorded but has not been given a live performance for many years. Rheinberger's (1839–1901) Christmas cantata *Der Stern von Bethlehem* is an engaging work, and it would be worth examining his other choral pieces. The choral works of Bruch (1838–1920) and Reger, at one time very popular, have slipped out of the repertory, and are unfortunately out of print, but both composers are now out of copyright. Spohr's bicentenary (he was born in 1784) brought a certain resurgence of interest in his choral works. If you enjoy early romantic music, *The Last Judgement* and *The Fall of Babylon* may well suit you. Gounod's *St Cecilia Mass* is steadily gaining a following, and we may see a revival of his many other choral works, including *Mors et vita*.

British romantic music has, until recently, had a bad press. Even the great works by Stanford and Parry have failed to satisfy music scholars and critics, but the tide is turning, and as the recording companies continue to release recordings of their works, together with the early (Parry-like) works of Elgar, so the case for reviving nineteenth-century British music grows. Do take a look at the scores – the best works of Parry and Stanford are very good indeed. It is somewhat harder to make a case for their predecessors, Sullivan and Sterndale Bennett, because the Victorian tone of the convoluted texts they set are so alien to the twentieth century. Sullivan's *The Golden Legend*[1] is certainly worth reviving, but like all such enterprises, it must be done with love and enthusiasm – Victorian music must not be presented as a series of museum pieces.

Modern music

The twentieth century is very rich in choral works, particularly choral works suitable for moderate and large sized choirs with orchestral accompaniment. British music includes famous and less well-known works by Elgar, Delius, Walton, Britten, Tippett and many more. In most European countries and in the USA there has been a constant outpouring of choral works, too many of which have been performed once or twice only, and then neglected. In an area so vast, it is only possible to mention a few works.

Larger choral societies could well tackle Roussel's *Psalm 80*, the *Book with the seven seals*, by Schmidt (1874–1939), or Fricker's mighty *Vision of Judgement*. Hindemith's *Requiem* is a solid but melodious work, as is Frank Martin's *In terra pax*, which is a moving oratorio, and one of his greatest works. Howells's *Hymnus Paradisi* is one of the most hauntingly beautiful pieces to emerge from this country during the twentieth century. America has contributed a vast corpus of choral works; an ambitious choir could well start with the short *Lament for Beowulf* by Howard Hanson, (1896–1981) which is written in a late romantic, but rhythmically vital idiom. Penderecki's scores may tax even the best choirs, but are rewarding works, nevertheless; his recent *Te Deum* was heard in this country in 1984.

For smaller choirs there are numerous works by British composers such as Rawsthorne and Britten, as well as a host of pieces by foreign composers, not all of which are in the regular repertory. Among the living British composers, Paul Patterson (b. 1947) is one of the liveliest writers of choral works; other larger works such as Wilfred Joseph's (b. 1927) *Requiem*, Gordon Crosse's (b. 1937) *Changes*, Geoffrey Burgon's (b. 1941) *Requiem*, William Mathias's (b. 1934) *Lux Aeterna* and Michael Berkeley's (b. 1948) *Or shall we die?* have all been commercially recorded.

[1]The work was broadcast live in 1986 on Radio 3, conducted by Sir Charles Mackerras.

Composers

BACH, *Johann Sebastian* (*1685–1750*)

Bach's career falls fairly neatly into three phases: the first from 1708 when he was employed as court organist, and later as director of the court orchestra, at Weimar; the second from 1717 when he worked as director of music at Cöthen; and the third when he became cantor at St Thomas's Church, Leipzig. From these three different periods come the greater part of his organ music, orchestral and keyboard music, and church music respectively.

Bach composed almost two hundred church cantatas for services at St Thomas's, Leipzig (not a large number compared to the one thousand or so composed by his contemporary Telemann) and also the *Magnificat** (1723), the Passions according to *St John** (1723) and *St Matthew** (1729), the six cantatas which we group together as the *Christmas Oratorio** (1734), the *Easter Oratorio* (1725), four short masses (settings of the Kyrie and Gloria only) and the *Mass in B Minor** (1733). The latter collection of movements were never performed complete in Bach's lifetime, since Bach would have had no opportunity to mount a performance of a Roman Catholic mass in a Lutheran church.

Bach also wrote secular cantatas, including the *'Coffee' cantata* (no. 211) and *'Peasant' cantata* (no. 212), and six motets for choir (almost certainly with continuo accompaniment although it is not specified) which were possibly composed as funeral anthems.

The church cantatas are settings of words of a contemplative nature and were designed to complement the scriptural text or sermon on a particular Sunday; after an opening chorus of an elaborate nature, a sequence of recitatives and da capo arias is rounded off by a chorale.

The two passion settings are among the supreme choral achievements of any age: the *St John Passion* is arguably less well structured than its companion, while the recitatives for Christ are simply accompanied by continuo; the *St Matthew Passion* is altogether on a grander scale, and here Christ's words are accompanied by a 'halo' of strings.

BANTOCK, *Granville* (*1868–1946*)

Bantock wrote a vast amount of orchestral and choral music, much of which is unperformed today. His part songs are still occasionally sung, but the three symphonies for unaccompanied voices, and the large works for choir and orchestra are neglected.

The three symphonies are *Atalanta in Calydon* (1911), *Vanity of Vanities* (1913) and *A Pageant of Human Life* (1913). These works rely on choral texture and colouring, and are highly effective in performance even if they are perhaps not melodically inspired.

Bantock's large scale pieces include

the gigantic *Omar Khayyam*, based on Fitzgerald's translations, which was performed in three separate parts in Birmingham (1906), Cardiff (1907) and Birmingham (1909), *The Fire Worshippers* (1892) and *The Song of Songs* (1922), all of which are scored for soloists, chorus and orchestra; as well as *Sea Wanderers* (1906), *Song of Liberty* (1914) and *Prometheus Unbound* (1936) for chorus and orchestra without soloists.

BARBER, Samuel (1910–1981)

Barber's neo-romantic style has not always found its admirers – the audience and critics alike were unenthusiastic about his opera *Anthony and Cleopatra* (1966). Certain works, however, have remained deservedly popular, such as the *Adagio for Strings*, which Barber later rewrote as an *Agnus Dei* for chorus and organ (1967). Of his choral music the three unaccompanied pieces *Reincarnations* (1940) are very approachable. Barber's setting of Spender's *A stopwatch and an ordinance Map* for male voices, brass and timpani, of the same year, is however written in a more dissonant idiom. Works with orchestra include the impressive *Prayers of Kierkegaard* (1954) and *The Lovers* (1971), to poems by Neruda.

BARTÓK, Béla (1881–1945)

Bartók collected folk music in his native Hungary and its bordering countries; the folk idiom was an inspiration to him in many of his freely composed works. He published various collections of folk songs, both genuine and 'composed', including *Four Old Hungarian Folk Songs* for male voices (1912), *Four Slovak Folk Songs* for mixed choir and piano (1917) and *Four Slovanic Folk Songs* for male voices and piano (1917). In 1935, Bartók published a collection of 27 two- and three-part choruses which were intended for childrens' voices; again they are based on Hungarian folk tunes and are devised for educational use.

The large-scale *Cantata Profana** (sometimes called *The Enchanted Stags*) (1930) is scored for tenor soloist, double choir and orchestra. The text is in Hungarian, but versions in German and English have been published. *Three Village Scenes* (1926) for womens' voices and chamber ensemble are settings of Slovakian texts.

BAX, Arnold (1883–1953)

Bax described himself as a 'brazen romantic' and his music is romantic in the broadest sense of the word; it is highly chromatic and sensual but also 'impressionistic'. Of Bax's choral works only a few unaccompanied pieces have stayed in the repertory, but the revival in 1983 for the centenary celebrations on Radio 3 of *Enchanted Summer* (1910), scored for two sopranos, chorus and orchestra, on verses from Shelley's *Prometheus*, showed him to be a master of orchestration and choral effect. Most of this work is for three-part female semichorus and includes some of his most delicate and difficult writing. *To the name above every other name* (1923) sets a poem by Crashaw and is arguably less successful in its overblown gestures, and short choral sentences. *Walsinghame* (1926) is a gentle piece, a loose set of variations on a theme for tenor, chorus and orchestra.

The works for unaccompanied choir include the impressive and masterly *Mater ora filium* (1921) for double choir and the deeply felt *This Worldes Joie* (1922), as well as the settings of the *Magnificat* (1948), *Nunc Dimittis* (1944), *Te Deum* (1944) and *Gloria* (1945) which are less interesting. The carol *Of a rose I sing* has an accompaniment of harp, cello and bass.

BEETHOVEN, Ludwig van (1770–1827)

Beethoven was not the first composer to add voices to a symphony, but when he composed a vocal finale to his Symphony no 9 in D minor (*Choral Symphony**), he established a model for all subsequent composers. The finale of his ninth symphony is a setting of Schiller's *Ode to Joy* scored for four soloists and chorus; the vocal writing is particularly taxing and puts great demands on the stamina of the performers, mainly because it lies so high for the sopranos and basses.

An earlier work may have been a model for the choral finale, the *Choral Fantasia**, of 1807. This work also consists of a set of variations on a simple diatonic melody; soloists and chorus are joined by a pianist who has a long preamble before the choir sings.

Beethoven's two mass settings stand in much the same relationship to each other as the *Choral Fantasia* and the Symphony no 9; the first mass, in C, is a Haydenesque affair, composed for Prince Esterházy, Haydn's patron, whilst the second the *Missa Solemnis**, is a gigantic work of epic proportions, and like the ninth symphony is demanding to sing, for the same reasons. With this work, Beethoven steps outside the church and into the concert hall, establishing the trend to perform masses as concert works.

Other choral works with orchestra include *Der Glorreiche Augenblick* composed to celebrate the Congress of Vienna in 1814, and two early cantatas from the year 1790, the cantata on the death of Emperor Joseph II (which includes a melody later used in the finale of the opera *Fidelio*), and the cantata on the accession of Emperor Leopold II. The oratorio, *Christ on the Mount of Olives** was once very popular in Britain, where it was performed under the title of *Engedi*, with a new text telling the story of David. Beethoven also made a setting of Goethe's *Calm sea and prosperous voyage* (1815) for chorus and orchestra; his other cantatas and shorter choral works are rarely heard.

BELLINI, Vincenzo (1801–35)

Bellini is best known as a composer of operas, but he also wrote choral works including settings of the mass. Bellini's masses are of the type referred to as Messa di gloria, that is, a setting of the Kyrie and Gloria only. His *Mass in A* (major and minor) is scored for soloists, chorus and orchestra; it is an attractive work, but the best music is given to the soloists. Many of Bellini's other choral works remain unpublished.

BERKELEY, Lennox (b. 1903)

Berkeley was greatly influenced by French music, and while studying in Paris met Ravel. Berkeley's music is written in a genial French idiom and includes many choral works, a number of which were composed for the Roman Catholic church. Two works with small orchestra are the cantata to words by Donne, *Batter my heart* (1926) for soprano, chorus and instruments, and *Signs in the Dark* (1967) for choir and strings. On a grander scale is Berkeley's *Magnificat*, composed in 1968; his church music also includes a number of anthems with organ, such as *The Lord is my shepherd* and the popular *Missa Brevis* (1959). Unaccompanied choral pieces include a *Mass* (1964), three Latin motets (1972) and the taxing *Hill of the Graces* (1975), which is an extended setting of verses from Spenser's *Faerie Queen*.

Berkeley's full scale oratorio *Jonah* was first heard at the Leeds Festival in 1935, but was not a great success; it is an impressive and lyrical score.

BERLIOZ, Hector (1803–69)

Almost everything Berlioz composed was written in a flamboyant style and on a grand scale, not least the large choral works. On a visit to London he was impressed by massed choirs of children singing in St Paul's Cathedral, but he was also fired by the turbulent times in which he lived, and by the extravagant cantatas of his immediate contemporaries, Gossec (1734–1829), Leseur (1760–1837) and Mehul (1763–1817). Out of this post-revolutionary melting-pot came Berlioz's epic works, the first of which was the requiem, *Grande messe des morts** (1837), which he scored for four brass bands in addition to the full orchestra. However, there are many moments of repose in the work, including the striking Hostias, with its famous chords scored unusually for flutes and trombone.

The *Te Deum* (1855) is also a large piece, calling for many harps and timpani as well as organ and full orchestra; the one soloist, as in the *Grande messe des morts*, is a tenor. The *Symphonie funèbre et triomphale** was written for open air performance (on the march) in 1840 for the tenth anniversary of the July Revolution; the enormous wind band is augmented by a choir (added in a later re-working of the score) who join in the glorious finale.

Shakespeare was always an inspiration to Berlioz, particularly so when he fell in love with the actress Harriet Smithson, whom he first saw playing Ophelia and Juliet in Paris in 1827. The purely orchestral *Symphonie fantastique* (1830) was written in the first floods of despairing passion for her. The later choral symphony, *Romeo and Juliet** (1839) is a hybrid work which fails to tell the complete story of the play. The chorus takes part in only some of the movements, the others being purely orchestral.

The oratorio *The Childhood of Christ** (1854) is unusual in that it traces the story of the child Jesus *after* the nativity and follows the family's flight into Egypt. The work also relies on orchestral movements, including a march of Roman soldiers, to carry the action forward. The famous Shepherd's chorus comes in Part Two; Berlioz passed this movement off as a re-discovered essay by a seventeenth-century composer, and actually fooled everyone by it.

Goethe's *Faust* has inspired a number of romantic composers, and Berlioz's *Damnation of Faust** was first heard in 1846. This colourful score is actually a re-working of his *Eight Scenes from Goethe's Faust*, originally composed in 1829. Berlioz takes liberties with the action of the play in order to make room for the colourful and spectacular; these include a swift change of scene to Hungary to incorporate the *Hungarian March (Rákóczky March)*. All of the above works were premiered in Paris.

The sequel to the *Symphonie fantastique, Lélio** (1832) has a choir in two of its six movements. Berlioz's other works for choir are smaller and include the setting of Hugo's *Sara la baigneuse* (1834) and the *Méditation religeuse* (1831); both works require orchestra. Berlioz intended to write a choral work called *The Last days of the world* but never did so.

BERNSTEIN, Leonard (b. 1918)

Bernstein's *Chichester Psalms** are frequently performed, but his other choral music is less well known. His third symphony *Kaddish* (1963) is a choral symphony scored for soprano, female speaker, chorus and boy's choir. A short religious piece with organ accompaniment, *Hashkivenu*, appeared in 1945, and his writing for the stage (apart from his musicals) includes

Choruses from The Lark for soloists, chorus, drums and bells, a series of items written as incidental music to Anouilh's play. The *Mass* of 1971 is an extravagant theatre piece for singers, players and dancers, and not a straight-forward setting of the mass.

BIZET, Georges (1838–75)

Bizet failed to complete many of his works, and among the incomplete essays are many choral works, cantatas and smaller pieces. His *Te Deum* of 1858 is youthful and melodically rather naive, but has gained a certain popularity recently. The cantata which won the Prix de Rome in 1857 is unfortunately lost. Concert performances of Bizet's famous opera *Carmen* (1875) provide the chorus with plenty to sing, although some editions play havoc with the story line!

BLISS, Arthur (1891–1975)

Arthur Bliss succeeded Bax as Master of the Queen's Musick in 1953. He began his composing career as an *enfant terrible*, but his music mellowed over the ensuing years. The *Pastoral: Lie strewn the white flocks* (1928) was his first choral work with orchestra (two flutes, timpani and strings only) and is written in an engaging melodic style. *Morning Heroes* (1930) is a grander piece scored for reciter, chorus and orchestra; it was Bliss's response to the effects of war, and was written as a tribute to his brother and those who fell in World War I. It is a setting of a variety of disparate texts, including poems by Walt Whitman, and *Spring Offensive* by Wilfred Owen. *The Beatitudes* for soprano, tenor, chorus and orchestra, was written in 1962 for performance at Coventry Cathedral, and deserves to be better known. *The Golden Cantata* (1964) is scored for tenor, chorus and orchestra, but *The world is charged with the grandeur of God* (1969), a setting of three Hopkins poems, written at the request of Peter Pears, is for chorus, two flutes and brass only. *The Shield of Faith* (1974) is for chorus and organ.

BRAHMS, Johannes (1833–97)

The mighty *German Requiem** of Brahms has overshadowed his other works for chorus and orchestra. The requiem was first performed complete in 1869. It is not a setting of the Latin text, but words from the Lutheran Bible. Two other works which are frequently performed are the *Alto Rhapsody* (1869), on a text by Goethe, for alto soloist, male chorus and orchestra, and the *Schiksalslied* (Song of Destiny*), on a text by Hölderlin, composed in 1871 for chorus and orchestra. The cantata *Rinaldo* (1869) for tenor, male chorus and orchestra, *Triumphlied* (1872) and *Nänie* (1881), both for chorus and orchestra, and the *Gesang der Parzen* (Song of the Fates (1883)) are less frequently heard but equally impressive.

Brahms also wrote a considerable number of part-songs: the *Liebeslieder* and *Neue Liebeslieder Waltzer* (with piano accompaniment) are justly popular; the four songs for female voices, two horns and harp (op. 17) represent Brahms at his most romantic, as does the *Geistliches Lied* for voices and organ. Other works include unaccompanied songs and motets for female or mixed voices, of which the motets opus 29 and 74 and the *Fest-und Gedenksprüche* (Festival and Commemoration Sentences), a set of three songs for eight-part chorus, are perhaps the strongest. Brahms also wrote *Deutsche Volkslieder* which are four-part settings of folk tunes, two sets of *Lieder* for chorus, two sets of *Lieder* for chorus, two sets of *Lieder und Romanzen*, and the *Marienlieder* ('Song of Mary').

BRIDGE, Frank (1879–1941)

Bridge was chiefly a composer of chamber and orchestral music, but a few of his choral works are worthy of revival. *A Prayer* (1916) is a setting of words by St Thomas à Kempis, and has recently been commercially recorded. A larger work from the same year, *For God, King and Right*, is no longer in print. Bridge composed a few part songs, five of which have been published, together with a few lighter pieces for two- and three-part womens' chorus.

BRITTEN, Benjamin (1913–76)

Although the majority of Britten's early works with opus numbers are instrumental, it was the growing body of choral works, songs, and (later) operas, which confirmed his stature as one of Britain's great composers. Choral works do, however, appear among his first published works, including *A Boy was Born*, a masterly set of variations on an original theme, written in 1933. The earlier *Hymn to the Virgin* was written when Britten was only seventeen. Other works from these early years include the set of songs *Friday afternoons* (1933–35) written for the school where his brother taught, and a few other miscellaneous part-songs (without opus numbers).

During the period of his friendship with W. H. Auden and his circle, Britten wrote a number of works which have now slipped from the repertory, including *Ballad of Heroes* (1939) for tenor, chorus and orchestra, with words by Auden. Auden also provided the poem for the well known *Hymn to St Cecilia* (1942) for unaccompanied choir. The popular *Ceremony of Carols* for treble voices was first heard in 1942 at Norwich Castle. It has subsequently been arrranged for mixed choir, by Julius Harrison; both versions can be accompanied by harp or piano.

Rejoice in the Lamb (1943), like the *Hymn to St Cecilia*, falls into short movements; it is scored for four soloists, chorus and organ, but there is also a version for small orchestra by Imogen Holst. The poem, written by Christopher Smart, is neatly and succinctly conveyed by Britten in some of his most inventive music. The secular cantata *St Nicolas** was written for the centenary of Lancing College in 1948, but first performed at Aldeburgh. In the following year, Britten composed the *Spring Symphony**, which was given its first performance in Amsterdam, under van Beinum. Both works have established themselves in the regular choral repertory, particularly *St Nicolas*, which is scored for more modest forces. The *Five Flower Songs* for unaccompanied choir were written in 1950 as a twenty-fifth wedding anniversary present; they make a very satisfying set of contrasting pieces, as do the *Choral Dances* arranged by the composer from his opera *Gloriana*.

In response to a commission from Basle University, Britten composed his *Cantata Academica** in 1959, a setting of Latin texts from the charter of the university, and other orations. Another occasional piece was the *War Requiem**, written for the opening of the newly built cathedral at Coventry in 1962. In this magnificent work, Britten followed an example set by Vaughan Williams in his *Dona nobis pacem**: Vaughan Williams juxtaposed war poems by Walt Whitman with Latin words from the requiem mass, and Britten sets the entire *missa pro defunctis* (requiem mass) together with poems by the war poet Wilfred Owen. This gigantic work is a towering and moving achievement.

The *Cantata Misericordia** for tenor, baritone, chorus and small orchestra is a setting in Latin of the story of the Good Samaritan; this is a particularly apt text as the work, first performed in Geneva in 1963, was written for the centenary celebrations of the Red Cross. *The Golden Vanity* (1966), a vaudeville, was written for the Vienna Boys' Choir, and is one of a number of works Britten wrote for children's choirs. *The Children's Crusade* (1968) was composed for the Wandsworth School Choir with whom Britten had a thriving working relationship; it is a very dissonant setting of the poem by Brecht, in a translation by Hans Keller. It was written for the fiftieth anniversary of the Save the Children Fund, and was premiered at St Paul's Cathedral in 1969.

Britten's last two choral works were *Sacred and Profane* (1975), settings of medieval texts composed for the Wilbye Consort, and another work for children, the *Welcome Ode* (1976). An earlier work written for schools was *Psalm 150* (1962), and among Britten's other sacred works is the *Missa Brevis* for unbroken voices, specially composed for Westminster Cathedral in 1959. Britten also composed two settings of the *Te Deum* (1936 and 1944), the *Hymn to St Peter* (1955), *Antiphon* (1956) and *Jubilate* (1961), all with organ accompaniment. Of his secular works in a lighter vein, *The Ballad of Little Musgrave and Lady Barnard* for male voices and piano is brilliantly witty.

BRUCKNER, *Anton (1824–96)*

Bruckner was a devout Roman Catholic and the music he wrote for the church in the early stages of his career is an important part of his output: themes from these sacred pieces subsequently appeared in his symphonies. The three numbered settings of the mass pre-date the most important symphonies, and were written while he was organist at Linz Cathedral (before 1868). There are a number of early unnumbered masses (some of which are unpublished) and two settings of the requiem: one for male voices and organ, and one for four soloists, mixed chorus and orchestra (1849).

The three numbered masses are great choral works and all but the first hold a secure place in the repertory today. The D minor mass (no. 1) has been overshadowed by the second mass, in E minor, which has all the harmonic and chromatic excitement of the best of the motets. This mass is scored for choir and wind band, and was first performed in 1869 outside Linz Cathedral. Like Liszt and Gounod, Bruckner was trying to emulate the music of Palestrina, and the E minor mass is his most concentrated essay in this mould. The third mass, in F minor, is a fully symphonic affair for soloists, chorus and orchestra; it was composed in 1868, but subsequently revised.

Two later works composed by Bruckner, the *Te Deum* (1884) and a setting of *Psalm 150* (1892), were not intended for church performance. Both works are short (about twenty minutes each), and were written at the same time as the seventh and ninth symphonies respectively. Soloists are required for the *Te Deum*, but not for *Psalm 150*.

Bruckner's motets, which are almost all available in a single volume, are short masterpieces which encapsulate the very essence of his harmonic writing. Some of them are accompanied by trombones and organ. A few secular pieces for male voices are not readily available.

BUXTEHUDE, Dietrich (1637–1707)

Buxtehude was appointed to the Marienkirche, Lubeck, at the age of 31, and such was the fame of his organ playing, that Bach walked over two hundred miles from Arnstadt to Lübeck to hear him play! Also celebrated were the evening concerts (Abendmusiken) which Buxtehude presented annually, and for which he wrote many of his choral works. Buxtehude's music points the way to Bach: his cantatas are obvious precursors to Bach's great series, but they are shorter, being made up of briefer sections. His most typical and attractive works include *Alles was ihr tut, Jesu meine Freude* and a setting of the *Magnificat*. His *Missa Brevis* is written in the old style (in polyphony) and consists of Kyrie and Gloria only.

BYRD, William (1543–1623)

William Byrd remained a Roman Catholic even after the Reformation. With Thomas Tallis he was both joint organist of the Chapel Royal, and joint holder of the monopoly of music printing, which was granted to them by Elizabeth I in 1575. Byrd wrote works in English and Latin, mostly in a complex and highly charged polyphonic style.

Byrd's works include madrigals and three mass settings for three, four, and five voices respectively, which were probably written in the 1590s. A book of *Cantiones sacrae* including works by Tallis and Byrd appeared in 1575; two further books were published by Byrd alone in 1589 and 1591. Settings of texts for use in the mass were published with the title *Gradualia* in 1605 and 1607, and Byrd's final volume of *Psalmes, Songs and Sonnets* appeared in 1611.

CARISSIMI, Giacomo (1605–74)

Carissimi was the first composer of oratorios. The very first work which may be called an oratorio was in fact Cavalieri's sacred opera *La Rappresentazione di anima e di corpo* (1600), which was written in Italian, but Carissimi's oratorios were written in Latin, and take subjects from the Old Testament.

The words, however, were of foremost importance and Carissimi preferred arioso to recitative or aria. Carissimi's oratorios have no set pattern, but are in one continuous movement, divided into short sections, which speed the drama along. The chorus sometimes takes the role of narrator, and sometimes takes part in the action. *Jephtha**, written before 1650, is Carissimi's best oratorio; others include *Jonah,* and *The Judgement of Solomon.* Carissimi also wrote masses and motets, some in an old-fashioned style, including the last known setting based on the tune *L'homme armé.*

CHARPENTIER, Marc-Antoine (c. 1645–1704)

Charpentier studied with Carissimi in Rome, and like his master wrote oratorios in Latin for concerts of sacred music. His oratorios include *Judith** and *The Judgement of Solomon.* Other sacred music written for church performance includes the famous *Te Deum*, a *Magnificat*, and various motets. Charpentier's *Messe de minuit* for performance on Christmas Eve sets the Latin mass to the tunes of old French carols.

CHERUBINI, Luigi (1760–1842)

Cherubini was an important figure in his day and remained a popular composer well into the nineteenth century. Beethoven admired him, and as director of the Paris *conservatoire* he influenced many composers, including the young Berlioz, with whom he was in frequent disagreement. Cherubini's two settings of the requiem are still performed today; the first is in C minor for mixed chorus, soloists and orchestra, and the second is for male voices only (with orchestra) and was composed in 1836. The four mass settings are rarely performed, but deserve revival and are at present being commercially recorded. Cherubini's music lacks the breadth of Beethoven's, and is cast in a classical, rather than a romantic mould.

COLERIDGE-TAYLOR, Samuel (1875–1912)

Coleridge-Taylor was only 23 when his cantata *Hiawatha's Wedding Feast** brought him spectacular and lasting success. Over the next few years he wrote two further settings of excerpts from Longfellow's poem, *The Death of Minnehaha* (1899), which is the slow movement of the trilogy, and *Hiawatha's Departure* (1900), the longest and least successful. His other cantatas have not remained in the repertory, but were very popular in their day. As with so much choral music of this period, the words and sentiments of the cantatas prove to be the greatest stumbling block to their general acceptance by a modern audience.

Other works include *The Blind Girl of Castél-Cuillé* (1901) – another Longfellow setting, the sacred cantata *The Atonement* (1903, Hereford), a setting of Samuel Taylor Coleridge's poem *Kubla Khan* (1906), *Endymion's Dream* (1910), *A Bon-bon Suite* (1909), and *A Tale of Old Japan* (1911). Five choral ballads for choir and piano (or orchestra) (1904) are further settings of Longfellow, and are written in a pleasant, 'drawing-room' style. Coleridge-Taylor's part-songs have disappeared from the repertory, and have been out of print for many years, but his setting of the *Morning and Evening Service in F* (1899) is sometimes performed.

COPLAND, Aaron (b. 1900)

Copland's *In the beginning* (1947) is one of the best unaccompanied twentieth-century works in the choral repertoire; it describes the creation in words taken from Genesis, and lasts about 17'. Other works include *Lark* (1938), for unaccompanied choir with baritone soloists, and *Las Agachadas* (1942), for unaccompanied chorus.

DALLAPICCOLA, Luigi (1904–75)

Dallapiccola's music in the 1930s followed the then-current trend for neo-classicism, but gradually Dallapiccola evolved a more chromatic style and by 1942 had adopted the twelve-note system. Before that he had written the passionate *Canti di prigionia** (1941), and the more traditional settings of sonnets by Michelangelo. Dallapiccola expressed his views on freedom in a later opera *Il Prigioniero*, and the choral *Canti di Liberazione** (1955); these works, together with the terse *Tempus destruendi – Tempus aedificandi* (1971) are written in a controlled but highly dissonant and individual idiom.

DAVIES, Peter Maxwell (b. 1934)

Peter Maxwell Davies studied music in Manchester at the same time as Harrison Birtwistle and Alexander Goehr. Together these three composers have become known as the 'Manchester school'. Maxwell Davies taught at various schools, including Cirencester Grammar from 1959 to 1962, and he attracted attention by his adventurous music making. Many of his works betray his interest in serialism (the twelve note technique), numerology and medieval music.

One of the first pieces to bring Maxwell Davies to public attention was the Christmas choral sequence *O magnum mysterium* (1960), written for Cirencester Grammar, and since then he has written a number of works for choirs, including many carols. His output is growing steadily and incorporates such diverse works as *Westerlings* (1976), a bravura piece for unaccompanied choir, *Solstice of Light* (1979) for amateur choir, but with a very difficult tenor solo and organ accompaniment, as well as a number of pieces for children. The latter include *Songs of Hoy* (1982) and *The Shepherd's Calendar** (1975), and operas for performance in schools. Many of Maxwell Davies's works have been specially written for performance at the St Magnus Festival in Orkney.

DEBUSSY, Claude (1862–1918)

Debussy's only published work for unaccompanied choir is *Trois Chansons de Charles d'Orléans,* which he completed in 1908. His large scale works for voices and orchestra include *L'enfant prodigue* (1884), with which he won the Prix de Rome, and *La damoiselle élue** (1888), which is for female chorus with soprano and mezzo soloists. His incidental music to the stage work based on D'Annunzio's play *The Martyrdom of St Sebastian** (1911) includes movements for chorus and orchestra.

DELIUS, Frederick (1862–1934)

Delius wrote music in almost every form (except symphonies) and his choral works are a significant part of his oeuvre. The first choral work to remain firmly in the repertory is *Appalachia* (1898–1903); this piece and most of his subsequent choral compositions have been recorded commercially, although they do not feature regularly in live concerts.

Sea Drift* (1903–4) sets a poem by Walt Whitman, and is scored for baritone, chorus and orchestra. Like most of Delius's scores, the orchestration is very heavy, and only by reducing the dynamic markings (or perhaps using editions prepared by Beecham) will the soloists and chorus be heard clearly. The gigantic *A Mass of Life** is not a liturgical work, but a setting of texts by Nietszche, in German, for four soloists, double chorus and an enor-

mous orchestra; it was first performed in English under Beecham in 1909.

Delius composed his *Songs of Sunset* between 1906 and 1907 for mezzo-soprano, baritone, chorus and orchestra; the poems are by Dowson, the friend of the composer Cyril Scott. Two choral works, both written in 1911, are *An Arabesk* for baritone, chorus and orchestra, and *The Song of the High Hills,* for wordless chorus and orchestra. Delius's non-liturgical *Requiem,* a short piece for soprano, baritone, chorus and orchestra, consists of settings of H. Simons: it is dedicated to the memory of all young artists who fell in the First World War.

One of Delius's final works, the *Songs of Farewell** (1930) for double choir and orchestra, was dictated to his amanuensis Eric Fenby. Delius also composed a number of short unaccompanied works and part-songs, most notably *On Craig Ddhu, The splendour falls on castle walls* (Tennyson), and the textless *Songs to be sung of a summer night on the water.*

DONIZETTI, Gaetano (1797–1848)

Like Rossini, Bellini and Verdi, Donizetti wrote sacred works in an operatic style. Most notable amongst Donizetti's numerous sacred works is the requiem written to commemorate the death of Bellini (1835); the solo writing is in the best *bel canto* tradition, but the choral sections are hardly distinguished, and include statutory, but pedestrian, fugues. The list of Donizetti's sacred and secular works is enormous, but most of it remains unpublished.

DUFAY, Guillaume (c. 1400–74)

The Franco-Flemish composer Dufay was one of the most significant composers of the fifteenth century. He worked for a time in Italy but finally settled in Cambrai. His works include settings of the mass which throughout his career show a changing approach to composition. In the later masses Dufay gives musical unity to the composition not merely by the use of the same cantus firmus in each movement, but also by using the same head motif to start each movement. One of Dufay's masses is based on the secular tune *L'Homme armé*.

Dufay also composed motets and chansons which show a dramatic development in style pointing the way to the Renaissance.

DUNSTABLE, John
(c. 1380–1453)
The English composer Dunstable was also a mathematician and astronomer. His fame seems to have spread abroad, as many of his works appear in continental manuscripts. Like Dufay, Dunstable's music bridges the gap between the Medieval period and the Renaissance. Of the 50 or so works credited to Dunstable, two complete mass settings are among the first examples in which musical material is shared by the movements, giving them musical unity.

Dunstable's motets are complex works, generally written for a number of voices each with their own words, and often organized in strict rhythmic patterns. English music of the early fifteenth century was noted for its use of thirds and fifths, making common chords, and Dunstable's music is typical of this English style.

DURUFLÉ, Maurice (1902–1986)
Duruflé's output is very small but includes several choral works which are frequently performed: the four *Motets on Plainsong Melodies* (1960), and the *Requiem* (1947), which is available in versions for organ or orchestral accompaniment. The *Requiem* bears a family resemblance to Fauré's *Requiem* as both works call for soprano and baritone soloists (who incidentally sing exactly the same portions in each work). Another mass, *Cum jubilo* (1966) is scored for baritone soloist and male voice choir with orchestra (or organ).

DVOŘÁK, Antonín (1841–1904)
Dvořák was one of the many nineteenth-century composers who visited England and wrote choral works for performance there; a number of his pieces were translated into English and published by Novello and Co.

A short piece which is seldom heard and little known outside Czechoslovakia is the *Hymnus: The heirs of the white mountain*, composed for chorus and orchestra in 1873. However, Dvořák's setting of the *Stabat Mater* (1880) was popular in Victorian and Edwardian England, although it is not so frequently performed nowadays; it is a fine work, containing many beautiful passages. His other sacred works include the *Mass in D* originally written for soloists, choir and organ (1887) for local performance, but later scored for full orchestra and published in London in 1893. Dvořák's *Requiem* was composed on a grand scale for performance in Birmingham in 1891.

Two works on Czech subjects by Dvořák have now slipped from the repertory, the secular cantata *The Spectre's Bride* (1885), and the oratorio *St Ludmilla*, which was given its first English performance in Leeds in 1886. Both of these works are worthy of revival.

Dvořák took up his appointment as director of the National Conservatory of Music in New York in 1892, and specifically for America wrote a *Te Deum* (1892) for soprano, baritone and chorus, and the cantata *The American Flag* (1895).

He composed a number of part-songs throughout his life including a few for male voices only. The *Songs of Nature* for mixed voices (1882) are the most charming and popular.

DYSON, *George (1883–1964)*

Dyson's name is familiar to church musicians who regularly perform his settings of the Magnificat and Nunc Dimittis. His cantata *The Canterbury Pilgrims*, based on Chaucer (in a modern translation), was first performed in 1931 at Winchester, where Dyson was director of music at Winchester College – it was once very popular, and is well worth reviving. His other works include *In honour of the City of London* (1928) (a text also set by Walton), *St Paul's Voyage to Melita* (Hereford, 1933), *Quo Vadis?* (Hereford, Part One 1939, Part Two 1949), and *Nebuchadnezzar* (Worcester, 1935) – written after Walton's *Belshazzar's Feast**, in apparent imitation.

The hauntingly beautiful *Hierusalem* (1956), a setting of a sixteenth-century poem for soprano solo, mixed chorus and strings, with optional harp and organ, has recently been revived.

ELGAR, *Edward (1857–1934)*

Parry and Stanford were writing some of their best choral music when Elgar, self-taught and in his thirties, began composing large-scale cantatas in the same mould: *The Black Knight* (1892), *The Light of Life* (1896), *King Olaf* (1896), *The Banner of St George* (1897) and *Caractacus* (1898). The subject matter and texts of some of these works make them barely palatable today, while the patriotic fervour of much of the music hardly compares with that of Elgar's next choral work, *The Dream of Gerontius**. The earlier works may be derivative, but Elgar found his own voice in two works of 1899: the song cycle *Sea Pictures* and the orchestral *Enigma Variations*.

The Dream of Gerontius was heard in 1900. It was first performed under Hans Richter in Birmingham but the performance was shaky and ineffective; only when the work achieved success in Germany two years later, attracting the attention of Richard Strauss, did it begin to establish itself in England. Two other oratorios followed, *The Apostles** (1903) and *The Kingdom** (1906) which were part of a projected, but never completed, trilogy on biblical texts. In 1912 Elgar made a setting of O'Shaughnessy's poem *The Music Makers**; he quotes from his own music in it, as well as from the *Marseillaise* and *Rule Britannia*.

Recent commercial recordings of the *Coronation Ode** (1902, but revised in 1911 to include the *Pomp and Circumstance* march tune 'Land of Hope and Glory') and *The Spirit of England** have confirmed that these are both rather patriotic, overblown works. However the latter (in three sections, *The Fourth of August* (1917), *To Women* (1915) and *For the Fallen* (1915)) certainly contains some impressive music.

Elgar's smaller choral pieces include two psalm settings: *Psalm 29, Great is the Lord*, scored for organ or orchestra, and *Psalm 48* for baritone, chorus and organ. An earlier *Te Deum and Benedictus* (1897) were subsequently orchestrated, and short pieces include a lovely *Ave Verum* and various anthems. Elgar also composed secular choral music, often in a lighter vein; his best known work in this genre is probably *From the Bavarian Highlands* (1895) for chorus and piano or orchestra (three were later arranged for orchestra alone). His partsongs are some of the best examples of their kind, particularly the op. 53 and 71 sets.

FAURÉ, *Gabriel (1845–1924)*

One of the most poignant settings of the requiem mass was written by

Fauré, in 1877, and is scored for small orchestra, chorus, and soprano and baritone soloists. Fauré does not set the colourful text of the *Dies Irae*, but instead concentrates on a subdued setting of reflective words, including the final *In Paradisum*. Another mass, the *Messe Basse* (without a *Gloria* or *Credo*) for female voices and harmonium (or organ) dates from 1881, and the short *Cantique de Jean Racine*, for chorus and organ, was written in 1865. Fauré composed various Marian anthems (*Ave Maria*, etc.) and other pieces for church use. His secular works include a *Madrigal* (1883) for chorus and orchestra (or solo voices and piano).

FINZI, Gerald (1901–56)

Finzi's output was not extensive, and most of it is now available on commercial discs. He was not only successful with smaller pieces, including his songs, but was quite brilliant on a larger scale. The *Cello Concerto* (1955) confirms this, as does the cantata, *Intimations of Immortality*, a setting of stanzas from Wordsworth's poem for tenor, chorus and orchestra (revised 1950). Other large choral works are *For St Cecilia* (1947), a ceremonial ode for tenor, chorus and orchestra, and *In Terra Pax* (1954) written to words by Bridges. This short Christmas cantata was originally written for string orchestra with soprano and baritone soloists, harp and cymbals, but was subsequently re-orchestrated in 1956. Other choral pieces which Finzi wrote for organ accompaniment but later orchestrated are *Lo', the full final sacrifice* (1946) and *Magnificat* (1952).

Unaccompanied works by Finzi include seven part-songs to poems by Bridges (1934–7) and *White flowering days*, written in 1953 as part of *A Garland for the Queen**. The anthem *God is gone up* is the second of *Three Anthems* (1948–53) for choir and organ.

FRANCK, César (1822–90)

Franck's oratorio *The Beatitudes* is a large scale work for soloists, chorus and orchestra, and a BBC studio recording a few years ago confirmed the view that it is a major piece and deserves more performances. The earlier *Redemption** was described by the composer as a 'poème symphonique' and is scored for female voices, speaker and orchestra; however nowadays only the orchestral portion of this work is performed. Two other biblical scenes, *Ruth* and *Rebecca*, are not known today, and neither is the cantata *Le tour de Babel*. An early mass setting for three voices was popular in Franck's lifetime.

FRICKER, Peter Racine (b. 1920)

Fricker was commissioned in 1958 to write a large choral work to celebrate the centenary of the Leeds Triennial Festival. The work was *The Vision of Judgement* to words by the eighth-century poet Cynewulf. This enormous score, with extra brass players augmenting the symphony orchestra, has not yet achieved the success it deserves; it is an obvious successor to Walton's *Belshazzar's Feast**, but is written in a less overtly popular style.

Smaller works for chorus are *Rollant et Oliver* (1949), *Ave Maris Stella* (1967), for tenor, male voices and piano, and various madrigals and motets. There is also a setting of the *Magnificat* (1968) for soloists, chorus and orchestra.

GABRIELI, Giovanni (1557–1612)

Gabrieli's earliest works were in the polyphonic style of his uncle and teacher, Andrea Gabrieli (*c.* 1510–86), whom he succeeded as organist of St Mark's in Venice. St Mark's boasted a large choir and Gabrieli became interested more in contrast than polyphony; he wrote works for various choirs spaced apart (*cori spezzati*) in the galleries of the church, accompanied by brass instruments. In these works he provided contrast in the size of the choirs, in pitch (choir one may use higher voices than choir two), and by writing sections for solo voices. Gabrieli was also influenced by opera and madrigal composers who concentrated on word painting. One of his most notable motets is *In Ecclesiis* for two choirs (one full, and one made up of soloists), brass ensemble and organ; solo passages are punctuated by full ensemble alleluias. Gabrieli taught the German composer Heinrich Schütz.

GESUALDO, Carlo (c. 1560–1615)

The scandal of the murder of Gesualdo's first wife and her lover in 1590 has coloured our view of Gesualdo the composer. Not all of his music is harmonically daring, but a number of his madrigals push harmony to the extremes of chromaticism. His sacred music (much of it written to atone for his misdeed) is rarely as outrageous and is notable for its restraint and beauty.

GIBBONS, Orlando (1583–1625)

Gibbons was a boy chorister at Kings, Cambridge, and became organist at the Chapel Royal in 1598, remaining in the post until his death. He graduated in music from both Oxford and Cambridge, and took a doctorate at Oxford in 1602. In 1623 he became organist at Westminster Abbey.

Gibbons wrote both anthems and madrigals, and his collection of the latter includes the famous madrigal, *The Silver Swan*. This is typical of Gibbons's work and more closely related to solo song than to the polyphonic Italian madrigal. His anthems range from those in the older polyphonic style, such as *O clap your hands* and *Hosanna to the song of David*, to the newer accompanied verse anthems, of which *This is the record of John* is the most famous.

GOUNOD, Charles (1818–93)

Gounod's *St Cecilia Mass* was once very popular, and there is every indication that it is once more entering the regular repertory. Most of his other sacred music is still forgotten, including his many mass settings (he wrote as many masses as he did operas); some of these are full scale orchestral affairs, while others are for unaccompanied choir. His *Requiem* (1895)[1] was his last work. Throughout his life, Gounod considered taking holy orders, but he never did so.

Gounod's oratorios and cantatas were much performed in Victorian England, where their pious style suited the taste of a public who welcomed many famous foreign composers to these shores. Gounod's motet *Gallia* was written for the opening of the London International Exposition in 1871, and his oratorio *The Redemption** was first heard in Birmingham in 1882; *Mors et Vita* was also given there in 1885. *The Redemption* was dedicated to Queen Victoria and contains much excellent music, although it is arguable that the one seminal theme which runs throughout the work is not strong enough to sustain interest. Perhaps professional performances of Gounod's oratorios will convince us that they are worthy of revival. His many part-songs, both sacred and secular, have also fallen out of favour although some of the sacred songs for solo voice (such as *Nazareth*) are still heard.

GRIEG, Edvard (1843–1907)

At least one short piece of choral music

[1] Edited and published after his death by H. Büsser.

by Grieg deserves to be better known, *Landkjending* (Land-sighting), written in 1872 (but subsequently revised) for baritone, male chorus and orchestra. This short work is most impressive. Grieg's incidental music to *Peer Gynt* (1875), *Sigurd Jorsalfar* (1872) and *Szenen aus Olav Trygvason* (1906) all include choral items. Most of his unaccompanied choral works are for male voices, but there are four psalm settings (1906) for baritone and mixed chorus.

HADLEY, Patrick (1899–1973)
After being taught at the Royal College of Music by Vaughan Williams and Adrian Boult, Hadley joined the teaching staff there, and later became a lecturer and subsequently Professor of Music at Cambridge (1938). His small output of compositions includes the popular anthem *My beloved spake*, as well as three large scale choral pieces – the symphonic ballad *The Trees so High* (1931) with baritone soloists, the cantata *La belle dame sans merci* to Keats's poem (1935) with tenor soloist, and *The Hills* (1944) to his own words, scored for soprano, tenor, and chorus – all with full orchestra.

HANDEL, George Frederic (1685–1759)
Unlike Bach, who was born in the same year, Handel did not stay in his native Germany, but travelled first to Italy and later to England, where he eventually took up residence and became naturalized in 1726. As a young man Handel worked in Hamburg as a composer of operas, although he also wrote a number of German cantatas and other sacred works, including a setting of the Passion on a text by Brockes (1716) at the same period. His trip to Italy in 1706 brought Handel in contact with the agile, florid music being written by composers working in Naples, Florence, Venice and Rome. Handel wrote

a number of pieces which show this Italian influence, including *Dixit Dominus* and *Nisi Dominus*, both written in Rome in 1707; (these form part of a recently reconstructed Vespers).

Handel became Kapellmeister to the Elector of Hanover in 1710 and visited England for the first time in that year. He returned to England in 1711 and stayed there, becoming court composer to Queen Anne, George I (his old patron, the Elector of Hanover) and George II. For royal and special occasions he composed four coronation anthems for George II in 1727, and also odes for the birthday of Queen Anne (1713 or 1714), an *Ode for St Cecilia's Day** (1739), the eleven Chandos Anthems* (1717–18) for James Brydges, the Duke of Chandos, the Foundling Hospital anthem (1749), the funeral anthem for Queen Caroline *The Ways of Zion do mourn* (1737), and festive pieces such as the *Utrecht Te Deum and Jubilate* (1713) and the *Dettingen Te Deum and Jubilate* of 1743.

Handel's success in London as an opera composer began to wane as the public became less enamoured of this Italian entertainment. When he produced *Haman and Mordecai* in 1732 as a concert piece with the title *Esther**, English oratorio was born. In a succession of similar works from *Esther* to *Jephtha** (1752) Handel became again the most popular and successful composer working in the capital. The oratorios written after *Esther* were: *Deborah* (1733), *Athalia* (1733), *Alexander's Feast** (1736), *Saul** (1739), *Israel in Egypt** (1739), *L'Allegro ed Il Penseroso** (1740), *Messiah** (1741), *Samson** (1743), *Semele** (1744), *Joseph and his brethren* (1744), *Hercules* (1745), *Belshazzar** (1745), *Occasional Oratorio** (1746), *Judas Maccabaeus** (1747), *Joshua** (1748), *Alexander Balus** (1749), *Susanna* (1749), *Solomon** (1749), *Theodora* (1750), *The Choice of Hercules*

(1751), and *Jephtha** (1752). Another oratorio, *The Triumph of Time and Truth*, which was performed in 1757, was a re-working of an earlier Italian oratorio.

HARRIS, Roy (1898–1979)

Harris's early music is dissonant and austere, but his musical language mellowed as he came under the influence of folk music. While teaching at Westminster Choir School he composed his *Symphony for Voices* (1935) to poems by Whitman – a deeply satisfying and well-wrought composition. The folk song influence is prominent in his fourth symphony (1940) – a *Folksong Symphony* for chorus and orchestra – and the *Folk Fantasy for Festivals* (1956) for chorus and piano which includes parts for folk singers.

HAYDN, Joseph (1732–1809)

Haydn earned for himself the title of 'father of the symphony' and it is his orchestral and chamber works which form the main part of his output. However, of his twelve settings of the mass, six date from the period 1796–1802 and are among the outstanding achievements of his maturity, together with the oratorios *The Creation** (1798) and *The Seasons** (1801). These two works were both inspired by performances Haydn heard in England of Handel's oratorios, and both were premiered in Vienna.

Of Haydn's mass settings, the early *Nicolaimesse* (1772) is one of the most charming, while the *Saint Cecilia Mass* (1766) is a cantata mass, that is, a mass which is divided into short movements. The final six masses, all written in a through-composed symphonic style, include the justly popular *Nelson Mass** (1798), the *Paukenmesse** (1796) and one of Haydn's last works, the *Harmoniemesse** (1802).

Haydn's other choral works include an early oratorio, *Il Ritorno di Tobia* (The return of Tobias), which consists in the main of a sequence of arias, but also contains the chorus generally taken out of context and given new words – *Insanae et vanae curae*. He also made a setting of the *Stabat Mater* (1767), three settings of the *Salve Regina*, and two settings of the *Te Deum* (the second, in C, in 1800), together with about twenty other miscellaneous sacred works, various secular pieces and part songs. His *Seven last words** was originally written for orchestra, and later turned into a choral work with words by Baron van Swieten (1796).

HENZE, Hans Werner (b. 1926)

One of the most successful and prolific composers of his generation, Henze has written music in many different mediums. Vocal music forms a major part of his output and includes *Five Madrigals* to poems by Villon composed in 1947 for chorus and eleven instruments, *The Muses of Sicily* (1966) and other cantatas, and the requiem for Che Guevara *Das Floss der Medusa*, which received a stormy reception in 1968. A recent choral work for unaccompanied choir *Orpheus behind the wire* was written in 1984.

HINDEMITH, Paul (1895–1963)

Hindemith was a notable teacher, conductor and theorist as well as being a very fluent composer; he could play every instrument of the orchestra and he composed a sonata for each of them. During the 1920s he wrote many works for children and amateur players and singers; the term 'Gebrauchsmusik' (music for use) embraces these works, which are written in an approachable style.

But not all of Hindemith's works

had to be functional, and his later composition needed no such justification. The *Requiem: When lilacs last in the door-yard bloom'd* (1946) is a setting of Walt Whitman poems and was written to a commission from Robert Shaw and the Collegiate Chorale, following Hindemith's move to America in 1940. It is written in a 'romantic' style, although he would not have used this description himself. A choral piece which is in a more gritty mood is his *Apparebit repentina dies* (1947), a setting of a medieval Latin text for chorus and brass.

Hindemith also wrote other cantatas and oratorios including *Das Unaufhörliche* (1931), a number of unaccompanied motets and madrigals, the *Six Chansons* (1939) to poems by Rilke, and works for male and female choirs. His difficult unaccompanied setting of the *Mass* dates from 1963; it was his last composition.

HOLST, Gustav (1874–1934)

Holst's orchestral suite *The Planets* is one of the most popular orchestral works in the repertory; in the final movement, *Neptune, the mystic*, a wordless female chorus helps to establish an ethereal mood, eventually fading into the distance, unaccompanied. One choral work by Holst, *The Hymn of Jesus** (1917) has achieved a great success; it is an evocative work scored for double choir, semi-chorus and orchestra. Holst's masterly setting of Whitman's *Ode to Death* was premiered at the Leeds Festival in 1922, but has not been regularly heard since. Neither the *First Choral Symphony* (1924) (there is no second) to poems by Keats, nor the short *Choral Fantasia* for soprano, chorus and small orchestra, which is a setting of a Bridges poem, are often performed.

Of Holst's other works for choir and instruments, *King Estmere* (1903), an early work, was given its first broadcast performance in 1983 conducted by Norman Del Mar. *The Cloud Messenger* for chorus and orchestra is rarely performed. Holst also set Eastern texts in his own translations, four sets of *Hymns from the Rig Veda*; the first set for chorus and orchestra, the second for female voices and orchestra, the third for female voices and harp, and the fourth for male voices, brass, percussion and strings. Holst wrote various part-songs, carols and anthems with instrumental accompaniment, including another Whitman setting, the *Dirge for two veterans* (1914) for male voices, brass and percussion. Of his many unaccompanied choral works *This have I done for my true love* (1916) and *The Evening Watch* (1924) are notable, and his folk song arrangements include the well known set of *Six Choral Folk Songs* (1916).

HONEGGER, Arthur (1892–1955)

Honegger was born of Swiss parents in Le Havre, France. He became a member of the group of French composers known as *Les Six*, but always cultivated his own style. The dramatic oratorio *Le Roi David** (1921) is a stirring, episodic work for narrator, soprano, mezzo-soprano and tenor soloists, chorus and fifteen players, although it was later re-orchestrated for full orchestra. Another work which relies on narration is *Joan of Arc at the stake** (1938), a stage work more often performed as a concert cantata.

Honegger's *Christmas Cantata* (1953) is a rather engaging piece which makes use of traditional melodies, and the choir is augmented by a children's chorus. A piece which deserves a hearing is the rarely performed *Cantique de Cantiques* (1926) for chorus and full orchestra.

HOWELLS, Herbert
(1892–1983)

Howells's anthems and motets are frequently heard in churches throughout the country, together with his settings of the morning and evening services. His anthems include *A spotless rose* (1919), *My eyes for beauty pine* (1925), and *Like as the hart* (1941). His musical style did not radically alter during his lifetime, and is readily identifiable by its bittersweet harmony and melodic turns of phrase.

The *Requiem* (published 1981) for unaccompanied choir (a setting of various texts including psalm 23) dates from 1936, and represents the composer's first outpourings of grief on the death of his son, who died at the age of nine from spinal meningitis. Music from the *Requiem* was re-used in the large scale *Hymnus Paradisi** for soprano and tenor soloists, chorus and orchestra, which was first performed in 1950 at the Three Choirs Festival. Another large work, the *Missa Sabrinensis* (1954, first performed at Worcester) confirmed that Howells was not merely a miniaturist. Both works – particularly the mass – are vocally demanding but very rewarding.

Earlier secular cantatas written by Howells are more traditional in style: *Sir Patrick Spens* (1918) for baritone, chorus and orchestra, and *A Kent Yeoman's wooing song* (1935) for soprano, baritone, chorus and orchestra. Later works include an *English Mass* (1956) scored for chorus, organ and strings, which was written for liturgical use, and a *Stabat Mater* (1963), scored for tenor, chorus and orchestra. One of Howells's most moving works is the motet he wrote on the death of President Kennedy, *Take him earth for cherishing* (1964) – an inspired and poignant composition.

IRELAND, John (1879–1962)

Ireland was a pupil of Stanford. He wrote only one large-scale choral and orchestral piece, the impressive cantata *These things shall be* (1937), a setting of words by J. A. Symonds, with baritone soloist. The unaccompanied part song *The Hills* was Ireland's contribution to *A Garland for the Queen** (1953). His church music includes settings of the service, the popular anthem *Greater love* (1912) and an early *Vexilla Regis* (1898) for choir and brass.

IVES, Charles (1874–1954)

Charles Ives worked in insurance and was in the happy position of being able to pay for the publication of his own works. Although he was thoroughly trained in music and initially composed works in a traditional style, he quickly developed a revolutionary approach to composition in which he anticipated many devices of the twentieth-century *avant-garde*.

Ives composed numerous songs and choral pieces, many of the latter scored for unison voices and piano. The cantata *The Celestial Country* was composed in 1899, and is typical of Ives's eccentric but engaging style. Ives also set a number of psalms, and incorporates a chorus in his *Symphony no. 4* (1909–16).

JANÁČEK, Leoš (1854–1928)

In all his vocal works, Janáček made a particular effort to match his musical rhythms with those of the spoken language; he made a special study of folk song and speech. This fact makes it essential to perform Janáček's works in the vernacular, which has of course been a barrier to their wider acceptance.

Janáček's best known choral work is the *Glagolitic Mass** (1926); the text is in old church Slavonic (but available in a Latin version); the title of the work is taken from the old Slavonic alphabet. His other works for chorus and orchestra include the cantata *Amarus* (1897, but subsequently revised), and a shorter work, *Eternal Gospel* (1914). *Okěnaš* (1901), a setting of the Lord's Prayer, was written to accompany *tableaux vivants* representing a cycle of pictures by the Polish artist Josef Krzesz-Mecina, and is scored for chorus, harp and organ. Janáček's *Elegy on the death of my daughter Olga* is a poignant piece for choir and piano.

Janáček wrote many choruses for male voices to Moravian texts, and although short, a number of them, *Kantor Halfar* (1906), and *The Czech Legion* (1918) for example, are masterpieces. *The Wolf's Trail* (1916) for female voices and piano is a striking and dramatic piece, as is the unaccompanied *Kašpar Ruckỳ* (1916), also for female voices. *Říkadla* ('Nursery Rhymes') (1927) is a collection of eighteen pieces for two sopranos, two altos, three tenors and two basses with instrumental accompaniment. There are female voices in the otherwise solo cantata for tenor and piano, *The Diary of one who disappeared* (1917).

Janáček also wrote a number of sacred works. His *Mass in E flat* (1908) for voices and organ is incomplete, but performable as it stands.

JANNEQUIN, *Clément* (c. 1484–1558)

Jannequin was a French composer who worked at various cathedrals and royal chapels in France, but died a pauper under the impecunious Henry II. Jannequin's most notable compositions are his dramatic and programmatic chansons. These works are really quite extended and include the famous *La guerre*, which describes the battle of Marignan, and *Le chant des oiseaux*, a catalogue of birdsong; both pieces employ onomatopoeic word painting.

JOSQUIN DES PRES (c. 1440–1521)

Josquin was one of the greatest Franco-Flemish composers; he sang and worked at various times in Italy in the Papal chapel, but settled in Cambrai and died at Condé. He was a pupil of Ockeghem and composed music in a more expressive style than that of his immediate predecessors. Josquin's twenty mass settings are in a more conservative style, but became very popular; they were published by Petrucci, the first publisher of music.

Josquin wrote over one hundred motets which are notable for their expressive writing. In his secular music he paid particular attention to the text, and wrote in a free style in an attempt to be true to the poetry. In a letter written to the Duke of Ferrara (for whom Josquin worked) in 1499, the writer suggests that the Duke employ the composer Isaac (*c.* 1450–1517) instead of Josquin, but admits that 'Josquin composes better, but he does it when it suits him, and not when one wants him to'.

JOUBERT, *John (b. 1927)*

After winning Novello's anthem competition in 1952 with *O Lorde, the Maker of Al Thing*, Joubert sprang before the public as a leading composer of choral music. Since then he has written a large number of works for choir including the cantata *Urbs beata* (1963), the choral symphony *The Choir Invisible* (1968) and the oratorio *The Raising of Lazarus* (1971) – each scored for soloists, chorus and orchestra. Many of his other works are short and modestly scored; *The Holy Mountain* (1964) is a brief work for choir and two pianos written in a direct musical idiom characteristic of much of Joubert's writing. The motets *Pro Pace* (1956–9) for unaccompanied chorus are moving and impressive, while the carols *Torches* and *There is no rose* are perennial favourites. Joubert has also written secular music, including the ballad cantata

Leaves of Life for soloists, chorus and piano.

KODÁLY, Zoltán (1882–1967)

Kodály, and his contemporary Bartók, both made collections of Hungarian folk songs and absorbed folk music into their own compositions. Kodály wrote a large amount of music for amateur singers; many of these pieces are arrangements of folk melodies. He also developed his own system of teaching children, the Kodály method, which is something like our Tonic Sol-fa, with hand signals for each of the degrees of the scale. Kodály collected together graded pieces in volumes to help teach children this method of sight singing, the *Bicinia Hungarica*.

Among Kodály's works for unaccompanied mixed choir are the superb *Jesus and the traders*, and the extended *Hymn of Zrinyi* (1954) for baritone and mixed choir. There are also numerous songs for high voices and male voices, and a few works specifically written for children. Many of these are available in English, but the Hungarian speech rhythms cause problems of word stress in translation.

Two of Kodály's large scale choral and orchestral works are established in the repertory: the *Psalmus Hungaricus** (1923) with tenor soloists, and the *Missa Brevis**, written during the bombing of Budapest in 1945. This mass can also be performed in its original version for choir and organ only; there are short solos for three sopranos, alto, tenor and bass. The *Te Deum* (1936) for soloists, chorus and orchestra is not often heard, but is a solid and enjoyable piece. Kodály made a setting of O'Shaughnessy's poem *The Music Makers** for chorus and orchestra in 1964; it is not on the scale of Elgar's masterpiece.

LAMBERT, Constant (1905–51)

Rio Grande* was incredibly popular after its first performance in 1929, and seems to have returned to the repertory recently, but Lambert's other choral works are not frequently performed. The best-known, *Summer's Last Will and Testament* (1935) is a sombre piece, described as a masque, with words by Thomas Nashe, for baritone, chorus and orchestra.

LASSUS, Orlandus (1532–94)

Lassus had such a beautiful singing voice as a boy that he was three times kidnapped by rival choirs; he was a chorister at Mons, Rome and Antwerp, and finally employed as singer, then choirmaster, in Munich. Lassus was greatly honoured in his lifetime, and was the last and greatest of the line of Flemish composers of the Netherland school. He composed over two thousand works, including some sixty settings of the mass and almost six hundred motets. His secular works include French chansons, Italian madrigals, and German part-songs. Lassus's music may be compared with that of Palestrina, but Lassus allows himself greater freedom of expression, and is always attentive to the text.

LIGETI, György (b. 1923)

Ligeti's early works were influenced by Hungarian folk music, but already his use of dense harmonies and clusters of notes pointed the way to his future development. He settled in Cologne in 1956 and studied electronic music there. His *Requiem* (1965) for soloists, double choir and orchestra is fiendishly difficult for the choir who sing in two movements only. *Lux aeterna* for sixteen voices uses a text from the requiem mass; the work relies on an ever changing sustained texture of voices. *Clocks and Clouds*, which uses a text written by the composer, is scored for female voices and orchestra, and dates from 1973.

LISZT, Franz (1811–86)

Like Berlioz, Liszt composed works for chorus and orchestra which he called symphonies; Liszt's two symphonies have a greater claim to their titles as they both have three movements, that is, a classical symphony format without the dance movement. *A Faust Symphony* appeared in 1857, and is scored for tenor soloist and male chorus who sing at the end of the third movement. In the *Dante Symphony* (1856) female voices sing the Magnificat at the close of the second movement, Liszt's representation of Paradise (Heaven). It was Wagner, to whom the work is dedicated, who suggested a setting of the Magnificat to Liszt; he said that no composer could adequately portray Paradise in music.

Both of Liszt's symphonies are mainly orchestral; his oratorios, on the other hand, are not. *The Legend of St Elisabeth* was first heard in 1865 and was subsequently published in English by Novello & Co. *Christus** dates from 1867 and was heard in a complete version in this country during the Liszt Festival of 1977 and subsequently at a Promenade concert. Both works have been recorded commercially.

Of Liszt's various settings of the mass, the small scale *Missa Choralis* is scored for choir and organ; in this work Liszt sets out to recapture the style of Palestrina, although the harmonies are unashamedly romantic. Another successful work for choir and organ is the *Via Crucis** of 1879, which is a series of meditations on the fourteen stations of the cross.

Two large scale mass settings, the so-called *Gran Mass* of 1867 and the *Hungarian Coronation Mass*, are scored for soloists, chorus and orchestra, as is the setting of *Psalm 13*. Other psalm settings are for more modest forces – male voices and organ. A *Requiem* for male voices with soloists is scored for ad lib brass band. There are many other smaller pieces on sacred and secular texts, including *Chor der Engel* (1849) for mixed voices and harp, on a Goethe text; some of these pieces are very short and, frankly, uninteresting.

LOTTI, Antonio (c. 1667–1740)

Lotti lived and died in Venice, working throughout his life at St Mark's. He composed operas, oratorios, masses, and motets, and a number of settings of the words from the Creed which begin 'Crucifixus etiam pro nobis'. The chromatic style of these latter pieces with their discords and expressive modulations have ensured for them a place in the repertory; the best known is the *Crucifixus* for eight-part choir.

MACHAUT, Guillaume de (c. 1300–77)

The French composer Machaut was the great composer of the new music of the fourteenth century, the 'Ars nova'. His works are mainly secular (he was also a poet) and include motets and over one hundred secular songs, almost all of which are monophonic.[1] His *Messe de Notre Dame* is the first complete four-part setting of the mass by one composer (an earlier complete mass, the *Tournai Mass*, is a compilation).

MAHLER, Gustav (1860–1911)

The ten monumental symphonies of Mahler form the main body of his output. His other compositions include many songs which are mostly settings of poems from the collection *Des Knaben Wunderhorn*; the melodies and texts of some of these songs appear in Mahler's symphonies. The second, third and eighth symphonies are scored for orchestra with soloists and chorus; the fourth symphony requires a solo soprano, but no chorus. In Mahler's

[1] A single unaccompanied line of music.

second symphony, *Resurrection*, the chorus join in during the final pages of the work singing Klopstock's *Resurrection Ode*; the soloists are soprano and alto. In the third symphony, the alto soloist is accompanied by a female chorus who sing a Wunderhorn poem, while a boys' choir imitate bells. The eighth symphony is the so-called *Symphony of a Thousand**, which is fully choral; Part One is a setting of the Latin hymn 'Veni creator spiritus', and Part Two, a setting of the final scene from Goethe's *Faust*. This work is scored for eight soloists, double choir, boys' chorus and a vast orchestra.

Mahler's early cantata *Das klagende Lied** ('The Song of Lamentation') was completed in 1880 but was subsequently revised; at this stage Part One Das Waldmärchen was rejected by the composer. Hence performances of *Das klagende Lied* generally consist of Part Two and Three only, although Part One has now been published.

MARTIN, Frank (1890–1974)

The Swiss composer Frank Martin adopted the twelve tone technique of composition in the early 1930s, but his music is basically tonal. It sounds a little like Hindemith, but nevertheless has a distinctive quality of its own, and is arguably more melodic. A *Mass* for unaccompanied double chorus dates from 1926 and is not typical of Martin's output; the oratorio *Le vin herbé* (1941) is based on the Tristan and Isolde legend and is scored for twelve solo voices and small ensemble. *In terra pax* (1944) was commissioned by Radio Geneva for performance on Armistice Day and is a full scale work for five soloists, double choir and orchestra, including two pianos – it deserves to be better known. *Golgotha* dates from 1948 and tells the Passion story in seven 'pictures' interspersed with meditations from the works of St

Augustine. Late works with orchestra are *Pilate* (1964), which is a cantata, and the *Requiem* (1972).

On a smaller scale are the unaccompanied *Songs of Ariel* (1951), arranged by the composer from his opera *Der Sturm*.

MARTINŮ, Bohuslav (1890–1959)

Martinů was born, and spent the early part of his life, in a bell tower in the city of Polička in Bohemia. He was musically precocious and throughout his life wrote readily in all forms, often producing four or five major works in a year. Choral music forms a large part of his output, and the works are deeply rooted in the folk music of his native land. But while his fragmentary phrases may remind us of the music of Janáček, Martinů's music has a disarming tunefulness which recommends it.

Of the works for chorus and orchestra, Martinů's cantata *Kytice* (Bouquet) (1937) is very attractive; it is scored for mixed choir and children's choir with orchestra. The atmospheric *Field Mass*, written for open air performance in 1939, is scored for male voices, wind, harmonium and percussion. Martinů's oratorio *The Epic of Gilgamesh* (1955) is a concise piece for narrator, soprano, tenor, baritone and bass, chorus and orchestra. Other works with accompaniment include three unusual pieces for choir and small instrumental forces: *The opening of the Wells* (1955) for speaker, female voices and ensemble, *Legend of smoke from potato fires* (1956) for solo voices, mixed chorus, wind ensemble, accordian and piano, and *Mikeš of the mountains* (1959) for solo voices, mixed chorus, strings and piano. Inevitably these works are best performed in Czech as the language and the musical rhythms go hand in hand. Other accompanied works include the *Prophecy of Isaiah* (1959) for solo voices, male choir, trumpet, viola, piano and timpani.

Martinů also wrote pieces for a variety of unaccompanied choirs: male voices, female voices, children's voices and mixed choir. Two sets of madrigals for mixed voices are delightful, as is the extended work *The Romance of the Dandelions* (1957), for soprano, tenor, and mixed chorus.

MASSENET, *Jules (1842–1912)*
Massenet's fame rests on his operas, of which *Manon* (1885) and *Werther* (1892) are the most popular. A few of his dramatic works are on religious themes and include the 'drame sacré' *Marie-Magdeleine* (1873), and the 'légende sacré' *La Vierge* (1880); the oratorio *La Terre Promise* (1900), is based on biblical texts. Massenet also composed sacred and secular cantatas, and a requiem.

MENDELSSOHN, *Felix (1809–47)*
Mendelssohn made frequent visits to England, and was often a visitor to the Royal Household. His first oratorio *St Paul** was premiered in Düsseldorf in 1836, and on the strength of its successful British premiere the following year, Mendelssohn was asked to write an oratorio for the Birmingham Festival. This was *Elijah** which was performed there (in English) in 1846, conducted by the composer – it was a huge success. Like other composers who visited England, Mendelssohn was inspired by the performances of Handel's oratorios, and *Elijah* owes as much to Handel as *St Paul* had to Bach. A third oratorio, *Christus**, was left incomplete.

Mendelssohn wrote a large amount of choral music including a 'choral symphony', the symphony no 2 in B♭, known as the *Lobgesang** (Hymn of Praise), written in 1840. After three orchestral movements Mendelssohn added a choral cantata which shares musical themes with the previous movements; despite this, the choral section of the work does not grow out of the rest of the symphony as is the case with the finale of Beethoven's ninth symphony. Mendelssohn's other large scale choral works include *Lauda Sion* (1846) and *Die erste Walpurgisnacht* (1832). The incidental music to *A Midsummer Night's Dream* includes sections for female voices.

Mendelssohn wrote many choral works on a smaller scale. *Hear my prayer* (1844) for soprano soloist, chorus and organ includes the famous solo 'O for the wings of a dove'; it was originally written in German. His religious motets include *Festgesang*, written for the same celebration as his second symphony. The third of these motets is the tune we know as 'Hark the herald angels sing'. Mendelssohn's many part-songs include light pieces specially written for his friends to sing out of doors.

An early setting of the *Te Deum* was published in 1976; it is scored for double choir and continuo (organ), and betrays the influence of Bach, whose music Mendelssohn studied and championed.

MESSIAEN, *Olivier (b. 1908)*
Messiaen is one of the most influential composers of the twentieth century. His musical style and the theories behind his compositions have made a deep impression on his pupils and on countless others who have heard his music. Vocal music plays a large part in his output, but the works for choir are few. They include the short unaccompanied motet *O sacrum convivium* (1937), the *Trois petites liturgies de la Présence Divine* (1944) for female voices and small orchestra, the unaccompanied

Cinq Rechants* (1949) which is a bravura piece for twelve singers, and *La Transifiguration de Notre Seigneur Jésus-Christ* (1969) for chorus and full orchestra. An early mass setting (1933) remains unpublished, and is perhaps lost.

MILHAUD, Darius (1892–1974)

Milhaud was one of a group of composers called 'The Six' (*Les Six*), the others being Auric (1899-1983), Durey (1888-1979), Honegger, Poulenc and Germaine Tailleferre (1892–1983). These composers were considered responsible for a renaissance of French music in the twentieth century. Milhaud was undoubtedly the most prolific of them all, writing hundreds of works in all forms, including the large-scale opera *Christopher Columbus* (1930).

Choral works figure largely in his output, and include his third symphony for large orchestra which consists of a setting of the *Te Deum* (1946), and his sixth symphony, which is scored for wordless chorus, with oboe and cello. Large choral works with orchestral accompaniment include a setting of *Psalm 136* (1919), and a number of cantatas – *Cantate pour louer le Seigneur* (1928), and *Cantate de la croix de charité*, *Cantate sur des textes de Chaucer* and *Cantate de l'initiation*, all composed in 1960. A late choral and orchestral work, *Pacem in terris* op 404 (1963) is a choral symphony to words by Pope John XXIII.

Among Milhaud's works for unaccompanied choir are settings of Claudel (*Cantique du Rhône*, 1936; *Les deux cités*, 1937; *Cantate de la guerre*, 1940), as well as settings of Rilke (*Quatrains valaisans*, 1939), Jorge Guillen (*Huit poèmes*, 1958), and the concise *Naissance de Vénus* (1949) to words by Jules Supervieille.

Milhaud's work is uneven, but he has a sure ear, and an inventiveness that is prodigious.

MOERAN, Ernest John (1894–1950)

Two sets of unaccompanied choral works by Moeran are outstanding in the part song repertory: *Songs of Springtime* (1934) and *Phyllida and Corydon* (1934). In the same year he also wrote the beautiful *Nocturne* for baritone, chorus and orchestra.

MONTEVERDI, Claudio (1567–1643)

Monteverdi worked in Mantua and later at St Mark's Venice. He heard Peri's opera *Orfeo* in 1600 and composed his own setting in 1607. Monteverdi was mainly concerned with operatic compositions throughout his life, but sadly, all but three operas have been lost. From 1587 he published volumes of Italian madrigals which became increasingly more 'modern'; Monteverdi abandoned the polyphonic unaccompanied style of the late sixteenth century and employed daring chromatic harmony and effects, eventually embracing instruments in works which are almost cantatas. The *Madrigali spirituali* are settings of sacred words.

Three of Monteverdi's settings of the mass are unusual in being written in the old fashioned 'stile antico' (ancient style), but the more familiar, *Gloria, Magnificat* (two settings), *Beatus Vir* and other psalm texts, together with the *Vespers* (1610) are in the most polished 'modern' idiom.

MOZART, Wolfgang Amadeus (1756–91)

Mozart wrote the majority of his church music for performance in Salzburg. After 1781, when he resigned from his post as Konzertmeister to Archbishop Colloredo, he composed only two settings of the mass, both incomplete (the *C Minor Mass* K427 and the *Requiem*), and very little other sacred music. The short *Ave verum* dates from 1791.

Although his appointment under the Archbishop gave Mozart a livelihood, he hated the restrictions imposed upon him. These restrictions included a specification that his mass settings should not be too long, and Mozart was forced to write short settings of both the Gloria and Creed, which are the two wordiest portions of the mass. Mozart adopted a symphonic approach in these movements, writing in a modified sonata form, which proves as satisfactory in performance as the more lengthy cantata-masses of his predecessors.

Mozart's *Mass in F* K192 is one of the most successful of these early Salzburg compositions. It makes use of a four-note phrase to the words 'Credo, credo', which was later to turn up again as the opening motif of the finale of the *Jupiter Symphony*. Other masses, such as the setting in D, K194, are even more succinct. The scoring of Mozart's masses is for string orchestra (sometimes without violas) with the occasional addition of trumpets and timpani. The *Coronation Mass* K317* is on a slightly grander scale and is scored for fuller orchestra. A *Mass in C* (sometimes called *Missa Solemnis*) K337, is less interesting.

Other music from Mozart's Salzburg years includes settings of the Vespers (including the *Vesperae solennes de confessore* K339 (1780)), of the litanies (including *Litaniae Lauretanae* K195 (1774)), of the psalm *Dixit Dominus* (1774) and the *Te Deum* (1769), as well as many shorter pieces.

The great *C Minor Mass* K427 (1782) was abandoned and left incomplete. It was later adapted to Italian words as the oratorio *Davidde Penitente* on a text probably written by Mozart's opera librettist, Da Ponte. Why Mozart began this cantata-mass in separate movements is a mystery; it may have been as a result of a vow which Mozart is said to have made, that if he married Constanze Weber he would write a mass for her and her sister to sing. The two soprano parts are certainly suitably florid and athletic! Mozart completed only the Kyrie, Gloria, part of the Credo, Sanctus and Benedictus. A completion of this mass using material from other Mozart works gained some currency earlier this century, but most modern performances give only those portions which Mozart is known to have completed for this particular work.

Mozart's *Requiem** is also incomplete, and was a commission from a nobleman who wanted to pass the work off as his own. When Mozart died he was under the delusion that he was being poisoned, and was in fact writing his own requiem! While working on the *Requiem* Mozart gave directions for the completion of the work to his pupil Süssmayr, who was asked to deliver the score and bring the money to Mozart's impoverished wife. A recent edition by Richard Maunder offers only the portions of the *Requiem* which Mozart actually set. Maunder has therefore had to compose his own ending to the Lacrymosa which breaks off in Mozart's manuscript after the eighth bar.

MUSSORGSKY, *Modest* (*1839–1881*)

Mussorgsky was one of the group of Russian composers known as 'The Five' or 'The Mighty Handful'. The five were Balakirev (1837–1910), Borodin (1833–87), Cui (1853–1918), Rimsky-Korsakov and Mussorgsky. Like his fellow composers, Mussorgsky wrote music inspired by Russian folk tales and history, but unlike them he was very concerned that his choral writing should reflect Russian speech inflexion. His operas (including *Boris Godunov*, 1874) and songs are remarkable and revolutionary in this respect. His music was also harmonically daring, which is why Rimsky-Korsakov re-composed a number of Mussorgky's scores, including *St John's Night on the Bare Mountain*.

Although *St John's Night on the Bare Mountain* has become well known in Rimsky-Korsakov's arrangement, it began life as a section of the opera-ballet *Mlada* (1872). Mussorgsky then reworked it into his opera *Sorotchinsky Fair* (1877) where it was scored for baritone soloist, chorus and orchestra.

Mussorgsky's other choral works include the less interesting *Destruction of Sennacharib* (1867, revised 1874) for chorus and orchestra, *Joshua*, and a set of Russian folksongs for mixed unaccompanied voices (1880).

NIELSEN, Carl (1865–1931)

Springtime in Funen (Fynsk Foraar) (1921) is one of Nielsen's sunniest compositions and would surely be popular with English-speaking choral societies were it not for the text which is written in Danish; it is scored for mixed choir, children's choir and orchestra, with soprano, tenor and baritone soloists. His other cantatas include *Sleep* (1904) on a Danish text by Johannes Jorgensen, and *Hymnus Amoris* (1897) written in Latin and scored for soprano, tenor and baritone, chorus, children's choir and orchestra. Although Nielsen composed many occasional cantatas few have been heard outside Denmark. His *Three Motets* op. 55 (1929) are settings of Latin texts.

OBRECHT, Jacob (1450/51–1505)

Obrecht was born on St Cecilia's Day, 22 November – but we cannot be certain in which year! This Franco-Flemish composer worked mainly in the Netherlands but died in Ferrara of plague. He composed 26 mass settings, in which he indulges in mathematical intricacies not apparent to the ear, and in no way detrimental to the beauty of his music. Obrecht's 30 or so motets point the way towards Josquin in their expressiveness. His secular pieces include settings of Dutch popular tunes.

OCKEGHEM, Johannes (c. 1425–97)

Ockeghem was a Franco-Flemish composer who worked in the Netherlands and later at the French court, where he died. He was the teacher of Josquin and was given the title 'Prince of Music' in his day. His ten masses include works based on plainsong (cantus firmus masses) – not always on a sacred melody – as well as freely composed settings; some of these rely on very complex canonic writing. Ockeghem also wrote motets and chansons, and his *Requiem Mass* is the earliest extant setting.

ORFF, Carl (1895–1982)

Orff's popular cantata *Carmina Burana** (1937) is the first part of a trilogy of similar works called simply *Trionfi*. The melodies and motor rhythms of this first cantata are considerably more spontaneous and attractive than those of *Catulli Carmina* (1943), scored for four pianos and percussion, on poems (in Latin) by Catullus, and *Trionfo di Afrodite* (1953), the third part. Many other works of Orff combine drama, music and dance, and *Carmina Burana* itself is often staged on the continent. Most of Orff's works reduce music to its bare essentials; rhythmic percussion and dramatic declamation take the place of melody and accompaniment, often to great effect.

Orff's *Schulwerk* (1930–33) inaugurated a major advance in the way music was taught to children in German schools. Once again it is the use of motor rhythms and percussion with an element of improvisation that makes up the body of the work; all children can take part in this kind of music making. The use of drone basses, ostinato rhythms and parallel lines of melody arguably take us back to the roots of folk music. Other pieces for chorus with or without instruments by Orff include *Stücke* (1969) for speaking chorus.

PALESTRINA, *Giovanni Pierluigida (c. 1525–94)*

Palestrina took his name from his birthplace; he spent his early life in the service of the church as a chorister, and later as a member of the Papal Chapel. His music has been studied for many years because it is a model of polyphonic writing: the polyphony is well organized and all dissonances are prepared and resolved, so that the music flows in a continuous stream of sound. It is rather conservative, however, and Palestrina's contemporaries, such as Victoria, wrote more overtly expressive music. His output was enormous: 105 mass settings, 250 motets (including the rather sensuous setting of the *Song of Solomon*), nearly 70 offertories in five-voice motet style, thirteen complete settings of the *Lamentations*, 45 hymns and 35 magnificats, all but one of the latter alternating plainsong with polyphony.

Palestrina also composed litanies and other sacred works, the famous (but untypical) *Stabat Mater* and many madrigals. His mass settings include a *Requiem* (only the Kyrie, Offertory, Sanctus and Agnus Dei are set), and the famous *Missa Papae Marcelli*, supposedly submitted to Pope Marcellus. Pope Marcellus and the Council of Trent, who met occasionally between 1545 and 1563, wanted to ban polyphonic settings of sacred texts because the words were not easily intelligible. Palestrina composed his *Missa Papae Marcelli* in a free style (not based on pre-existing material) and proved that it was possible to make the text clear even in a polyphonic composition. Other Palestrina masses use the 'parody' technique (quoting passages from his own or other composer's works) and some are rather old-fashioned *cantus firmus* masses based on plainsong melodies.

PARRY, *Hubert (1848–1918)*

The performance of Parry's *Prometheus Unbound* in 1880 is generally considered to be a landmark in the English musical renaissance: with this cantata Parry established a new school of British choral writing. The work had a mixed reception, but the critics recognised Parry's 'new' voice, and in retrospect we can see in his noble grandeur, pre-echoes of Elgar and Vaughan Williams. Parry was an uneven composer, and it is characteristic of his choral works that the oratorios are less successful than the cantatas, and that the shorter works are much the best. The brief *Blest Pair of Sirens** (1887) is arguably his finest achievement.

After *Prometheus Unbound* came a succession of choral works: *The Glories of our Blood and State* (1883), a short and successful work; *L'Allegro ed il Pensieroso* (1890), a setting of Milton; *De Profundis* (1891); *Invocation to Music* (1895) on a text by Bridges; *The Pied*

Piper (1905) and others. Parry's sacred music includes three oratorios: *Judith* (1888), *Job* (1892) and *King Saul* (1897). They tend to be undramatic but contain some striking music; an alto air from *Judith* is the tune we know as the hymn 'Dear Lord and Father of mankind'.

Parry's sacred cantatas include *The Soul's Ransom* (1906), a very fine work, and *An Ode on the Nativity* (1912) for soprano, chorus and orchestra on a text by Dunbar. His anthems (including *I was glad*, written for the coronation of Edward VII, 1902) are among the most loved in the repertory; many of his part-songs, including the *Songs of Farewell** (1918) are outstanding.

Parry and Stanford have been overshadowed by their many pupils, but their works provided the groundwork on which their pupils built; we need to be more familiar with the works of Parry and Stanford in order to re-assess their stature.

PENDERECKI, Krysztof (b. 1933)

In a number of his works Penderecki explored different sound worlds, and one of the first pieces to bring him to the public attention was the *Psalms of David* (1958) for chorus and percussion. With the gigantic *St Luke Passion** (1965) he consolidated his style and demonstrated his control of large forces; this deeply impressive work brings us close to Bach despite the disparity of musical idiom. Penderecki's other choral works include *Dies Irae* (1967) and *Utrenja* (1971), which are both large scale works for choir and orchestra, *Canticum canticorum* (1972) scored for chorus and chamber orchestra, *Eclog* (1972) for six male voices, the *Magnificat* (1974) for boys' voices, chorus and orchestra, and the *Te Deum* (1979) for soloists, chorus and orchestra. He has recently completed a *Polish Requiem*. In recent years Penderecki has become more traditional in his compositions and has sometimes returned to the style of the nineteenth century.

PERGOLESI, Giovanni Battista (1710–36)

The Pergolesi Collected Edition published in the 1930s and 1940s included a number of works now known not to have been composed by Pergolesi; there was a craze at one time to enhance his fame by crediting works to him. The famous *Stabat Mater* for female soloists and female choir is authentic; however, the *Magnificat* performed under his name is now thought to be composed by Durante (1684–1755). Pergolesi also composed settings of the mass, including the *Missa Romana*, and other church music.

POULENC, Francis (1899–1963)

Poulenc's choral music has found a regular niche in the repertory of large and small choir alike. His setting of the *Gloria* for soprano, chorus and orchestra (1959) is very popular and an easier work than the *Stabat Mater* for soprano, five-part chorus and orchestra (1950). Poulenc is adept at expressing the text in music; at some times it is poignant and lyrical, and at others, spiky and rhythmically vital. Other works with orchestra include the cantata *Sécheresse* of 1937.

Most of Poulenc's other choral works are for unaccompanied choir or choir with organ: the four Christmas and Easter motets are frequently heard. Other works on sacred texts are: *Litanies à la vierge noire* (1936) for female voices and organ, a *Mass* (1937) for unaccompanied choir, *Quatre petites prières de Saint Francois d'Assise* (1948) for male voices, and the *Laudes de Saint Antoine de Padoue* (1957–59), also for male voices. Secular choral works include the *Sept Chansons* (1936), and *Figure Humaine** (1943) for twelve-voice choir, which is an extended deeply impressive cantata. *Un soir de neige* (1944), is a chamber cantata for six-voice choir. There is a choir in his ballet *Les Biches* (1924).

PROKOFIEV, *Serge* (1891–1953)

Prokofiev's works for chorus and orchestra include two cantatas for the anniversary of the October Revolution, and another unpublished cantata, *Ballad of an unknown boy*. An early cantata *They are seven* for tenor, chorus and orchestra, composed in 1918 was later revised in 1933. A choral work, almost unknown in this country, is *Songs of our times*, which dates from 1937, just two years before Prokofiev's popular *Alexander Nevsky** (1939), the mainly orchestral cantata drawn from the incidental music Prokofiev had written to Eisenstein's film. Another choral work with minimum choral participation is *Winter Bonfire* (1950) for reciter, boys' chorus and orchestra. One of Prokofiev's most ambitious scores is the oratorio *On Guard of Peace* for mezzo soprano, reciters, chorus, boys' chorus and orchestra, which he wrote in 1950.

PUCCINI, *Giacomo (1858–1924)*

Puccini devoted his life to the composition of operas, which include some of the most performed works in the repertory. As a young man of twenty-two, as his final exercise at the Instituto Musicale Pacini in Lucca, Puccini composed the *Messa di Gloria* (1880); although the work is light and sometimes a little naive, it has a freshness which recommends it. Some of the solo 'arias' give an idea of the composer's gift for melody: the theme from

the Agnus Dei was in fact used again in the second act of *Manon Lescaut*, where it is called a madrigal. A *Requiem* by Puccini has also been published; it is a short work for STB chorus and organ or harmonium. He also wrote two secular cantatas in 1877 and 1897 respectively.

PURCELL, *Henry (1659–95)*

Purcell was a chorister at the Chapel Royal and later a pupil of Humfrey (1647–74) and Blow (1649–1708); he became organist of Westminster Abbey in 1679 in succession to Blow. Purcell assimilated the new styles of music which were coming to England from the continent – the broad dotted stride of French music, and the jaunty florid Italian style. He incorporated both of these in his secular as well as his sacred music.

Purcell composed a number of large works for special occasions; these odes include the first St Cecilia's Day ode of 1683, *Welcome to all the pleasures, Come ye sons of art** for Queen Mary's birthday in 1694, and another St Cecilia ode, *Hail bright Cecilia* (1692). His other choral works are mainly anthems; some of them are verse anthems (such as *Rejoice in the Lord alway* – see Bell Anthem) and others are full anthems.

The motet *Jehova quam multi sunt* is written in Latin, and like other such works of the period in Latin, we do not know for what purpose it was written. Purcell also set the funeral sentences, and made two settings of *Thou knowest Lord the secrets of our hearts*, one of which was performed at the funeral of Queen Mary with two brass pieces in 1694. Purcell also wrote a complete setting of the Service in B♭ (ten numbers in all), a *Magnificat* and *Nunc Dimittis* in G minor, and a *Te Deum* and *Jubilate* in D for St Cecilia's Day, 1694.

RACHMANINOV, Sergei (1873-1943)

Rachmaninov composed two settings of Russian liturgical texts for unaccompanied chorus, and both have become better known over recent years. His setting of the *Vespers* (1915), and the *Liturgy of St John Chrisostom* (1910), both in Russian, are written in a sonorous chordal idiom, fully exploiting the lowest range of the choir. Rachmaninov wrote both works in the idiom of Russian orthodox church music, and they are not as harmonically adventurous as his instrumental compositions.

Rachmaninov's choral works with orchestra, however, are written in a fully charged romantic language, and include *The Bells** (1913), a setting of poems by Edgar Allen Poe in a Russian adaptation. The work is in four movements; the third was originally written for double choir, but was later simplified for four-part chorus. Other choral works include *Three Russian Songs* (1926) for chorus and orchestra, and the cantata *Spring* for baritone, chorus and orchestra, which dates from 1902.

RAVEL, Maurice (1875-1937)

Ravel's unaccompanied *Trois chansons* (1915) to his own words, are often included in chamber choir concerts; they are his only exclusively choral pieces. The ballet *Daphnis and Chloe** (1912) has a wordless chorus as part of its colourful orchestration.

RAWSTHORNE, Alan (1905-71)

Rawsthorne was one of the most individual British composers of this century; his musical style is sometimes uncompromising, but he has a characteristic voice. His choral works, some of which are scored for small forces, are well worth investigating as they are not heard frequently. They include *A Canticle of Man* (1952) for baritone,

chorus, flute and strings, *Lament for a Sparrow* (1962) to a Latin poem by Catullus for chorus and harp, *Carmen Vitale* (1963) for soprano, chorus and orchestra on an English text, and *The God in the Cave* (1966) for chorus and orchestra. Unaccompanied works include *Four Seasonal Songs* (1955), *A Rose for Lidice* (1956) and *The Oxen* (1965) on a poem by Thomas Hardy. Rawsthorne contributed *Canzonet* to the collection *A Garland for the Queen* (1953).

REGER, Max (1873-1916)

The organ music of Reger has always held a place in the repertory, but his vast output of orchestral and chamber music, piano music, songs and vocal music is generally neglected outside Germany. Reger writes in a richly chromatic idiom influenced by the music of Wagner. His choral works include choruses for unaccompanied choir, many of which are for male voices. His jubilant setting of *Psalm 100* for chorus and orchestra dates from 1909 and two last choral pieces are impressive – *Der Einsiedler* and *Requiem* (a setting of a poem by Hebbel) composed in 1915. (Reger also wrote two movements of a Latin requiem mass).

RIMSKY-KORSAKOV, Nikolai (1844-1908)

Rimsky-Korsakov is best known for his colourful orchestral scores, but throughout his life he wrote choruses for unaccompanied choir, both sacred and secular, as well as works from the Russian liturgy, including eight settings of verses from the Liturgy of St John Chrisostom. His choral works with orchestra include *Svitezyanka* for soprano, tenor and mixed chorus, *The Song of Oleg the Wise* for male voices, *From Homer* for female voices, and two folk song settings; one of these, *Slava*, is based on the theme Mussorgsky used in the coronation scene in his opera *Boris Godunov*.

ROBERTON, *Hugh* (*1874–1952*)

Hugh Roberton was a prodigious composer and arranger of choral music; he was a choral conductor and wrote many works for his own choirs. In 1906 he founded the Glasgow Orpheus Choir. The short part-song *All in the April evening* is his best known work.

ROREM, *Ned (b. 1923)*

Rorem is both a writer and a composer and has always responded sympathetically to the texts he has set to music. His many choral works include *From an unknown past* (1951), *Little Prayers* (1973), *In Time of Pestilence* (1973), *Three Motets on Poems of Gerard Manley Hopkins* (1973), and *Three Christmas Songs* (1978), all for unaccompanied chorus. He has also composed a *Missa Brevis* (1974) and secular works.

ROSSINI, *Gioachino* (*1792–1868*)

Rossini composed operas between 1810 and 1829, ending with *William Tell*, and then retired from the stage, writing very little during the remaining forty years of his life. His two most famous sacred works date from this latter period of his life, when he also collected together many small chamber works and songs which he called the 'sins of my old age'. Rossini's setting of the *Stabat Mater** dates from 1842; he had half composed the work and left it to the Italian conductor Tadolini to complete, but later rescued it and completed it himself, just before its publication. The *Stabat Mater* is very operatic in style and requires operatic soloists (including a tenor with a top D flat!), but the gaiety of the melodies seems to be at odds with the gravity of the text. The same is also true of the *Petite Messe Solennelle** (Paris, 1864); this is hardly a small work (since it lasts at least 80 minutes!) and is certainly not solemn. It was originally written for soloists, chorus and an accompaniment of two pianists and harmonium; it is very effective in this form, but Rossini later orchestrated it.

Rossini's *Messa di gloria* dates from 1821. It is scored for soloists, chorus and orchestera, but the choir participates only in the Kyrie and final fugue; again the solo parts are very operatic. He also wrote a number of secular cantatas, and smaller sacred works. Among Rossini's short secular works are *I Gondolieri* and *Toast pour le nouvel an*.

ROUSSEL, *Albert (1869–1937)*

Roussel's music has not found a wide audience, and of his 50 or so scores, only one or two are regularly performed. Most of his vocal music consists of solo songs, but the *Madrigal aux muses* (1923) is for unaccompanied three-part women's chorus, and his opus 37 is a setting of *Psalm 80* for tenor, chorus and orchestra; this splendid score was first heard in Paris in 1929.

RUBBRA, *Edmund (1901–1986)*

Rubbra, like Parry and Stanford, was both a scholar (he was Senior Lecturer of Music at Oxford 1947–68) and a composer. A staunch Roman Catholic, Rubbra wrote most of his choral works on sacred texts. His two mass settings, *Missa Cantuariensis* (1945) for double choir, and *Missa in honorem Sancti Dominici* (1948) for SATB chorus with occasional divisions, are both frequently heard in the context of church services. Rubbra's other sacred works include two settings of the *Te Deum* (1951 – for the Festival of Britain, and 1962), a *Festival Gloria* (1957) and a three-part *Mass* (1958). His ninth symphony, *Sin-*

fonia Sacra (subtitled *The Resurrection*), is scored for soprano, baritone, chorus and orchestra, and uses texts from various sources on the subject of Christ's death and ascension. Rubbra's secular works include the *Five Motets* (1934), *Five Madrigals* (1940) and *Two Madrigals* (1941), all of which are unaccompanied.

SAINT-SAËNS, Camille
(1835–1921)

Saint-Saëns was equally at home with all branches of composition, but today he is chiefly remembered for his orchestral rather than his choral works. His two unaccompanied choruses, op. 68, are popular with chamber choirs, and his *Mass* op. 4 has been recorded commercially by Worcester Cathedral Choir. The *Oratorio de Noël* (1858) is scored for soloists, chorus, harp, organ and string quartet, and is written in an attractive, pastoral idiom. Two full scale oratorios, *Le Déluge* (1875) and *The Promised Land* (1913) are largely forgotten, although the orchestral prelude to the former is sometimes heard. The Saint-Saens *Requiem*, op. 54, is a fine piece, scored for soloists, chorus and small orchestra (without clarinets, trumpets or percussion).

SCARLATTI, Alessandro
(1660–1725)

Alessandro Scarlatti was an opera composer working mainly in Naples; his son, Domenico (1685–1757) was the famous composer of numerous keyboard sonatas. Alessandro composed oratorios in a very operatic style, relying on the vocal dexterity of his soloists, and giving a subordinate role to the chorus. Two of his ten masses were written in the new style, that is, divided up into movements, breaking up the text into arias and choruses; the

remaining masses were written in the old style. Scarlatti also wrote madrigals and solo voice cantatas.

SCHOENBERG, Arnold
(1874–1951)

Schoenberg's early works, written at the turn of the century, are overtly romantic. His chromatic style pushed romantic harmony as far as it would go, and he felt he had exhausted its possibilities when he developed the twelve-tone system. His works written in this idiom had a far reaching effect on the music of this century, and his pupils Berg and Webern perfected the technique in their own styles, further influencing successive generations of composers. Schoenberg's enormous *Gurrelieder** (1911) is cast in the romantic mould, but includes the first use of Sprechstimme (song-speech in which the singer does not rest on a note, but glides from one to another in a speech style). The short unaccompanied *Friede auf Erden* (1907) has sufficiently shifting harmonies to give a hint of the atonal music which is to come.

Schoenberg employed his twelve-tone (serial) principles most strictly in the *Piano Pieces* of 1923, and other works from that period. His choral music at that time is also serial: *Four pieces* for mixed voices op. 27 (1925), *Two Satires* op. 28 (1925), and *Six pieces* for male voices op. 35 (1930). His other works are *Kol nidre* (1938) for speaker, chorus and orchestra, *A Survivor from Warsaw* (1947) for speaker, men's chorus and orchestra, and his opus 50, which consists of three works: the unaccompanied *Dreimal tausend Jahre* (1949) and *De profundis* (1950), in Hebrew, and the incomplete *Modern Psalm* (1950) for chorus and orchestra. In his later works, Schoenberg relaxed the serial technique, but his music remained atonal.

SCHUBERT, Franz (1797–1828)

Schubert's settings of the mass have always given editors a headache! – he often altered the sequence of words, and in the case of the Creed, even omitted sections of the text. Some editions of these works have restored the missing words, making nonsense of the music. Schubert wrote six numbered masses: no. 1 in F (1814), no. 2 in G (1815), no. 3 in B flat (1815), no. 4 in C (1816), no. 5 in A flat (1822) and no. 6 in E flat (1828). The first setting is rarely performed, but the second is one of Schubert's most popular works. The A flat (often referred to as the 'Missa Solemnis') and E flat settings are large-scale, mature works. Schubert's *Deutsches Messe*, written in 1827, is a simple setting of non-liturgical German words by Johann Philipp Neumann, which reflect on the text of the mass.

Schubert's list of sacred works is quite large, including the oratorio *Lazarus* (1820), and settings of *Salve Regina*, the *Magnificat* (1815), *Tantum ergo* and *Stabat Mater* (1815). The latter uses a German paraphrase of the original Latin, by Klopstock. Smaller pieces, both secular and sacred, for mixed choir and male or female chorus are among Schubert's best works. Particularly notable are the setting of *Psalm 23* for female voices and piano, and the haunting *Ständchen* for alto solo and male voices with piano, which captures the spirit of the most outstanding of Schubert's solo songs. The incidental music to the play *Rosamunde* includes three choruses with orchestra.

SCHUMAN, William (b. 1910)

Schuman was taught for a while by Roy Harris, who helped bring his music before the public. His output is mainly symphonic. The *Carols of Death* for unaccompanied chorus (1958), which are settings of Whitman, are stark and impressive; less austere are the *Te Deum* (1944), also for unaccompanied choir, and two secular cantatas, *This is Our Time* (1940) and *A Free Song* (1942), both with orchestra.

SCHUMANN, Robert (1810–56)

When Schumann began publishing his first keyboard works in the 1830s he was considered a 'modern' composer, establishing new trends in romantic music. His piano music and songs have found a regular place in the repertory, and the symphonies are frequently performed, but Schumann's choral works are largely unknown. Arguably he is less successful when working on a large canvas, and in a work such as the (incomplete) *Scenes from Goethe's Faust* (1853) – which is perhaps his best choral work – he is only at ease in short movements. The secular oratorio *Paradise and the Peri* (1843) on a text arranged by the composer from *Lalla Rookh* by Thomas Moore is of less interest, as is *Der Rose Pilgefahrt* (1851) (The Pilgrimage of the Rose). The short *Requiem für Mignon* with words from Goethe's *Wilhelm Meister* captures the mood of the best of Schumann's songs, and is well worth hearing. Two sacred works written toward the end of his life, the *Requiem* (1852) and *Mass* (1853) are four-square and dull. However, Schumann's part-songs for unaccompanied choir are more successful, and include the splendid op. 141 for double choir which ends with a striking setting of Goethe's *Talismane*.

SCHÜTZ, Heinrich (1585–1672)

Schütz bridges the gap between the choral polyphony of the Venetian school and the contrapuntal music of Bach. He was sent to Italy to study under Giovanni Gabrieli from 1609–12, and he brought back with him to Germany the new Italian style of writing pieces for several choirs, with vocal contrast and word-painting. After a further visit to Italy in 1628 and trips to Copenhagen, he settled, and eventually died, in Dresden.

Schütz's large scale choral works include three settings of the Passion which influenced Bach, although they are unaccompanied and written in an archaic style with the narrator singing plainsong. He also set the *Seven Last Words** (in German), and composed a *Christmas Oratorio** (1664) in an Italian style with instrumental accompaniment. Schütz's other publications include the *Psalms of David* (1619), *Canticum Sacrum* (1625) and various volumes of *Symphonia Sacrae* and *Kleine Geistliche Konzerte*.

SESSIONS, Roger (1896–1985)

As a teacher Sessions has been a major influence on many American composers. He himself came under the spell of Stravinsky and of his teacher, Bloch, but soon assimilated the music of Schoenberg and the Second Viennese School. His requiem *When lilacs last in the door-yard bloom'd* (1970) for soprano, alto, baritone, chorus and orchestra is a highly charged and dissonant score of great stature.

SHOSTAKOVICH, Dimitri (1906–75)

Three of Shostakovich's symphonies are choral: the symphony no. 2 'October Revolution' (1927) has a choral finale, which is a setting of words by A. Bezimensky; the third symphony 'First of May' (1930) which celebrates the workers' holiday, is in one movement which ends with a choral setting of a poem by S. Kirsanov; and the symphony no. 13 'Babi Yar' (1962) sets five poems by Yevtushenko for bass soloist and male voice choir, including the title poem which offended the Soviet authorities. The symphony no. 14 is a song cycle on poems about death for soprano, baritone, percussion and string orchestra, but does not employ chorus.

Two cantatas by Shostakovich, *Poems on the homeland* (1947) and *The Sun shines over our mother land* (1952), are rather patriotic compositions of only moderate distinction, but the oratorio *Song of the Forests* for tenor, baritone, mixed chorus, children's chorus and orchestra is a fine work, which was composed in 1949 and awarded the Stalin Prize. *The Execution of Stepan Razin* (1964) for baritone, chorus and orchestra is also impressive; it is based on another Yevtushenko poem. His shorter works for unaccompanied choir include *Ten poems to words by Revolutionary poets* for mixed choir (1951) and a set of ballads for male voices called *Faithfulness* (1970).

SIBELIUS, Jean (1865–1957)

Although we do not associate the name of Sibelius with choral music, his list of choral pieces is quite extensive. Unfortunately, most of them set texts in Finnish, and translations have been made into German, but not, as yet, into English. His first large scale success was a choral symphony *Kullervo* (1892), scored for soprano and baritone with a male voice choir. The short choral piece *Rakastava* (*The Lover*) originally written for male voices but subsequently rescored for mixed voices, was then transformed into a piece for string orchestra. Sibelius composed a large number of part-songs, for male or mixed voices, and various cantatas, some for special occasions. Of the cantatas, *The origin of fire* (1910) and *The Liberated Queen* are the most significant.

SMETANA, Bedřich (1824–84)

There is sufficient chorus work in Smetana's opera *The Bartered Bride* to justify the many performances of concert versions which this opera enjoys. Of Smetana's many specifically choral works almost nothing is known in this country. *The Czech Song* (1878) for chorus and orchestra is a short work, and has been recorded commercially.

SPOHR, *Louis (1784–1851)*

Spohr's music was so well loved and revered in the early nineteenth century both abroad and in England, that Novello and Co. placed his name (together with Bach, Mozart and others) on the covers of their vocal scores. (Incidentally, the Mikado's song in the Sullivan operetta links Spohr's name with the great, in the line 'with Bach interwoven with Spohr and Beethoven . . .')

Two of Spohr's most successful oratorios were *The Last Judgement* and *Calvary*. The first was extremely popular in Britain where it was performed in English. The music, however, sounds to our ears rather like over-chromatic Mendelssohn. Another oratorio, *The Fall of Babylon*, was broadcast by the BBC as part of the Spohr bicentenary celebrations. Not all of Spohr's music is in the same mould – his *Mass* for five solo voices and double choir is quite sonorous and splendid, if melodically unremarkable. Spohr also composed a large number of sacred and secular cantatas, and a few part-songs. It is arguable that his operas, notably *Faust* and *Jessonda*, are more worthy of revival. The chamber *Nonet* is Spohr's most attractive and enduring composition.

STANFORD, *Charles Villiers (1852–1924)*

Stanford became Professor of Music at Cambridge in 1887, while still teaching at the Royal College of Music, where he had taught since 1883. Among his pupils were Vaughan Williams, Holst, Coleridge-Taylor, Ireland, Bridge, Butterworth, Bliss, Howells, Moeran, Boughton and Benjamin. Stanford wrote music in all forms, including operas, symphonies and many choral works, both with and without orchestra, many for church use. His part-songs, together with those of his contemporary Parry, are some of the finest ever written, and the most notable are *The Blue Bird* and the opus 119 collection.

Stanford's secular works are perhaps the more successful. *The Songs of the Sea* (Leeds, 1904) for baritone and male chorus, and *The Songs of the Fleet* (Leeds, 1910) for baritone and mixed chorus have recently been given a new lease of life by a recording made by the baritone Benjamin Luxon. *The Revenge – a Ballad of the Fleet* (Leeds, 1886), to words by Tennyson, for chorus and orchestra, was once very popular, as were *The Voyage of Maeldune* (Leeds, 1889) also on a Tennyson text, and *Phaudrig Crohoore* (Norwich, 1896). Stanford's sacred works are well-wrought and in need of re-appraisal; they include a *Mass* (1894) for soloists, chorus and orchestra, a *Requiem* (Birmingham, 1897) for soloists, chorus and orchestra, and a particularly impressive setting of the *Stabat Mater* (Leeds, 1907). His oratorio *Eden* (Birmingham, 1891) is rather long and dull. Stanford also wrote three odes in very different moods: the *Elegiac Ode* (Norwich, 1884) on a Whitman text, the *Ode to Wellington* (1908) on a Tennyson text, and the *Ode to Discord* (1908), which is a tongue-in-cheek parody beginning 'Hence loathèd melody' in imitation of Milton.

Stanford's numerous sacred pieces for church use include settings of the Communion Services and the Evening Canticles which are among the most loved music in the Church of England.

The three motets, op. 51, which include *Beati quorum*, are superb pieces, as is the isolated *Magnificat* in B♭ for double choir which dates from 1918. Other anthems include the jubilant *Ye choirs of new Jerusalem* and *The Lord is my shepherd*.

STRAUSS, *Richard (1864–1949)*

Strauss began his career as a conductor of his own orchestral pieces, but gradually it was his operatic compositions which consolidated his fame and fortune. Throughout his career he also wrote songs, mainly for his wife to sing while he played the accompaniment. A handful of unaccompanied choral works include: the *Deutsches Motet* (1913) on a poem by Rückert, the *Zwei Gesänge* op. 34 (*Der Abend* and *Hymne* by Schiller and Rückert respectively), choruses op. 42 and 45 for male voices, and two more extended works, *Die Göttin in Putzimmer* (Rückert) which dates from 1935, and *An dem Baum Daphne* (1943) which is scored for mixed chorus and boy's chorus, and based on material from the opera *Daphne*. His other choral works with orchestra, including *Wandrers Sturmlied*, are neglected.

STRAVINSKY, *Igor (1882–1971)*

Stravinsky composed music in a variety of very different styles throughout his career, moving from a romantic style in his early works, through a period of neo-classicism, and finally writing works in a twelve-tone idiom. His short early cantata *The king of the stars* (1912) for male voices and orchestra was composed around the time of the great ballets (*Petrouchka* was first heard in 1911).

The opera-oratorio *Oedipus Rex* was composed in 1927, and has been successful as a stage and concert work.

Two other stage works, the choral ballets *Les Noces** and *Perséphone** appeared in 1923 and 1933 respectively. The *Symphony of Psalms** (1930) is one of Stravinsky's most approachable scores; in it he leaves behind the iconoclasm of *The Rite of Spring* and the jazz music of *The Soldier's Tale*, setting three psalm texts for chorus and orchestra (without violins) in a melodious and subdued style. The cantata *Babel* (1953) for male voices and narrator, and the works that followed it, were all written in a dissonant idiom inspired by Stravinsky's study of Webern and the twelve-tone technique. The *Mass* of 1948 for mixed chorus (strictly speaking a wholly male choir with boys as trebles and altos) is scored for a wind ensemble of ten instruments. Stravinsky wanted to emulate the mass settings of Mozart, but did so by going back to the chanting style of the orthodox church.

In *Canticum Sacrum** (1955), written for Venice, Stravinsky indulges in various thematic contrapuntal devices, which are not particularly apparent to the listener. *Threni** (1958) and *A Sermon, a narrative and a prayer** (1961) are both scored for full orchestra and chorus, the first requiring six soloists, and the second written for speaker, alto and tenor. *Requiem canticles* (1966) is Stravinsky's last choral work, and is less astringent than its predecessors. Other choral works include settings of the *Ave Maria, Lord's Prayer* and *Credo* (all revised 1949), and *The Dove Descending* (1962), an anthem to words by T. S. Eliot.

SULLIVAN, *Arthur (1842–1900)*

Sullivan's fame today rests on the operettas he wrote in collaboration with W. S. Gilbert. All of his sacred music has fallen from the repertory, as have all the operettas not written with Gilbert.

The choral festivals in Britain gave nineteenth-century composers many opportunities, and it was at Birmingham in 1864 that the masque *Kenilworth* brought Sullivan's name to the fore. The first performances of his next works were events of great social importance and musical success: the oratorio *The Prodigal Son* (Worcester, 1869), the cantata *On Shore and Sea* (1871) to words by Tennyson, the oratorios *The Light of the World* (Birmingham, 1873) and *The Martyr of Antioch* (Leeds, 1880), and the cantata *The Golden Legend* (Leeds, 1886) with a libretto after Longfellow. Sullivan also wrote two *Te Deum* settings (1872 and 1900): the first, written for the festival held at the Crystal Palace to celebrate the recovery of the Prince of Wales, quotes the hymn 'O God our help in ages past', and the second, to celebrate the victorious end to the South African war.

Sullivan's oratorios are sometimes rather dull and undramatic, like the music of so many composers writing in Victorian England. His cantatas, on the other hand, are more successful, and *The Golden Legend* is worthy of revival.

SZYMANOWSKI, Karol (1882–1937)

Born in the Russian Ukraine, Szymanowski became the foremost composer in Poland in the early twentieth century, and his music is, at present, enjoying a new wave of popularity. The first *Violin Concerto* is well established in the repertory, and the *Stabat Mater* is gaining ground. This beautiful work is scored for soprano, alto and baritone, chorus and orchestra.

Other choral works with orchestra are *Veni Creator* (1930) and *Litany to the Virgin Mary* (1933) for soprano, and female chorus, His Symphony no. 3 'The Song of the Night' completed in 1916 also includes chorus with tenor or soprano soloist.

TALLIS, Thomas (c. 1505–85)

Together with Byrd, Tallis held the monopoly on music printing in England from 1575, and was also joint organist of the Chapel Royal with Byrd. Both composers wrote works in Latin and English, continuing to write Latin works even after the Act of Uniformity of 1549, which abolished Latin in English church services, replacing it with the Common Prayer Book. Tallis's many polyphonic works are notable for their use of dissonance, particularly at the end of a piece – the so-called 'Tallis cadence'. Many of his works reach great heights of complexity, and the best example of this is the forty-voice motet *Spem in alium**, which is scored for eight five-part choirs. Tallis's 'canon' is one of the psalm tunes he published in 1567; another from the same collections became the theme for Vaughan Williams's *Fantasia on a theme of Thomas Tallis*

TAVENER, John (b. 1944)

Tavener came to public notice in the 1960s with the cantata *The Whale**, performed at the inaugural concert of the London Sinfonietta in 1968, and the *Celtic Requiem** (1969) which juxtaposes words from the requiem mass with children's singing games. *Ultimos Ritos* (1972), first performed in the Netherlands in 1974, is a setting of words by St John of the Cross, a poet who has influenced Tavener; *Coplas* (1970) is another St John of the Cross setting. In 1972 Tavener wrote another requiem setting, the *Little Requiem for Father Malachy*. In 1978 he was admitted into the Russian Orthodox church, and recent works have reflected this: the *Great Canon of St Andrew of Crete* (1981) and the *Liturgy of St John Chry-*

sostom. A recent carol – *The Lamb* (1982), a setting of Blake's poem 'Little lamb who made thee?' – has proved very popular.

TAVERNER, *John* (c. *1490–1545/6*)

In 1526 Taverner became Master of the Choristers at Cardinal College (now Christ Church) Oxford, at the invitation of Cardinal Wolsey. At the college he became involved with heretics and was subsequently forced to return to Lincoln, where he spent the rest of his life. Taverner's music is extremely florid, and his masses written for feast days at the college are masterpieces of early Tudor music. Masses such as *Missa corona spinea* for six-part choir were written in elaborate and florid polyphony; the plainsong theme runs throughout the piece in longer value notes. His simpler mass, *Western Wind*, is the first English mass to be based on a secular theme, and this particular theme was also used as the basis of masses by Tye (*c.* 1505-72) and White (*c.* 1538–74). Taverner wrote a number of motets (including *Dum transisset*), settings of the *Magnificat* which alternate plainsong and polyphony, and various secular works.

TCHAIKOVSKY, *Peter* (*1840–93*)

Most of Tchaikovsky's choral music was written for the Russian Orthodox church, and includes the *Vespers* (1881), *Three Cherubic Hymns* (1884) and *Six Church Songs* (1885), which contain the famous 'Hymn to the Trinity'. A recent publication of some of these anthems in transliteration and translation have made them available to a wider public. Like much of the music written for the Russian Orthodox church, Tchaikovsky's religious works are harmonically conservative.

TELEMANN, *George Philipp* (*1681–1767*)

Telemann was a contemporary of Bach and Handel, and like Bach was employed as a church musician; he worked in Hamburg from 1721. Telemann composed well over one thousand cantatas for church services, and over 40 settings of the passion, as well as many oratorios, masses, motets and secular compositions. His phenomenal output included operas as well as chamber works and many concertos. Telemann's musical idiom is attractive but rarely as distinguished as that of Bach or Handel. His secular work *Die Tageszeiten* (1759) is a sequence of four short cantatas, one about each of the seasons of the year. His oratorio *Der Tag der Gerichts* was written in 1762; he also set two parts of Klopstock's *Messias*.

THOMPSON, *Randall* (*1899–1984*)

Randall Thompson is best known for his choral music written in an approachable, melodic idiom – his *Alleluia* (1940) has become a popular favourite with smaller choirs. *The Peaceable Kingdom* (1936) is on a much larger scale and is scored for unaccompanied choir; its text is taken from Isaiah. Thompson has also written a *Mass* (1956), *Requiem* (1958), and a *Passion according to St Luke* (1965).

THOMSON, *Virgil (b. 1896)*

The music critic and composer Virgil Thomson has written music in a wide variety of styles, and achieved notoriety with his operas to libretti by Gertrude Stein. His works for choir include two masses – *Missa Brevis* for male voices (1925) and *Missa Brevis* (1936) for female voices and percussion – a requiem (*Missa pro defunctis*, 1960) for chorus and orchestra, and a cantata on poems by Edward Lear for soloist, chorus and orchestra (1974).

TIPPETT, Michael (b. 1905)

Tippett's first oratorio *A Child of our Time** was first performed in 1941 and soon established a place in the choral repertory. The text, by the composer, tells the true story of a Jewish boy who shoots a Nazi official; in retaliation the oppressors wreak vengeance on the Jews in a fierce pogrom. Tippett does not specify events and the work becomes a parable for all men of any time. As a modern equivalent of Bach's chorales Tippett uses negro spirituals to comment on the action.

The Mask of Time is the third large scale work by Tippett; it was given its first performance in Boston and heard for the first time in this country at a Promenade concert in the same year, 1984. The words are by the composer with extracts from Yeats and other writers. The choral writing (in at least six parts) is as taxing as the music in his *Vision of St Augustine** (1965), which takes its text from St Augustine and the Bible. The texture of this work is florid and demanding for soloist (baritone) and choir alike, and is written in an astringent musical idiom.

Tippett's other choral works are all on a smaller scale but include a few unaccompanied pieces of great distinction: *The weeping babe* (1944), two madrigals, *The Source* (Edward Thomas) and *The Windhover* (Gerard Manley Hopkins) (1942), the motet, *Plebs angelica* for double choir (1943), the madrigal, *Dance clarion air* (1952), and *Four Songs from the British Isles* (1956).

Two works written for school performance are *The Crown of the Year* (1958) scored for unbroken voices and instruments, and *The Shires Suite* for full choir and orchestra composed for the Leicestershire Schools Symphony Orchestra between 1965 and 1970.

TOMKINS, John (1572–1656)

Tomkins was a pupil of Byrd and organist at the Chapel Royal from 1621. He was one of the last English composers to write madrigals; his single volume of madrigals was published in 1622 and contains *Too much I once lamented* and *See, see the shepherds' Queen*, which both use 'fa-la' refrains, and the moving *When David heard that Absalom was slain*. Tomkins's anthems are more numerous; a volume *Musica Deo sacra et ecclesiae anglicanae*, issued after his death (1668) collected all his anthems together in one publication.

VAUGHAN WILLIAMS, Ralph (1872–1958)

Vaughan Williams's first work for chorus and orchestra was the setting of Whitman's poem *Toward the unknown region* (1905), and this, together with the large scale *Sea Symphony** (1910), also to Whitman poems, established the composer's reputation as one of the foremost choral composers of his generation. The *Sea Symphony* made a great impact on all who heard it and it has remained one of Vaughan Williams's most impressive compositions, although the echoes of Elgar betray Vaughan Williams's roots. Choral works continued to play an important part in his oeuvre throughout his career.

The *Mass in G minor* (1921) for unaccompanied choir shows Vaughan Williams as a master of counterpoint and polyphony, in which he was influenced by his study of Tudor composers. There is also more than a hint of folksong melody in his music, because Vaughan Williams collected folk songs in the early part of the century. Despite its title, *Sancta Civitas* (1925) is a setting of English texts, for tenor, baritone, chorus and orchestra, as is *Dona nobis pacem* (1936). The latter, scored for soprano, baritone, chorus and orchestra, is a setting of Whitman poems and biblical words, and is a penetrating plea for peace. A setting of the *Benedicite* dates from 1929. The *Five Tudor Portraits* of 1935 have never achieved great success, perhaps because Skelton's poems are rather too wordy. On the other hand, the *Serenade to Music**, written originally for sixteen solo voices and later arranged for choir, is one of Vaughan Williams's most popular works. It is a setting of words from Shakespeare's *The Merchant of Venice*, and was written in 1938 for Henry Wood's golden jubilee.

Vaughan Williams's other works for chorus and orchestra include *An Oxford Elegy* (1949) on a poem by Matthew Arnold, for speaker, mainly wordless choir, and orchestra, and *Flos Campi* (1925) for solo viola, wordless choir and small orchestra. *The Sons of Light* (1950) has recently been recorded and is an impressive cantata, which was composed for the Schools Music Association of Great Britain. *Hodie** (1954) is a Christmas cantata which deserves many more performances than it achieves.

There are many other works of a less ambitious kind which are available in both orchestrated and organ only versions: *Te Deum* (1928), *Te Deum* (1937), *The voice out of the whirlwind* (1947) and *Epithalamion* (1957); as well as various works written specifically for choir and organ, such as *O clap your hands* (1920), which also includes brass, *A vision of aeroplanes* (1956) and *A choral flourish* (1956). Vaughan Williams's anthems include *O how amiable* (1934) and the unaccompanied *O taste and see* (1952), written for the coronation of Queen Elizabeth I. Other unaccompanied works include *O vos omnes*, the well-known and rather difficult *Three Shakespeare songs* and *Silence and Music*. Vaughan Williams also published numerous arrangements of folk songs including the *Wassail Song*, which is the fifth of the *Five English Folk Songs* (1913). He also composed carols and hymns, and edited the English Hymnal (1906).

VERDI, Giuseppe (1813–1901)

Verdi devoted his career to the composition of operas, but he was sometimes called upon to write occasional pieces, such as the *Hymn of the Nations*, intended for performance in England in 1862. He was one of seven composers who joined together to write a requiem for Rossini. The project came to nothing, but Verdi used his 'Libera me' movement in the subsequent *Requiem** written after the death of Manzoni. This is one of the finest settings of the requiem, and by far the most popular. It was first performed on the anniversary to Manzoni's death in 1874.

Among Verdi's last compositions were the *Four Sacred Pieces** for chorus and orchestra; the first two were written just before his last opera, *Falstaff*, and the final two, just after. An unaccompanied setting of the *Lord's Prayer* in Dante's version dates from 1880.

VICTORIA, Tomás Luis de (1549–1611)

Victoria has been called the 'Spanish Palestrina'; he worked in Rome before taking up an appointment as choirmaster in Madrid. Like Palestrina, who was an almost exact contemporary, Victoria perfected the art of polyphonic writing, but allowed himself greater freedom of expression and was altogether more emotional. Victoria composed over twenty masses, including two requiems, more than 40 motets, and several works for Holy Week, but no secular music of any kind.

VIVALDI, Antonio (1678–1741)

Vivaldi was employed as chorus master at the Ospedale della Pietà in Venice, which was an orphanage for girls. It was for his pupils there that he wrote many of his concertos and almost all of his church music. The famous setting of the *Gloria* for two sopranos, alto, chorus, oboe, trumpet and strings, is Vivaldi's most frequently performed choral work; there is another setting of the same text in D, and a third in C. The final movement of both D major settings 'Cum sancto spiritu' is a borrowing from a contemporary composer, Ruggieri. Vivaldi's other church works include settings of the *Magnificat*, psalms, *Dixit Dominum, Laudate pueri* and various motets. Of Vivaldi's oratorios, all but *Juditha Triumphans* (1716) are lost.

WAGNER, Richard (1813–83)

Wagner composed only a few choral works (not, of course, including his operas). His biblical scene *Das Liebesmahl der Apostel (The love-feast of the Apostles)* is a setting of his own words, scored for male voices and orchestra: the first half of the work is for unaccompanied choir. The work dates from 1843, the year his opera *The Flying Dutchman* was first performed in Dresden.

WALTON, William (1902–83)

Walton's *Belshazzar's Feast** has gained a permanent place in the repertory since its premiere in Leeds in 1931, in spite of the large forces required. Its success has rather overshadowed his other choral works, particularly since his style of competition remained fairly constant throughout his creative life, so that pieces written since *Belshazzar's Feast* inevitably sound like imitations of it. Walton's other major choral works are *In honour of the City of London* (1937), the *Te Deum* (1953), which was written specially for the coronation of Queen Elizabeth II, and the *Gloria* (1961) written for the 125th anniversary of the Huddersfield Choral Society.

Walton wrote church music throughout his career, starting at the age of fifteen with *A Litany* 'Drop, drop, slow tears' (1917), which is his earliest extant composition. Other sacred music includes the wedding anthem *Set me as a seal* (1938), the motet *Where does the uttered music go?* – written on a Masefield text in 1946 for the unveiling of the memorial window to Sir Henry Wood in St Sepulchre, Holborn – *The Twelve* (1965), an extended anthem to words by W. H. Auden for choir and organ (later orchestrated) and the *Missa Brevis* (1966). In 1974 Walton wrote the unaccompanied *Cantico del sole*, a setting of a prayer by St Francis of Assisi, as a commission for the 24th Cork International Choral and Folk Dance Festival. Various short carols by Walton have been included in popular carol collections.

WEBER, Carl Maria von (1786–1826)

Weber composed three settings of the mass, and a large number of secular works for choir, both with and without orchestra. None of these are often performed nowadays, although Novello vocal scores of the *Mass in G* can still be found lurking on library shelves! This mass, dating from 1819, was written for a celebration, and is known as the *Jubelmesse*. An earlier mass in E♮ is less interesting; the third mass is in C.

WEBERN, Anton (1883–1945)

Webern studied privately with Schoenberg from 1904 to 1908. His works are all extremely brief and condensed, some movements lasting only a few seconds. An early chorus for unaccompanied choir, *Entflieht auf leichten Kähnen* bears the opus number 2, and is a setting of a poem by Stefan George. In 1924 he adopted the twelve-tone method of composition. His other choral works are settings of poems by Hildegard Jone: *Das Augenlicht* for chorus and orchestra and two cantatas (1939 and 1943), and of Goethe (Lieder op 19).

WEELKES, Thomas (c. 1575–1623)

Thomas Weelkes was one of the foremost English madrigalists. He was organist at Winchester, and later, Chichester, cathedrals, where he was often in trouble for being drunk and disorderly. Weelkes contributed *As Vesta was from Latmos hill descending* to the *Triumphs of Oriana** (1601), and published three books of madrigals, and one of *Ayres or Phantasticke Spirites for Three Voices*. His colourful setting of words in *Like two proud armies* and *Mars in a fury* is perhaps overshadowed by the melodic invention of *Thule, the period of cosmography*. *O care thou wilt despatch me* is a more poignant madrigal in a highly charged emotional style. Weelkes's sacred music, anthems and settings of the service include *When David heard* and a fine six-part *Hosanna to the Son of David*.

WEILL, Kurt (1900–50)

Kurt Weill's musicals are among the most popular works of their kind, and songs such as 'Mack the knife' from *Die Dreigroschenoper* (1928) (*The Threepenny Opera*) have become classics. From the same period came two other Brecht settings; the *Berlin Requiem* (1928) for three male soloists, chorus and fifteen instruments, and a cantata which tells the story of the Lindberg flight (1929), which is a re-working of a radio score. Weill's early *Recordare* (1923) for mixed chorus and children's choir is a very impressive setting of the Latin text.

WESLEY, Samuel (1766–1837)

Samuel Wesley came from a remarkable family: his uncle, John Wesley (1703–91) was the founder of Methodism, his nephew Charles was a Roman Catholic composer and organist, his brother Charles (1757–1834) was a composer, and his illegitimate son, Samuel Sebastian was another composer, even more famous than Samuel himself. Samuel Wesley wrote music in Latin for the Roman Catholic church, including several masses and the eight-part anthem *In exitu Israel*. He also wrote anthems and music for services in English, as well as many glees and part-songs.

WESLEY, Samuel Sebastian (1810–76)

No doubt Samuel Wesley's son was given the name Sebastian because of his father's love and championship of Bach's music. S. S. Wesley's anthems for the Church of England have long held a firm place in the repertory together with his *Magnificat* and *Nunc Dimittis* in E. His anthems range from the multi-movement works such as *Ascribe unto the Lord* and *Blessed be the God and Father* (which includes the duet 'Love one another') to the short *Wash me thoroughly*, but they all share the same romantic harmony and dramatic fervour. The long anthem *The Wilder-*

ness was later orchestrated, as was *Ascribe unto the Lord*. S. S. Wesley devoted much effort to improving the quality of church music. He also composed a few secular pieces, including glees.

See also WESLEY, Samuel.

WILBYE, *John (1574–1638)*

John Wilbye was an English composer mainly in the employ of noble families. He was one of the outstanding madrigal composers, and contributed *The Lady Oriana* to the 1601 collection *The Triumphs of Oriana*. His other madrigals, which were published in two volumes in 1598 and 1609, include: the four-part *Adieu sweet Amaryllis*, the five-part *Flora gave me fairest flowers*, the six-part *Sweet honey sucking bee*, and the harmonically daring *Draw on sweet night*. Wilbye also wrote a little sacred music.

WILLIAMSON, *Malcolm (b. 1931)*

The Australian-born composer Malcolm Williamson was appointed Master of the Queen's Musick in 1975. He has written a large number of works in all forms, and choral music has been a significant part of his *oeuvre*. His musical language is very eclectic. The *Symphony for Voices* (1962) is a very tightly-organized composition for unaccompanied choir, and other unaccompanied works include the choral dances from the chamber opera *English Eccentrics* (1964), based on Edith Sitwell's book, which are very witty and entertaining. Williamson wrote *The Brilliant and the Dark*, a cantata for female voices and orchestra, for the National Federation of Women's Institutes in 1966. *In Place of Belief* (1970), with words by Lagerqvist, is scored for choir and piano (four hands). Most recently, Williamson's *Mass of Christ the King** (1977) has been proving popular with choral societies in this country.

WOLF, *Hugo (1860–1903)*

Hugo Wolf composed over three hundred songs, mainly in short bursts of creative energy during the 1880s and 1890s. Choral works do not form a significant part of his output, but include the *Sechs geistliche Lieder* for unaccompanied chorus, which are among the best short German choral pieces of their kind. Other choruses for male voices have been lost. Of Wolf's accompanied choral works, a few short pieces with orchestra, such as the *Elfenlied* (1891) on Shakespearean texts, for female choir, and *Morgenhymnus* (1897), for mixed voices, are well worth hearing.

Works

Acis and Galatea

Handel's* *Acis and Galatea* is best described as a masque: it was written for modest forces in 1718 for performance at Cannons, the home of the Earl of Caernarvon, later Duke of Chandos. The libretto was culled from the writings of various men, including John Gay and Alexander Pope. Acis is killed by the monster Polyphemus, but Galatea uses her divine powers to turn him into a fountain. Among the famous arias in the work are 'O ruddier than the cherry' and 'Love in her eyes sits playing'; the chorus which begins Part Two, 'Wretched lovers', is one of Handel's finest. (Handel also wrote a cantata for three solo voices and orchestra in Italian, *Acis, Galatea e Polifemo* (1708)).

S, T, T, B: Chorus
o.2rec.2.o.o. – o.o.o.o. – cont –
  strings
Duration: 96′

African Sanctus

David Fanshawe (b. 1942) made his first trip to Africa in 1969, and while there he conceived the idea of a work that would combine traditional African music and western music of his own composition; he wanted to create a work that would praise God. It was not until the spring of 1972 that the *African Sanctus* was written, and the first performance was given by the Saltarello Choir at St John's Smith Square later that year. Since then the work itself has been revised, and Fanshawe has been the subject of a television documentary and considerable publicity. The 'pop' rhythms and electric instruments add an extra layer above the 'authentic' tribal music on tape.

S: Chorus
Timp – perc – piano – tape
Optional: elec guitar, elec bass guitar,
  rock drums, ethnic drums, elec
  organ
Duration: 60′

Alexander Balus

After the success of *Judas Maccabaeus*, Handel* turned again to the same librettist, Thomas Morell, who found another incident from the Book of Maccabaeu (chapters 10 and 11). *Alexander Balus* was first performed at Covent Garden in 1748, but was never a success in Handel's day, although it contains much fine music. The title role of Alexander Balus, King of Syria, was written for a castrato.

S, S, A, T, B, B: Chorus
2.2.0.1. – 2.2.0.0. – timp – harp –
  mandolin – cont – strings
Duration: –

Alexander Nevsky

Prokofiev* based his cantata *Alexander Nevsky* on the score he had written in 1938 for the film of the same name directed by the great Soviet film-maker Sergei Eisenstein. The hero of the film is the thirteenth-century Grand Prince of Novgororod, Alexander Yaroslavo-vich, who was granted the honorary title 'Nevsky' in commemoration of the victory over the Swedish troops on the bank of the River Neva on June 15 1242. The cantata has seven short movements, and is scored for mezzo soprano soloist, and chorus (who sing in all but the first movement). The climax of the cantata, and of the film, is the *Battle on the Ice* which took place on the frozen Lake Chudskoye. The last movement is a hymn of victory.

Ms: Chorus
2.picc.2.corA.2.bcl.tsax.2.dbn. –
4.3.3.1. – timp – perc – harp –
strings
Duration: 40 minutes

Alexander's Feast

Handel* composed a setting of Dry-den's *Ode for St Cecilia's Day* in 1736. It is an undramatic piece with verses in praise of music. At Alexander's Feast Old Timotheus demonstrates the power of music by conjuring up differ-ent moods with his playing; at the conclusion of the poem St Cecilia is honoured. The extra verses which were added to praise the saint were adapted from Newburgh Hamilton's *The Power of Music*.

S, S, T, B: Chorus
0.2rec.2.0.3. – 2.2.0.0. – timp – cont –
strings
Duration: 88'

The Apostles

The oratorio *The Apostles* was the first part of a projected trilogy by Elgar*, and was first performed at Birmingham in 1903. The second part of the trilogy was *The Kingdom*, and the third part, *The Last Judgement*, was never com-posed. The oratorio is scored for a large orchestra, but does not include the instrument called a shofar, which is referred to in the score – its fanfares are played by the trumpet. *The Apostles* tells of the calling of the Apostles, the Betrayal of Christ, and the Ascension; and the soloists portray the Blessed Virgin (also an angel), Mary Magdalen, St John, St Peter, Judas and Jesus. The plight of Judas is particularly well han-dled by Elgar; his extended aria (with chorus) before his death is extremely moving.

Various leitmotivs are used throughout *The Apostles* and *The King-dom*; for example, the opening phrase of the orchestral introduction repre-sents the spirit of the Lord. Elgar was a composer who was very responsive to his text, for example, at the words 'recovering of sight' (page 4 of the vocal score) he quotes from his own *The Light of Life*, which tells the story of Jesus's healing of the blind man. Elgar also quotes (perhaps subcons-ciously) from *The Dream of Gerontius* (vocal score, page 236, figure 212).

S, A, T, 3B: Chorus
2.picc.2.corA.2.bcl.2.dbn. – 4.4.3.1. –
timp – perc – 2 = 1 harp – organ –
strings
Duration: 120'

Appalachia

Appalachia is the old American Indian name for North America. Delius* as a young man spent a rather unhappy time in Florida working on an orange plantation. *Appalachia* is a set of varia-tions on an old slave song. The main portion of the work is scored for or-chestra alone, but Delius introduces voices in the final section. There is one line of music for a baritone which may either be sung as a solo or by the basses of the chorus.

Chorus
3.3.corA.3.bcl.3.dbn. – 6.3.3.1. – timp
– perc – 2 harps – strings
Duration: 33'

Bell Anthem

Bell Anthem is the name sometimes given to Purcell's* anthem Rejoice in the Lord alway because the opening string ritornello[1] features a repeated bell-like scale. This is one of Purcell's best verse anthems and is often performed with organ accompaniment in a shortened form. The full version is scored for strings and continuo.

AT, T, B: Chorus
cont – strings
Duration: 9′

[1] A ritornello is a 'little return' of basic material heard at the opening of a piece. It is often applied to baroque works whose structural form relies on this kind of rondo device.

The Bells

Rachmaninov* composed his four-movement choral symphony, The Bells, in 1913, and it was given its first performance in St Petersburg that year, with the composer conducting. The words are a Russian adaptation by Konstantin Balmont of a poem by Edgar Allen Poe. In the first movement silver bells are associated with youth, while in the second, golden bells invoke marriage (the soprano soloist figures prominently). The third movement is a scherzo for chorus, representing bells of terror; Rachmaninov made two versions of this. The slow finale conjures up the iron bells which toll at the approach of death.

S, T, Bar: Chorus
3(III = picc).3(III = corA).3(III = bcl).
    3(III = dbn). – 6.3.3.1. – timp – perc
    – cel – harp – piano – strings
Duration: 36′

Belshazzar

Handel's* oratorio Belshazzar, first performed at the Kings Theatre, London in 1745, is like an opera and is sometimes staged as one. Not only does it include stage directions in the score (as do some other oratorios) but it has extended passages of secco recitative, very much in the operatic tradition. The story tells how Belshazzar despoils the sacred vessels in the temple, and how the writing on the wall foretells his downfall. The character of Cyrus (a countertenor) figures strongly as Belshazzar's conqueror. The work opens with the customary overture which is followed by an extended accompanied recitative and aria – a format which Handel used again in Messiah.

S, As, A, T, T, B, B: Chorus
0.2.0.1. 0.2.0.0 – timp – cont – strings
Duration: 150′

Belshazzar's Feast

Walton* worked between 1929 and 1931 on the oratorio Belshazzar's Feast, increasing its size as he went. It eventually took the form of a large scale work for double choir and semi-chorus, baritone soloist and an enormous orchestra with extra offstage brass. It was first performed in 1931 at the Leeds Triennial Festival, conducted by Malcolm Sargent. The words were selected from the Bible by Osbert Sitwell; Walton had been a friend of the Sitwell family since his teens when he was a student at Christ Church Oxford.

The oratorio begins with a brass fanfare and the prophecy of Isaiah which foretells the captivity of the Israelites in Egypt. The plight of the captive Israelites is expressed in the setting of the psalm, 'By the waters of Babylon we sat down and wept'. The baritone then lists Babylon's riches and the chorus describes the feast at which Belshazzar presided. The profanation of the vessels from the temple brings down the wrath of God; the writing on the wall tells of the King's impending death, and with the shout 'slain', the chorus describes his fall. The final section is one of general rejoicing.

The jazz idiom, the melodic invention and the chromatic harmonies of the oratorio have assured it a place in the popular repertory; it must be performed by large choirs to have its full effect.

Bar: Chorus
2.picc.2.(corA[1]).3(II = Eb,III = bcl).
  asax.2.dbn. – 4.3.3.1. – timp – perc –
  2 harps – piano(ad lib) – organ –
  strings (+ 2 brass ensembles, each
  0.3.3.1.)
Duration: 34'
[1] corA only used in absence of asax

Blest Pair of Sirens
This short cantata by Parry* was first performed in 1887. It is a setting of Milton's poem *At a solemn music*, which begins with the lines, 'Blest pair of Sirens, pledges of heav'n's joy'. In the first sections of the work the choir is divided into eight parts, but over half the work is scored for straightforward four-part choir. A version of the piece was made by C. S. Lang in 1938 which reduces the choral writing to four parts throughout. *Blest pair of Sirens* is one of Parry's best works, and has always been popular. It is dedicated to Stanford and the members of the Bach Choir. Stanford quotes from the work in his own humorous *Ode to Discord*.

Chorus
2.2.2.2.dbn. – 4.3.3.1. – timp – organ
 – strings
Duration: 10'

Cantata Academica
Britten's* *Cantata Academica* was composed in 1960 and was dedicated to the University of Basle for the celebration of its 500th anniversary. The text is in Latin and the words were selected from the charter of the university together with orations in praise of Basle by Bernard Wyss. Britten divides the piece into two parts, each consisting of separate movements. The music is 'academic', relying heavily on fugues and canons. Part One begins with a chorale (corale) which re-appears at the end of the entire work. Part Two opens with a serial (twelve-tone) theme, which is harmonized conventionally, and this is followed by a choral fugue on a new theme. The twelfth movement is a canon for the four soloists.

S, A, T, B: Chorus
2(II = picc).2.2.2. – 4.2.3.1. – timp. –
  perc. – 2 harps(or 1) – piano (= cel
  ad lib) – strings
Duration: 22'

Cantata Misericordia
Benjamin Britten* composed the *Cantata Misericordia* for the centenary of the Red Cross, and it was first performed at a solemn ceremony in Geneva in 1963. The soloists were Peter Pears and Dietrich Fischer-Dieskau, and the conductor was Ernest Ansermet. The text is in Latin and tells the story of the Good Samaritan. The music is less tuneful than in many other Britten works and the chorus writing is demanding.

T, Bar: Chorus
0.0.0.0. – 0.0.0.0. –timp – harp –
  piano – strings
Duration: 20'

Cantata Profana
Bartók's* *Cantata Profana* is sometimes called *The Enchanted Stags* or *The Giant Stags*. It tells the story (a Romanian folk ballad) of a father whose nine sons were all lost in the forest while hunting a giant stag, and were all turned into stags themselves. The cantata is divided into three sections – in the first

the sons are transformed into stags, and in the second their father meets them in the forest. He asks them to come home, but they explain that they cannot as their antlers are too large to go through the door of a house. In the third part, the chorus repeat the story. The original text is in Hungarian, but it can also be sung in English. The work is scored for double choir.

Bartók composed the *Cantata Profana* in 1930, but withdrew it, intending to write a cycle of cantatas on folk legends: he abandoned the project. The first performance of the *Cantata Profana* was given in London by the BBC in 1934.

T, Bar: Chorus
3(III = picc).3.3(III = bcl).3(III = dbn). – 4.2.3.1. – timp – perc. – harp – strings
Duration: 20'

Canti di Liberazione
Dallapiccola* composed the *Canti di Liberazione* in 1955, although the idea for various works on the subject of freedom and liberty had been in his mind for some time. This particular work celebrates the liberation of Italy from Fascism. The *Canti di Liberazione* is in three parts and is a setting of texts by Sebastiano Castellio, and passages from the *Book of Exodus* and the *Confessions* of St Augustine. It is one of Dallapiccola's largest pieces, and is in a complex twelve-tone style.

Chorus
3(III = picc).2.corA.2.Eb.bcl.asax.tsax. 2.dbn – 4.3.3.0. cbtba. – timp – perc – cel – 2 harp – strings
Duration: 30'

Canti di Prigonia
Dallapiccola* composed the *Canti di Prigonia* between 1938 and 1941; it is related to his opera *Il Prigoniero* (*The Prisoner*) (1949). The work is in three

movements, each representing a particular prisoner: Mary Stuart, Beethoven and Savonarola. It uses a twelve-tone theme, and quotes the plainsong Dies irae melody.

1. Preghiera di Maria Stuarda
2. Invocazione di Boezio
3. Congedo di Girolamo Savonarola

Mixed chorus (1 and 3); female chorus (2)
2Timp* – perc – 2 harps – 2 pianos
Duration: 25'

* Second timpanist only required in no. 3.

Canticum Sacrum
Stravinsky's* cantata *Canticum Sacrum* was composed in 1955, and dedicated to the city of Venice and its patron saint, St Mark. The first movement is the dedication, and the five subsequent motets correspond to the five domes of St Mark's. The last motet is identical (note for note) to the first, but is written backwards. *Canticum Sacrum* was first performed a year after its composition at the Festival of Contemporary Music in Venice.

T, Bar: Chorus
1.2.corA.0.2.dbn – 0.4.4.0. – harp – organ – strings (violas and double bass only)
Duration: 17'

Carmina Burana
The songs in the medieval manuscript found at the Monastery of Benediktbeuern in Bavaria are known as *Carmina Burana*; the twentieth-century composer Carl Orff* selected poems from this manuscript for his secular cantata of the same name. The cantata was first performed in Frankfurt in 1937 and was a spectacular success; it is often performed in Germany as a stage work with dancing and action, but in England it is popular as a concert piece. The poems are in Latin and old

German, and are collected in the cantata into sections rejoicing in the pleasures of life: *Fortuna Imperatrix Mundi* (Fortune, Empress of the World), *Primo Vere* (Spring), *Uf dem Anger* (In the meadow), *In Taberna* (In the tavern), *Cour d'Amours* (The Court of Love), *Blanziflor et Helena,* and a final repeat of the opening chorus.

The cantata *Carmina Burana* properly forms the first of a trilogy of cantatas written over a number of years. The other two parts, *Catulli Carmina*, (1943), (to poems by Catullus) and *Trionfo di Afrodite*, (1952), are less musically interesting than *Carmina Burana*. Orff's music relies on motor rhythms, repetitive tunes, percussive effects, and general *joie de vivre*.

S, T, Bar: Chorus: Boys' chorus
3(II & III = picc).3(III = corA).3(III = Ebcl).2.dbn. – 4.3.3.1. – timp – perc – cel – 2 pianos – strings
Duration: 60′

Celtic Requiem

The text of John Tavener's* *Celtic Requiem* is a compilation of sentences from the requiem mass, poems by Vaughan, Newman and others, and the words of children's games – often parodied and distorted. The work was commissioned by the London Sinfonietta, and first performed by them in 1969.

S; Children's Chorus; Chorus
0.0.1.0. – 0.1.(= tpt.picc).1.0.Aeolian bagpipes – perc – piano – organ – elec guitar(= elec bass guitar) – strings
Duration: 23′

Chandos Anthems

In 1718 Handel* was appointed composer in residence to James Brydges, Earl of Caernarvon, who later became Duke of Chandos, at Cannons (his palace near Edgware). Handel composed eleven anthems to sacred texts between 1717 and 1718 and these are collectively known as the Chandos Anthems. These eleven anthems exist in a number of versions, but are usually scored for soloists, a chorus in three parts (without altos) and a small orchestra consisting of one oboe, one bassoon, strings (without violas) and continuo. Two of the anthems, *O come let us sing* and *The Lord is my right*, also have parts for two recorders. The Chandos Anthems each last for between twenty and thirty minutes. They are: *O be joyful in the Lord, In the Lord I put my trust, Have mercy upon me, O sing unto the Lord a new song, I will magnify thee, As pants the hart, My song shall be alway, O come let us sing unto the Lord, Praise the Lord with one consent, The Lord is my light,* and *Let God arise.*

Five other anthems have been called Chandos anthems erroneously.

O praise the Lord, ye angels of his   28′
A, B: Chorus 0.2.0.1. – 0.2.0.0. – cont – strings
This is the day which the Lord has made (Wedding anthem) (1734)   –
S, A, T, B: Chorus 0.2.0.1. – 2.2.0.0. – timp – cont – strings
Sing unto God, ye kingdoms of the earth (Wedding anthem) (1736)   19′
S, A, T, B: Chorus 0.2.0.(1). – 0.2.0.0. – timp – cont – strings
The king shall rejoice (Dettingen anthem) (1743)   –
A, B: Chorus 0.2.0.1. – 0.3.0.0. – timp – cont – strings
Blessed are they that consider the poor (Foundling Hospital anthem) (1749)
S, S, A, T: Chorus 0.2.0.(1). – 0.2.0.0. – timp – cont – strings

Chichester Psalms

Bernstein* composed his Chichester Psalms in 1965 for the Southern Choirs Festival, in which Chichester, Winchester and Salisbury cathderals join forces. The verses from six psalms are sung in Hebrew and are grouped into three movements. The second is a lyrical setting of Psalm 23 for boy alto and choir, with aggressive interruptions from Psalm 2, 'Why do the nations so furiously rage together'. The final movement begins with an instrumental prelude based on themes already heard in the work, which dissolves into a haunting melody written in an irregular rhythm.

Boy alto: Chorus
0.0.0.0. – 0.3.3.0. – timp – perc – 2 harps – strings *or* perc, harp and organ
Duration: 19'

A Child of Our Time

A Child of Our Time was first performed at London's Adelphi Theatre in March 1944. Walter Goehr conducted the Morley College Choir with the London Philharmonic Orchestra and soloists Joan Cross, Margaret MacArthur, Peter Pears and Owen Brannigan. Tippett* was at that time Director of Music at Morley College. With this oratorio he achieved his first notable success.

An ardent pacifist, Tippett identified with the oppressed – particularly those in East European countries overrun by Hitler – and for a long time he contemplated a subject for an opera that would give expression to his feelings. He might have written an opera on the subject of the Irish Easter Rising of 1916, but in 1938 an event occurred which became the catalyst for the projected work, no longer an opera but an oratorio.

In November 1938, in Paris, a young Jewish refugee, frustrated at his failure to help his family by getting them the correct papers, shot the German official von Rath; there followed the most brutal official Nazi pogrom. *A Child of Our Time* tells the story of this incident, but gives it a broader background than the specifically Nazi event it describes. The text of the oratorio, by the composer, presents the boy (the child of our time) thrown into conflict with the tyrant (the man of destiny).

The work is in three parts, in direct imitation of Handel's *Messiah*. The structure of choruses, recitatives and arias is modelled on Bach's passions. Tippett searched for a modern parallel to the Bach chorales, and found it in the negro spirituals, which speak to a wide variety of peoples regardless of their beliefs. The chorus and soloists tell the story, but they also comment on it and become involved in the action. In the latter section of part three Tippett provides a mood of consolation, as soloists and chorus join together and winter turns to spring.

S, A, T, B: Chorus
2.2.corA.2.2.cbn – 4.3.3.0. – timp – perc – strings
Duration: 70'

The Childhood of Christ (L'Enfance du Christ)

The Childhood of Christ by Berlioz* was first performed in Paris in 1854. The libretto, by the composer, is a dramatic account in three parts of the trials of Joseph and Mary in Bethlehem, their flight into Egypt, and their arrival at Saïs. Part one is called 'The dream of Herod': Christ has already been born, and Herod is haunted by a dream of a new king. Berlioz sets the scene of Jerusalem occupied by the Romans; there is a March by Night – Roman soldiers patrolling on night duty. Herod summons his soothsayers who perform a Cabalistic Dance (in $\frac{7}{4}$ time) and conjure up spirits to interpret the dream; hearing the interpretation Herod sends his men to kill all the young boys in Jerusalem (four-part male chorus). The scene changes to the Holy family in Bethlehem, where angels (four part female semi-chorus placed off-stage) warn them to escape.

Part two is the 'Flight into Egypt' and includes the famous chorus, the 'Shepherd's Farewell to the Holy Family'. Berlioz originally passed this piece off as the work of a seventeenth-century composer; such was the hazy knowledge of music history at the time that he succeeded in fooling the scholars! In part three, 'The Arrival at Saïs', the family seek shelter, and at last find comfort in the home of an Ishmaelite whose children entertain them with a trio for two flutes and harp. The final scene, a choral epilogue introduced by the narrator (tenor), is mostly unaccompanied and concludes with the narrator, angels (off-stage women) and full chorus repeating the word 'Amen'.

S, T, Bar, B, B: Chorus
2(II picc).2(II corA).2.2. –
  2.2.2cnt.3.0. – timp – harp – organ
  – strings
Duration: 97′

Choral Fantasia

Beethoven's* fantasy for piano, chorus and orchestra, the *Choral Fantasia* looks (and sounds) like a study for the final of the *Choral Symphony*; both compositions are variations on a simple diatonic melody. The words of the Fantasia are by C. Kuttner, and are in praise of music. The Fantasia begins with a long piano cadenza and an orchestral preamble before the choir enters. The *Choral Fantasia* was first heard in an 'epic' concert which also included the fourth piano concerto, and the fifth and sixth symphonies!

S, S, A, T, T, B: Chorus: solo piano
2.2.2.2. – 2.2.0.0. – timp – strings
Duration: 20′

Choral Symphony

Concert-going audiences recognize the title *Choral Symphony* to refer specifically to Beethoven's* symphony no. 9 in D minor. After three large orchestral movements Beethoven provided a grand finale which reiterated the main themes heard previously in the symphony, and introduced voices. The bass soloist begins with the lines 'O friends, not these sounds; let us raise a song of joy', and the orchestra plays the now famous melody which is the subject of variations throughout the finale, as the chorus and soloists sing Schiller's *Ode to Joy*. Beethoven had considered setting this poem for a number of years, and it is possible that the Choral Fantasia was a first attempt at choral variations, and hence a 'sketch' for the finale of the ninth symphony.

S, A, T, B: Chorus
2.picc.2.2.2.dbn. – 4.2.3.0. – timp –
  perc – strings
Duration: 68′

Christ on the Mount of Olives
(*Christus am Ölberg*)

Beethoven's* oratorio, *Christ on the Mount of Olives* was composed in 1803 (but later revised) and performed for the first time in Vienna in a concert which also included the second symphony and third piano concerto. The oratorio, which was Beethoven's only work of this type, was very successful and was performed a number of times in his lifetime. It is scored for soprano (Seraph), tenor (Jesus) and bass (Peter), and tells of the arrest of Christ: the chorus take the part of the soldiers and disciples. The final chorus considers Christ's resignation to his fate and looks towards his triumphant resurrection, 'Allelujah! Praise the Lord'. In the nineteenth century, the work was known in England as *Engedi*, and the libretto was altered to tell the story of David.

S, T, B: Chorus
2.2.2.2. − 2.2.3.0. − timp − strings
Duration: 53′

Christmas Oratorio

The work which we know as Bach's* *Christmas Oratorio* is in fact a collection of six church cantatas written for the festival days over the Christmas period from Christmas Day to the Epiphany; Christmas Day, December 26, December 27, January 1 (the Feast of Circumcision), the Sunday after the Feast of Circumcision, and January 6 (Epiphany). As six separate pieces they rank with the greatest of Bach's other (numbered) cantatas, but it is unreasonable to mount a performance of all six in one evening. Not only would six half-hour cantatas make a very long programme, but a performance of all six together would not reflect Bach's intentions. The different scoring of each cantata is yet another problem.

In each of the cantatas, the Evangelist is sung by the tenor, who relates the narrative of the gospels, while the arias are settings of texts reflecting on the action. The role of the chorus is similar to that in the settings of the passions: they comment on the action as well as taking part in it. There is, however, variety in the cantatas; for example, the second cantata opens not with the usual chorus, but with an orchestral sinfonia, the so-called Pastoral Symphony. Four of the cantatas end with an elborate chorale setting.

1. Jauchzet, frohlocket Duration: 28′
S, A, T, B; Chorus; 2.2(obd'a).o.1. − 0.3.0.0. − timp − cont − strings

2. Und es waren Hirten Duration: 31′
A, T, B; Chorus;
2.0.2obd'a.2obdc.0.0. − 0.0.0.0. − cont − strings

3. Herrscher des Himmels Duration 24′
S, A, T, B; Chorus; 2.2(obd'a.)o.o. − 0.3.0.0. − timp − cont − strings

4. Fallt mit Danken Duration 25′
S, (S), T, B; Chorus; 0.2.0.0. − 0.2. cor dc.0.0.0.0. − cont − str

5. Ehre sei dir, Gott gesungen Duration 27′
S, A, T, B; Chorus; 0.0.2 obd'a.0.0. − 0.0.0.0. − cont − strings

6. Herr, wenn die stolzen Feinde schnauben Duration 27′
S, A, T, B; Chorus; 0.2 (obd'a).0.0. − 0.3.0.0. − timp − cont − strings

Christmas Story

Schütz* published the Evangelist's part of his *Christmas Story* in 1664, but in order to monitor performances of the complete work, kept the other sections 'on hire'. The complete work consists of narration and *intermedii*, that is, scenes from the story. The title of the work is *Historia der Freuden und Gnädenreichen Geburt Gottes und Mariens Sohnes, Jesu Christ, Unseres Einigen Mittlers, Erlösen und Seligmachers* − 'The History of the joy and grace-abounding Birth of Jesus Christ, the Son of God and Mary, our Mediator, Redeemer and Saviour'. The *intermedii* introduce the angels, shepherds and wise men, whose parts are usually sung by soloists. The full chorus sing at the beginning and end of the work.

S, T, B: Chorus
2.0.0.1. − 0.2.2.0. − cont − strings
Duration: 50′

Christus

Listz's* oratorio *Christus* was finished in 1866 while Liszt was in Rome; parts of it were first performed there. The work was given its first complete performance in Weimar in 1873 with the composer conducting, and was later performed in Budapest. *Christus* is in three parts: *Weihnachtsoratorium* (Christmas oratorio), *Nach Epiphania* (scenes from the life of Christ), and *Passion und Auferstehung* (passion and resurrection). Throughout the work, Liszt quotes plainsong melodies which help to give musical unity to an otherwise rather sprawling work. *Christus* was popular in Liszt's lifetime but has since slipped from the repertory. It was however heard in London in 1977 as part of the Liszt Festival of that year, and has since been performed at a Promenade concert. Much of the music in the oratorio is for orchestra alone, including the march, 'The Three Holy Kings'.

S, A, T, Bar, B: Chorus
2.picc.2.corA.2.2. – 4.3.3.1. – timp –
perc – 2 harp – organ – strings
Duration: 153'

Christus is an incomplete oratorio by Mendelssohn, which he began writing in 1844. It was left uncompleted at his death, although one or two excerpts have been published.

The role of Christ in Bach's *St Matthew Passion* is referred to as *Christus*.

Cinq Rechants

Messiaen* composed his *Cinq Rechants* in 1948, immediately after the large scale *Turangalîla Symphony*. The *Cinq Rechants* are scored for twelve solo voices (3S, 3A, 3T, 3B) and set texts by the composer, mostly in a pseudo-Hindu language, although portions of the poems refer to the legend of Tristan and Isolde. Messiaen developed a system of rhythmic and dynamic organisation, and he explores this device throughout the work. He also exploits the possibilities of the vocalists, who alternate between speech and song.

Unaccompanied
Duration: 18'

Come ye sons of art

Purcell* composed six odes for the celebration of the birthday of Queen Mary II, wife of William III, and *Come ye sons of art* is the last of them. It was written for the Queen's 33rd birthday in 1694, and she died later the same year. The anonymous texts are undistinguished, but the solo numbers by Purcell are very fine, and include the famous alto duet *Sound the trumpet*. The chorus has very little to do, merely repeating melodies first sung by the soloist.

S, A, A, B: Chorus
2.2.0.0. – 0.2.0.0. – timp – cont –
strings
Duration: 25'

Coronation Anthems

Coronation anthems have been written for the crowning of our monarchs for hundreds of years. Purcell* and Blow wrote coronation anthems, but probably the most famous examples are the four composed for the coronation of George II in 1727 by Handel*. The four works and their placing in the service were: *The King shall rejoice* after the Recognition, *Zadok the Priest* at the Annointing, *Let thy hand be strengthened* after the Enthronement, and *My heart is inditing* after the Crowning of Queen Caroline. This final anthem includes the words 'Upon Thy right hand did stand the queen in vesture of gold, and the king shall have pleasure in thy beauty'. The anthem *Zadok the Priest* has been performed at all subsequent coronations.

1. *Zadok the Priest*   Duration: 6'
Chorus; 0.2.0.2. – 0.3.0.0. – timp –
cont – strings

2. *The King shall rejoice*   Duration: 11′
Chorus; 0.2.0.1 – 0.3.0.0. – timp –
cont – strings

3. *My heart is inditing*   Duration: 12′
Chorus; 0.2.0.(1). – 0.3.0.0. – timp –
cont – strings

4. *Let thy hand be strengthened*
Duration: 9′
Chorus; 0.2.0.(1). – 0.0.0.0. – cont –
strings

Coronation Mass

Mozart's* Mass in C, K 317, composed
in 1779, is called the *Coronation Mass*.
The origin of the title is not clear, but
the mass may have been associated
with the service held at Maria-Plain
near Salzburg each year. This service,
held on the fifth Sunday after Pentecost, commemorated the miraculous
crowning of an image of the Virgin,
and had been held regularly since 1751.

S, A, T, B: Chorus
0.2.0.2. – 2.2.3.0. – timp – organ –
strings (without violas)
Duration: 28′

Coronation Ode

Elgar's* *Coronation Ode* was commissioned for the Covent Garden gala
concert to be held in June 1902, but the
concert was cancelled as the King was
ill. The work was first heard later that
year at the Sheffield Festival. Elgar set
words by A. C. Benson, including the
lines 'Land of Hope and Glory' with
music from his *Pomp and Circumstance
March no. 1*.

S, A, T, B: Chorus
2.picc.2.2.bcl.2.dbn. – 4.3.3.1. – timp
– perc – harp – organ – strings
Duration: 28′

The Creation *(Die Schöpfung)*

When Haydn* visited London in 1791
and 1794 he heard the oratorios of
Handel performed there. Inspired by
their example, he set about composing
his own oratorio to English words,
although working from a German
translation. The text of *The Creation*
was selected from the book of Genesis
and supposedly from Milton's *Paradise
Lost*, by Baron van Swieten. The work
was first performed in Vienna in 1798.

Like the oratorios of Handel, *The
Creation* is in three parts. Part One
begins with an orchestral 'Representation of Chaos', which is an amazingly
daring piece of orchestral painting.
The chorus and soloists then describe
the creation. Part Two is concerned
with the creation of living things, and
Part Three devoted mainly to duets
between Adam and Eve on the first
morning.

The work is scored for three
soloists, who take the part of angels
(Gabriel, Uriel and Raphael) in the
early sections of the work; in Part
Three the bass and soprano assume the
roles of Adam and Eve. An alto soloist
is required for the final movement,
which is a chorus with interjections
from all four soloists.

There are many remarkable moments in the score. One very exciting
section comes near the beginning, as
the chorus reaches the words 'and
there was light'; on the word 'light'
they blaze into a loud chord of C
major, which makes a thrilling impact.
Two fine choruses end Parts One and
Two respectively: 'The Heavens are
telling', and 'Achieved is the glorious
work'. When the bass describes the
creation of various elements in Part
One (rain, snow, wind, etc.) Haydn
represents them in the orchestra before
the soloist mentions them. Haydn is a
master of the orchestra, and represents
the 'creeping worm' with notes on the
double bassoon. The arias and duets in
The Creation are among the best Haydn
ever wrote, and do not include a single
da capo movement.

S, A, T, B: Chorus
3.2.2.2.dbn. – 2.2.3.0. – timp – cont –
strings
Duration: 105'

Creation Mass

Haydn's* Mass in B flat composed in
1801 has the title *Creation Mass*. In the
'qui tollis' section of the *Gloria* Haydn
uses a theme from his oratorio *The
Creation*, and hence the nickname.

S, A, T, B: Chorus
0.2.2.2. – 2.2.0.0. – timp – cont –
strings
Duration: 50'

The Crucifixion

The Crucifixion was composed by
Stainer for Marylebone Parish Church
in 1887, and it is still regularly performed there every Good Friday. The
words were written and selected by the
Reverend J. Sparrow-Simpson, and
the short cantata is described as a
'meditation on the sacred Passion of
the Holy Redeemer'. It is a much mis-
understood work, and seems (to many)
to typify Victorian sacred music of the
most maudlin kind. However, the
work is intended as a meditation, and
not a fully blown Passion; it sets out to
express in simple terms the Easter
story, and to comment on it in solo
numbers (for tenor and baritone) and
in hymns for the congregation. Its
continued success owes much to the
directness of its music, while endless
poor performances cannot detract
from its merits.

T, B: Chorus
Organ
Duration: 65'

La Damoiselle Elue *(The Blessed Damozel)*

The cantata *La Damoiselle Elue* by
Debussy* is based on poems by Dante
Gabriel Rossetti. Debussy had recently
won the Prix de Rome and completed
the piece in 1888 while he was working
in Italy. The work is dedicated to a
fellow pupil, Paul Dukas. It is not
typical of Debussy's later style (he had
not yet written the *Prélude à l'après-midi
d'un faune*) but is nevertheless an attractive piece.

S, A: Female Chorus
3.2.corA.3.bcl.3. – 4.3.3.0. – 2 harps
– strings
Duration: 20'

The Damnation of Faust

Berlioz* was twenty-four when he first
read Goethe's *Faust*, in a French translation. He was so inspired by the play
that he composed *Eight Scenes from
Goethe's Faust*, and published them at
his own expense as his opus 1 in 1829.
In 1846 he reworked the material into
another cantata, *The Damnation of
Faust*. The first performance in Paris
was a failure, but Berlioz thought well
enough of the work to bring portions
of it to London when he conducted
there in 1848.

The words of the cantata were written by the composer in collaboration
with two other librettists. The work is
rather episodic; the first scene takes
place in Hungary to accommodate the
Rákóczky March. Notable passages in
the score include the *King of Thule's
Song*, the *Song of the Flea*, the mock
Amen chorus which the men sing in
the beer cellar, and the chorus of devils
in Part Four who sing gibberish
words. The cantata was first performed
complete in England in 1880; it soon
became very popular with choral societies. The *Damnation of Faust* makes
great demands upon conductor, orchestra and soloists – not least the
tenor who is required to sing a top C
sharp!

S, T, Bar, B
3(I,II,II picc).2(I & II corA).2.bcl.4.
– 4.2.2cnt.3.2. – 2 timp – perc – 2
harps – strings
Stage band: o.o.o.o. – 2.1.o.o.
Duration: 20'

Daphnis and Chloe

Ravel's* ballet *Daphnis and Chloe* was
produced in Paris by Diaghilev's Ballets Russes in 1912. It is based on the
story of two lovers, Daphnis and
Chloe, written by the Second Century
A.D. Latin writer, Longus. The complete ballet is scored for wordless chorus and orchestra; the two orchestral
suites which Ravel made from the ballet do not require voices. Other ballets
with chorus include Roussel's *Aeneas*
and Bartók's *The Miraculous Mandarin*.

Chorus
2(picc).picc.afl.2.corA.2.Ebcl.bcl.3.dbn.
– 4.4.3.1. – timp – perc – 2 harps –
cel – strings
Duration: 50'

The Dream of Gerontius

At one time Dvořák* considered setting Cardinal Newman's poem *The
Dream of Gerontius*, but never did so.
Elgar's setting dates from 1900, and
although the first performance at Birmingham under Hans Richter was not a
success (partly because the chorus had
found it difficult and were under-
rehearsed), a performance of the work
in Germany in 1902 went well and
brought the work and its composer to
the attention of Richard Strauss. If
Parry and Stanford had encouraged a
renaissance in British choral music, it
was surely Elgar who consolidated it.
Elgar wrote of Gerontius – 'this is the
best of me'.

The *Dream of Gerontius* is in two
parts; in Part One Gerontius is dying
with a Priest and his friends around his
bed; in Part Two Gerontius's soul is

guided by an Angel (sung by a mezzo
soprano) who brings him to the seat of
God. The choral sections probably
amount to less than one third of the
entire work, but include the exacting
and graphic Demons' chorus *Low born
clods of brute earth*, and the magnificent
double chorus *Praise to the Holiest*. The
work is scored for a semi-chorus as
well as double choir.

Ms, T, B: Chorus
3.2.corA.2.bcl.2.dbn. – 4.3.3.1. – timp
– perc – 2 harp – organ – strings
Duration: 100'

Easter Oratorio
(Ostern-Oratorium)

Bach* performed his *Easter Oratorio*
(BWV 249 'Kommt eilet und laufet') at
St Thomas' Leipzig in 1725 and on a
number of subsequent occasions. It is
an arrangement of a secular cantata
which had already been remodelled.
The cantata justifies its title 'oratorio'
by the fact that it has narrative sections
and characters (implied but not named)
although no Biblical text is used. Bach
also wrote an *Ascension Oratorio*, the
cantata no 11 'Lobet Gott in Seinen
Reichen'.

S, A, T, B: Chorus
1.2rec.o.obd'a.o.1. – o.3.o.o. – cont –
strings
Duration: 50'

The *Easter Oratorio* by Schütz was
composed in 1623; it is called the
'Resurrection Story' (Historia der
Auferstehung Jesu Christi).

S, S, A, A, T, T, B, B: Chorus
Organ – Strings
Duration: 50'

Elijah

Mendelssohn's* first oratorio *St Paul*
had been a great success at its first
English performance at Liverpool, and
Mendelssohn contemplated writing
another such work, this time on the

subject of Elijah. When Birmingham asked him for an oratorio Mendelssohn was encouraged to begin work. *Elijah* has been performed regularly since its triumphant first performance at the Birmingham Festival in 1846, although in recent years it has declined in popularity.

Elijah is arguably more dramatic than *St Paul*, and it is only towards the end of Part Two that the interest begins to wane; it is customary, but really unforgiveable, to cut movements from the end of the work; nevertheless, Elijah's aria 'For the mountains shall depart' is often omitted.

The work is in two parts. In Part One the people call for help in a land of drought; Elijah raises the widow's son, then presents himself to King Ahab and challenges the priests of Baal to a trial of fire between their god and the God of Israel. Fire descends from heaven at Elijah's call, and God sends rain to the drought-stricken land. In Part Two Elijah denounces King Ahab, but the Queen stirs up the people and Elijah goes into the wilderness in despair. He is tended by angels, and ascends to heaven in a chariot of fire.

S, A, T, B: Chorus
2.2.2.2. — 4.2.3.0.oph. — timp — organ — strings
Duration: 135'

Esther

Esther was Handel's* first oratorio. He composed a version of the work for performance in 1720, with the title *Haman and Mordecai*. The story is taken from the Book of Esther, but the text also seems to have been based on Racine's play of the same name.

S, S, A, 5T, B: Chorus
0.2rec.2.0.2. — 2.3.0.0. — timp – harp – cont – strings
Duration: 110'

Die erste Walpurgisnacht *(The first witches' Sabbath)*

Mendelssohn* composed this secular cantata in 1832 and revised it before its publication in 1844. The work was first performed in 1833 in Berlin. The text is by Goethe (whom Mendelssohn met in the 1820s), but is not a setting of the witches' Sabbath in Part One of *Faust*: in fact it is taken from a sketch Goethe made for the play. It gives an account of how the eve of May 1st, a feast day named after Saint Walpurga, an English missionary in Germany, passed into legend as a witches' Sabbath. The singers in the cantata are Druids who frighten off the Christians.

A, T, Bar, B: Chorus
2.picc.2.2.2. – 2.2.3.0. – timp – perc – strings
Duration: 34'

Figure Humaine

Poulenc described this work for double choir as a cantata. The two six-part choirs (with further divisions in the final section) sing poems by Paul Eluard, the *avant garde* poet who became known as the 'poet of the Resistance'. There are eight sections. They express the horror of the turbulent times in which it was written, reflecting on the steadfastness of the French women who survived the trials of war.

The work was commissioned by the director of the Discophiles record company and was composed in 1943. It is dedicated to 'Pablo Picasso whose work and life I admire'.

Unaccompanied
Duration: 20'

Flos campi

Flos campi means 'flower of the field' and is a quotation from the *Song of Solomon*. Each of the six sections of this work by Vaughan Williams* for viola solo, orchestra and wordless chorus is headed by a line from the *Song of Songs*. The viola soloist in the first performance in 1925 was Lionel Tertis.

Solo Viola: Chorus
1(picc).1.1.1. – 1.1.0.0. – perc – cel –
harp – strings
Duration: 20'

A Garland for the Queen

A Garland for the Queen is a collection of unaccompanied choral pieces by British composers commissioned by the Arts Council of Great Britain in 1953 to mark the occasion of the Coronation of Queen Elizabeth II. The idea was suggested by the madrigal collection *The Triumphs of Oriana*. The composers chosen to contribute to *A Garland for the Queen* were Bliss*, Bax* (Master of the Queen's Musicke), Tippett*, Vaughan Williams*, Berkeley*. Ireland*, Finzi*, Rawsthorne* and Rubbra*. Two composers not included, who made separate contributions were Britten*, who wrote the coronation opera *Gloriana*, and Walton*, who composed a *Te Deum* for the coronation service at Westminster Abbey.

Unaccompanied

Geographical Fugue

The *Geographical Fugue* is a four-part fugue for speakers, and it forms part of *Gesprochene Musik* by the Austrian-born (but later naturalized American) composer, Ernst Toch (1887–1964). The fugue is strictly worked out with the names of places and geographical features forming the text. In the first line the German pronunciation of the mountain 'Popocatapetel' has to be adopted to fit the rhythm of the music even when the work is performed in English!

A German Requiem

A German Requiem is the English title for Brahms's* *Ein Deutsches Requiem*. It is not a requiem in the liturgical sense, but rather a cantata to words from the German Bible. It is possible that Brahms got the idea from Schumann, or perhaps intended it in memory of him (Schumann died in 1856). Sketches for the *Requiem* date from the following year, and include the opening theme of the second movement which had been intended for a symphony (a symphony which in fact became the first piano concerto). Brahms was greatly distressed by the death of his mother in 1856 and it is supposed that the soprano solo (movement five) was added in memory of her. The first three movements were performed in Vienna in 1867, but the performance was somewhat marred by the timpanist, who played the pedal note so loudly throughout the fugue at the end of the third movement that he totally obliterated the chorus. Brahms conducted six movements of the work (omitting movement five) in 1868, and the work received its first complete performance in 1869 in Leipzig.

A German Requiem is scored for chorus (whose tenors are twice carried upwards to a top B flat), baritone solo (in movements two and six) and soprano solo (in movement five, which includes brief interjections from the choir). The choir figures in every movement and the short third movement, 'How lovely are thy dwellings' is often performed as an anthem in church services.

S, Bar: Chorus
2.picc.2.2.2.dbn. – 4.2.3.1. – timp –
harp – (organ) – strings
Duration: 70'

Glagolitic Mass

Janáček's* mass for solo voices, chorus, organ and orchestra was written in 1926. The word 'Glagolitic' refers to the language in which the work is set – an old Slav language not in use since the fifteenth century. The work may be performed in Latin, but this destroys the speech inflections suggested by Janáček's music. The mass opens with an orchestral movement (Introduction) and ends with two instrumental movements, an organ solo, and an orchestral Intrada. The chorus never have extended passages to sing, but instead interject with fragmentary bursts of melody; this may prove tiresome in rehearsal, but the whole work is one of the most colourful and rewarding in the choral repertory. The alto soloist sings only a few bars in the entire score.

S, A, T, B: Chorus
4(3picc).2.corA.3.bcl.3.dbn. – 4.4.3.1.
– timp – perc – cel – 2 harp –
organ – strings
Duration: 42′

Gothic Symphony

The Symphony no. 1 by the English composer Havergal Brian (1876–1972) is known as the *Gothic Symphony*: it was composed between 1919 and 1927 and is on an epic scale. Three purely orchestral movements are followed by a setting, in three movements, of the Te Deum in Latin, which is scored for four soloists, quadruple chorus, children's choir and an enormous orchestra including off-stage brass bands. The work was performed in London in 1961 under Sir Adrian Boult, and again in 1980 in a performance conducted by Ole Schmidt, with the boast that over eight hundred performers were taking part.

S, A, T, B Chrous; children's choir
four brass orchestras with timpani
minimum orchestra of: 2picc, 4fl, bass
fl, 4ob, corA, obd'a, bass ob, 3 Bbcl,
2Ebcl, 2basshorns, 2bcl, pedal cl,
3bsn, 2dbn – 8hn, 4cor, 5tpt,

basstpt, 3tentmb, bass tmb, dtbm,
2euph, 2basstba – 4timp – perc –
2harp – organ – cel – strings
Duration: 99′

Grande Messe des morts

Berlioz* composed his *Grande messe des morts* in 1837. It is conceived on the grandest scale. The score calls for four offstage brass bands which augment the orchestra for the first time at the words 'Tuba mirum', an effect which is heightened by timpani chords sounded simultaneously. However, comparatively few movements are as extrovert, and much of the music is soft and intimate; both the *Kyrie* and *Dies irae* begin softly. The *Quaerens me* section is scored for unaccompanied choir, and in the subdued *Offertorium* ('Domine Jesu Christe') the orchestra carry the burden of the argument while the chorus repeat just two notes in hushed tones. A remarkable piece of scoring occurs in the male voice chorus *Hostias*; between the phrases for the chorus, Berlioz writes orchestral chords for flutes and trombones, which provide moments of eerie repose.

The tenor soloist makes one appearance, singing the main melody of the *Sanctus*, which takes him up to a top B♮. The chorus consists of first and second sopranos, altos (who are only occasionally allocated their own line, for example in the *Sanctus*), first and second tenors, and basses (sometimes divided). The choir is thus mainly divided into three: women, tenors and basses.

T: Chorus
4.2.2corA.4.8. – 12.0.0.0. – 10 timp –
16 perc – strings – brass bands: (1).
0.0.4cnt.4.2. (2). 0.4.4.0. (3). 0.4.4.0.
(4). 0.4.4.4.
Duration: 90′

Gurrelieder

Schoenberg* composed the *Songs of*

Gurra between 1900 and 1911. This enormous work calls for a huge orchestra and a very large body of singers – three male voice choirs and an eight-part mixed chorus. The German text is taken from verses by the Danish writer J. P. Jacobsen, and relates stories from Danish history and legend. The six soloists required include a reciter; this was the first work in which Schoenberg used *Sprechgesang*[1] (speech song).

S, A, T, T, B, narrator: Chorus
8(4picc).5(2corA).7(2Ebcl,
2bcl).3.2dbn. – 10(4 Wagner
tubas).6.btpt.7.1. – timp – perc – cel
– 4harp – strings
Duration: 115′

[1] The pitches are indicated but are not to be sustained. They should be merely touched upon in a sing-song recitation.

Harmonie Mass

Haydn* composed his last mass setting in 1802; it is in B♭ and is called the *Harmoniemesse*. The term *harmonie* in German means wind band, and in this mass Haydn brings the wind instruments into prominence.

S, A, T, B: Chorus
1.2.2.2. – 2.2.0.0. – timp – cont –
strings
Duration: 50′

Heilig Mass

Haydn's* mass in B flat composed in 1796 has the title 'In hon. b. Bernardi de offida'; but is generally known as the *Heilig* (Holy) *Mass*. This is because Haydn quotes the German hymn, 'Heilig, Heilig, Heilig' in the *Sanctus* movement.

S, A, T, B: Chorus
0.2.2.2. – 0.2.0.0. – timp – cont –
strings
Duration: 40′

Hiawatha's Wedding Feast

This is the first of a trilogy of cantatas based on Longfellow's epic poem by the English composer Samuel Coleridge-Taylor*. The cantata was first performed in 1898 at the Royal College of Music and was a huge success. Indeed many of Coleridge-Taylor's compositions written in his twenties were very popular, and established him as one of the brightest hopes of English music. The other two cantatas, *The Death of Minnehaha* (1899) and *Hiawatha's Departure* (1900) lacked the freshness of inspiration of the earlier work. However the three cantatas were performed as a trilogy in 1900, and large scale semi-staged performances became very popular at the Royal Albert Hall.

Coleridge-Taylor's music at its best reminds us of Dvořák, but it tends to be more sentimental and falls rather too obviously into shortwinded sections. The aria 'Onaway, awake beloved' comes from the first cantata.

Hiawatha's Wedding Feast
T: Chorus
2.picc.2.2.2. – 4.2.3.1. – timp – perc –
harp – strings
Duration: 32′

The Death of Minnehaha
S, B: Chorus
2.picc.2.2.2. – 4.2.3.1. – timp – perc –
harp – strings
Duration: 40′

Hiawatha's Departure
S, T, B: Chorus
2.picc.2.2.2. – 4.2.3.1. – timp – perc –
harp – organ – strings
Duration: 40′

Hodie

Vaughan Williams's* Christmas cantata is called *Hodie* ('This Day') but despite the Latin title the texts are mainly in English, and include verses from the Bible as well as poems by Milton, Hardy and Herbert. The title refers to the Latin words from the

Vespers service of Christmas Day, which Vaughan Williams sets at the opening of the work. *Hodie* was completed in 1954 and first performed at the Three Choirs Festival that same year.

Two sections of the work, both for unaccompanied choir, have been extracted as carols in their own right, and appear in Book I of *Carols for Choirs: The blessed son of God*, and *No sad thought his soul affright*.

S, T, Bar: Trebles: Chorus
3(III = picc).2.corA.2.2.dbn. – 4.3.3.1. – timp – perc – cel – harp – piano – organ – strings
may be reduced to:
2(II picc).1.corA.2.2. – 2.2.3.1. – timp – perc – cel – piano – strings
Duration: 54'

Hodie Christus natus est – This day Christ was born – is also the text of many motets composed from the Middle Ages onwards. The most famous setting is probably by Sweelinck (1562–1621). The fourth of Poulenc's *Motets Pour le Temps de la Noël* is a setting of *Hodie Christus natus est*.

Hymn of Jesus

Holst* himself translated passages from the Apochryphal Acts of St John for his choral work *Hymn of Jesus*. This piece was composed in 1917, and is scored for double choir with female semi-chorus who punctuate the work with repeated *Amens*. At the beginning Holst quotes the plainsong words and melodies *Vexilla regis* and *Pange lingua*, and then the chorus burst in with the opening text of the *Hymn of Jesus* from the Acts of St John. Holst conducted the first private performance at the Royal College of Music in 1920, and also the first public performance at the Queen's Hall later that year. The work is dedicated to Vaughan Williams.

Chorus, female semi-chorus (SSA)
3(1picc).2.corA.2.2. – 4.2.3.0. – timp – perc – cel(piano) – organ – piano – strings
Duration: 22'

Hymnus Paradisi

The 'Hymn of Paradise' by Howells* was written in 1938 in memory of the composer's son, but not performed until 1950. The text, in Latin and English is taken from various sources including the mass of the dead, the burial service and psalms 23 and 121. Howells's son, Michael, died at the age of nine from spinal meningitis in 1935, and Howells composed an unaccompanied *Requiem* as an expression of his grief. He later reworked the material into the *Hymnus Paradisi* which remained unknown until Vaughan Williams persuaded Howells to offer it for performance at the Three Choirs Festival in Gloucester. The choral writing is no more complex than in some of Howells's church anthems, and is notable for its flowing lines and restrained beauty.

S, T: Chorus
2(II picc*).2.corA*.2.bcl*.2.dbn*. – 4.3.3.1. – timp – perc – harp – piano* – cel* – organ* – strings
(Instruments marked * are optional)
Duration: 50'

Israel in Egypt

Handel* composed *Israel in Egypt* immediately after finishing *Saul*, writing it in a great hurry for its first performance in April 1739. The work was conceived in three parts, with a straight adaptation of the funeral anthem *The Ways of Zion do mourn* standing as Part One. Handel had written the funeral anthem on the death of Queen Caroline, but modified the words to refer to the Israelites mourning the death of Joseph. The other two parts were composed in reverse order; in the correct order they are *Exodus* and *Moses's Song*. The words, possibly selected by Handel himself, are chosen from the Book of Exodus and the Psalms.

The funeral anthem was soon dropped, and Parts Two and Three performed alone. The work therefore now begins with a tenor recitative. *Israel in Egypt* was very popular in the nineteenth century; the majority of numbers in the score are choruses, some written for double choir, so the work has always appealed to large choral societies. In the first part the plagues are described: the frogs (alto aria), and the flies and lice, hail, darkness, and smiting of the first born (which are all choruses). In Part Two, the children of Israel sing their praise to God as the Egyptians are drowned in the Red Sea.

There are only seven solo numbers in this oratorio, consisting of two alto arias, one soprano aria, and duet for two sopranos, a tenor aria, a duet for alto and tenor, and a duet for two basses – *The Lord is a man of war*.

In his haste to complete the work, Handel borrowed music from his own and other composers' works for no fewer than sixteen of the thirty-nine numbers. But we misunderstand his methods if we consider this borrowing an easy option. Only when Handel copies note for note – *They loathed to drink of the river*, originally an organ fugue by Handel himself, and *Egypt was glad when they departed*, copied from an organ piece by Johann Caspar Kerll (d. 1693) – does he take a short cut. The other numbers are adaptations which involved considerable rewriting. *He led them through the deep* is an eight-voice version of a chorus Handel had written 30 years earlier in *Dixit Dominus*, where it is scored for five voices only. The 'Plague' choruses are adapted from a Serenata by Stradella composed in 1690, and other choruses are adapted from works by two composers who are sufficiently obscure to have given scholars the notion that their compositions are really the work of Handel himself in disguise – a *Te Deum* by Urio and a *Magnificat* by Erba.

The range of choral writing in *Israel in Egypt* is remarkable: *He sent a thick darkness* is a choral recitative; *But the waters overwhelmed their enemies* is notable for its drum rolls which represent the engulfing waves. Indeed the whole work is most carefully scored. A passage in the great chorus *The people shall hear* gives a pre-echo of *Surely he hath borne our griefs* from the *Messiah*.

S, S, A, T, B, B: Chorus
2.2.0.2. – 0.2.3.0. – timp – cont
  (organ & hpd) – strings
Duration: 97'

Italian Salad

Once very popular, the *Italian Salad* was originally written for unaccompanied male voices by the German conductor and composer of operettas, Richard Genée (1823–95). The work has as its text Italian musical terms (piano, allegro, etc.) which are represented in the music.

Unaccompanied
Duration: 6'

Jephtha

1. *Jephtha* was Handel's* last oratorio (the later *Triumph of Time and Truth* was merely an English adaptation of the Italian work *Il trionfo del Tempo della Verità* (*c.* 1707)). Handel composed the oratorio in 1751 by which time his eyesight was failing; he wrote in the score after the lines 'How dark, O Lord, are Thy decrees' that his sight was poor and that his face was giving him pain.

The oratorio, which has a libretto by

Morell, tells the story of Jephtha, a Judge of Israel and leader of the army, who makes a vow that if he is victorious in his fight against the Ammonites he will sacrifice whatever comes from his house to meet him first on his return. Jephtha's daughter, Iphis, is the unlucky victim, but an angel appears to proclaim that Iphis should be spared to devote herself to a life of celibacy in the service of God.

Jephtha contains many fine moments and is altogether one of Handel's greatest works. The recitative *Deeper and deeper still* and the aria *Waft her, angels*, both sung by Jephtha (tenor), come from Parts Two and Three of the oratorio respectively, although they are often performed as a pair in recitals and on record.

S, S, Ms, A, T, B: Chorus
1.2.0.2. – 2.2.0.0. – cont – strings
Duration: 135′

2. Carissimi composed his oratorio *Jephtha* just before 1650. It is a short work in Latin which tells the story as in Handel's oratorio (see above). At the end of Carissimi's oratorio the people mourn as Jephtha's daughter leaves to go into the mountains for a month to prepare for her death. The story is told by various soloists in turn who are described as 'Historicus' – narrator. The other characters are Jephtha (tenor) and his daughter (soprano).

S, A, T, B: Chorus
Cont – strings
Duration: 25′

Jerusalem

Parry's* unison setting of Blake's poem has, like *Land of Hope and Glory*, become one of the United Kingdom's national songs. It appears in many hymn books. Parry composed the work in 1916, and Elgar orchestrated it in 1924. *Jerusalem* is sung regularly at the Last Night of the Proms, having been introduced by Sir Malcolm Sargent in 1953.

Joan of Arc at the stake (*Jeanne d'Arc au bûcher*)

Jeanne d'Arc au bûcher is a play by Paul Claudel for which Honegger* provided the music, and it was first performed in Basle in 1938. The work was written at the request of the dancer and actress Ida Rubinstein. Some of the characters in the play have singing roles, and others have speaking parts. The story of Joan of Arc, who was burned at the stake in 1431, is told in eleven sections and a Prologue; Joan is tied to the stake and awaits her martyrdom while Brother Dominic reads to her (from a book) the events of her life. Honegger's music is directly appealing and the work was immensely popular in wartime France.

S, S, S, A, T, B; 4 speakers; chorus
2(1 picc).2.1.Ebcl.bcl.3sax.3.dbn. –
0.3.Dtpt.3.1. – timp – perc – cel –
ondes martenot – strings
Duration: 72′

Joshua

Handel's* oratorio *Joshua*, with its text by Thomas Morell based on the Bible, was first heard in 1748. It tells the story of the Children of Israel as they pass over the River Jordan into the land of Canaan, and of the destruction of Jericho. After a battle during which sun and moon are stopped in their course, Joshua is praised by the people, and he gives to Caleb (a captain of the tribe of Judah) lands promised him by Moses. Caleb bestows his daughter Achsah on the conqueror of the city of Debir. The city is then overthrown by the young warrior, Othniel, and it is to him that the chorus sing 'See the conquering hero comes'; Achsah sings the aria 'O had I jubel's lyre'. 'See the conquering hero comes' was also used by Handel in his oratorio *Judas Maccabbaeus*.

S, A, T, T, B: Chorus
2.2.0.1. – 2.3.0.0. – timp – cont – strings
Duration: 105'

Judas Maccabaeus

The text of Handel's* oratorio *Judas Maccabaeus* (Covent Garden, 1747) was written by the Rev. Thomas Morell, who took his story from the first Book of Maccabees in the Apocrypha. The work was written with an eye on current events – the English victory over the Young Pretender at Culloden in 1746. At the beginning of the oratorio the people mourn the death of Mattathias, the leader of the resistance against Synai domination. Judas Maccabaeus is appointed leader in Part One, he encourages his people in Part Two, and in Part Three returns victorious to Jerusalem. The chorus 'See the conquering hero comes' was borrowed from Handel's oratorio *Joshua* for a revival, probably in 1750. *Judas Maccabaeus* is less dramatic than most of the other oratorios but has always been very popular; in fact it is one of the few oratorios performed regularly since Handel's death to the present day.

S, A, A, T, B, B: Chorus
2.2.0.1. – 2.3.0.0. – timp – cont – strings
Duration: 100'

Judith

The oratorio *Judith* by Parry* was first performed at the Birmingham Festival in 1888. The melody of the hymn we know as 'Dear Lord and Father of mankind' is taken from an alto solo in the early pages of the work, 'Long since in Egypt's plenteous land' (v.s. p. 39).

2 Trebles, S, A, T, Bar, Bass: Chorus
2.2. 2. bcl. 2. cbn – 4.4.3.1. – timp – harp – organ – strings
Duration: 150'

Judith is also the subject of oratorios by M.-A. Charpentier and Thomas Arne (1761). Honegger wrote incidental music (Action musicale) to a play about Judith in 1926; it is scored for narrator, soprano and mezzo soprano soloists, with chorus and orchestra.

* 2.bcl.2.cbn.

The Kingdom

The Kingdom is the second of Elgar's* projected trilogy of oratorios (the first is *The Apostles*; the third was not composed), and was first performed at Birmingham in 1906. The text of the work was selected from the Bible by the composer; it is scored for four soloists, who play the parts of the Blessed Virgin, Mary Magdalen, St John and St Peter. *The Kingdom* tells the story of the Pentecost, the work and healing performed by Peter and John, and their arrest. Themes (leitmotives) are shared with *The Apostles*. The work begins with an extended orchestral prelude and ends with the Lord's Prayer. The extended solo passages include the duet for Peter and John ending with 'Turn ye again', and the beautiful soprano solo 'The sun goeth down'.

S, A, T, B: Chorus
3(I = picc).2.corA.2.bcl.2.dbn. – 4.3.3.1. – timp – perc – 2 harp – organ – strings
Duration: 104'

Das klagende Lied (*The Song of Lamentation*)

Mahler's* cantata *Das Klagende Lied* was completed in 1880 while the composer was a student in Vienna. The text is his own, and is taken from a story by Ludwig Bechstein. Mahler was sufficiently pleased with the cantata to regard it as his 'opus 1'. However, it was not performed until 1901, by which time he had revised it, omitting the first part (*Waldmärchen*); it is the two-part cantata which became widely known. In the 1930s the score of Part One was reconstructed for a few performances, but it was not until the original 1880 manuscript was found at Yale University in 1969 that performances of the original version were performed and recorded. The work relies on the frequent repetition of melodies (leitmotives) and it is arguable that in a performance of all three parts these become tiresome.

The story tells how a queen vowed to give her hand to whoever finds a certain flower in the forest. In Part One two brothers search for the flower, and on finding it, one kills the other. In Part Two, a minstrel finds the bones of the dead brother and makes a flute out of one of them; when he plays, the flute tells of the murder. In Part Three, the minstrel arrives as the brother is about to marry the queen and the flute tells its tale; the queen falls senseless as the castle collapses.

S, A, T: Chorus
3(III=picc).3(III=corA).3(II = Ebcl, III=bcl).3.(III=dbn). – 4.4.3.1. – timp, perc – 2 harps – strings
offstage: 2.picc.2.2.2.Ebcl. – 4.2(I&II=Flg).o.o. – timp – perc
Duration: 40'

L'allegro, il pensieroso ed il moderato

Milton's two poems *L'allegro* and *Il penseroso* extolling the virtues of mirth and melancholy respectively, were set by Handel* as an oratorio in 1740. The librettist Jennens compiled the text and provided a third part, *Il moderato*, which provides a middle course. Jennens alternates Milton's poems in the first two parts of the oratorio, providing contrast throughout. The oratorio includes the tenor aria 'Let me wander not unseen'. There is a great deal of excellent music in the score, and the choral writing is not over-demanding; the work deserves to be better known.

S, A, T, B: Chorus
1.2.0.2. – 1.2.0.0. – timp – cont – strings
Duration: 116'

Lauda per la Natività del Signore

Respighi composed his short Christmas cantata *Lauda per la Natività del Signore* in 1930; it is a lyrical piece written in an engaging pastoral idiom. The angel (soprano) announces the birth of Our Lord to the shepherds (chorus), who come to the manger, offering their cloaks to the child, led by the tenor soloist. Mary (alto) sings a lullaby to her child, and the work ends with a chorus of praise for the birth of the Saviour.

S, A, T: Chorus
2(II=picc).1.corA.0.2. – 0.0.0.0. – perc – piano (4 hands)
Duration: 25'

Lélio

Lélio has an alternative title, 'The return to life', and is Berlioz's* sequel to his *Symphonie Fantastique*. He composed the work in 1831, and gave it the opus number 14b (the *Symphonie* is opus 14), intending that it should be performed immediately after the *Symphonie*. The work is scored for narrator, two tenors, baritone and chorus, and is best described as a monodrama.

Narrator, 2T, Bar: Chorus
2(IIpic).2(IIcorA).2.2. – 4.2.cnt.3.1. –

2timp – perc – harp – piano (4
hands) – strings
Duration: 52'

Lobgesang *(Hymn of Praise)*

Mendelssohn's* symphony no. 2 in B♭
consists of three purely orchestral
movements (described by the composer as the 'sinfonia'), followed by a
choral finale – a cantata which com-
prises the greater part of the work.
Mendelssohn had accepted a commission to celebrate the 400th anniversary
of the invention of printing by Guten-
berg, and he decided to write a 'sym-
phony-cantata', selecting his own text
from the Bible. The work was first
performed in 1840 at St Thomas's
Church, Leipzig, conducted by the
composer. Mendelssohn conducted the
Hymn of Praise in Birmingham later
that same year, and revised it (adding a
new choral movement) before its publication. The duet and chorus 'I waited
for the Lord' is particularly well-
known, and is often used as an anthem.

S, S, T: Chorus
2.2.2.2. – 4.2.3.0. – timp – strings
Duration: 66'

Magnificat *(J. S. Bach)*

Bach* composed his *Magnificat* (BWV
243) for performance at St Thomas's
Leipzig for the service of Vespers on
Christmas Day 1723. He had originally
composed it in E♭ and included settings of Christmas texts interspersed
with the lines of the Magnificat, but
during the 1730s he revised the work,
omitting the Christmas numbers and
transposing it down to D.

Bach divides his text into choruses,
arias and duets, using the full orchestra
sparingly. He repeats the opening
music for the final chorus at the words
'Sicut erat in principio' ('As it was in
the beginning') – a common musical
pun.

S, S, A, T, B: Chorus
2.2(I&II = obd'a).o.1. – 0.3.0.0. –
timp – cont – strings
Duration: 30'

The Martyrdom of St Sebastian *(Le Martyre de St Sébastien)*

Debussy* composed incidental music
to the mystery play *Le Martyre de St
Sébastien* by D'Annunzio in 1911. The
music is usually performed in the concert hall in the arrangement by Inghel-
brecht, which was made with
Debussy's approval. This version calls
for a narrator to tell the story. The
original orchestration was by Debussy
and a fellow composer, Caplet
(1878–1925).

S, S, A: Chorus
4.2picc.2.corA.3.bcl.3.dbn. – 6.4.3.1.
– timp – perc – 3 harp – harmonium
– strings
Duration: 72' including narration

Mass in B Minor

We do not know why Bach*, in the
last years of his life, assembled and
published the movements which we
call the *Mass in B Minor*. As a Lutheran
in the service of the church he would
have had no opportunity to perform
the work complete, and in any case, a
piece of such length would have been
totally unacceptable in the context of a
religious service.

In 1733 Bach offered the first two
parts (Kyrie and Gloria) to the new
Elector of Saxony and asked him for a
post as court composer; Bach gained
the position some three years later. The
Kyrie and Gloria together form a *Missa*
– in other words a *Missa Brevis* as used
in the Lutheran church – and Bach
wrote four other such works. But for
some reason he decided to add movements to the 1733 *Missa* to form a
complete setting of the Ordinary of the

Roman Mass. The other movements are the Credo (Symbolum Nicenum – the Nicene Creed), Sanctus, and a final group of miscellaneous movements comprising Osanna, Benedictus, Agnus Dei and Dona nobis pacem. Many of the individual items were adapted from earlier cantatas and it is possible that very few pieces in the *Mass in B Minor* were written specifically for it. Some of the choruses seem to have been adapted from orchestral concertante works, a fact suggested by their florid lines and the lively nature of the orchestral accompaniment. The American scholar Joshua Rifkin has recently put forward the theory that this work (and others by Bach) would have originally been performed by solo singers who sang the arias as well as the choral sections.

S, S, A, T, B: Chorus
2.3(2 = obd'a).o.2. – o.cor d-c.3.o.o. –
timp – cont – strings
Duration: 130'

Mass of Christ the King

Williamson's* *Mass of Christ the King* was commissioned by the Three Choirs Festival and the Royal Philharmonic Orchestra to celebrate Her Majesty the Queen's Silver Jubilee, as well as marking the 250th anniversary of the Three Choirs Festival, but was performed incomplete at the 1977 Three Choirs Festival in Gloucester. It was subsequently completed and heard in its entirety the following year in Westminster Cathedral. Since then it has established itself as one of the major choral works written in the last decades.

S, S, T, Bar: Chorus, children's chorus.
3(II = picc,III = afl).3.(III = corA).2.
bcl.3(III = dbn). – 4.4.(4 = Dtpt).3.1.
– timp – perc – harp – strings
Duration: 70'

A Mass of Life (*Eine Messe des Lebens*)

Delius* composed his enormous *A Mass of Life* between 1904 and 1905. The work is a setting of selected passages from Nietzsche's *Also sprach Zarathustra* in German, but at the first complete performance in 1909, under Sir Thomas Beecham, it was sung in English. *A Mass of Life* is one of Delius's most extended compositions, and requires a large chorus since much of the writing is in eight parts.

S, A, T, B: Chorus
3(III = picc).3.bob(= corA)3.bcl.3.dbn.
– 6.4.3.1. – timp – perc – 2 harp –
strings
Duration: 110'

Messiah

Handel's* most successful oratorio, *Messiah* (incidentally, not 'The' *Messiah*), was first performed in Dublin in 1742 – the only one of his English oratorios not premiered in England. Handel wrote the work in just over twenty days in 1741, and declared 'I did see all heaven before me, and the great God himself.' The text, compiled by Jennens, from the Bible, presents the life of Christ in three parts: the Christmas story in Part One, the betrayal in Part Two, and the resurrection and afterlife in Part Three.

Messiah stands apart from Handel's other oratorios in a number of ways. It is not dramatic as is *Saul* or *Belshazzar*, and there are no characters. Since there is no 'action' there is little recitative, and most of what there is is accompanied (such as 'For behold, darkness shall cover the earth'). There are few da capo arias in *Messiah* (most of them are through-composed); this is a feature of the oratorios in general, and a fundamental departure from the conventions of opera of the period. 'He was despised' is a da capo aria, although the middle section is often omitted in performance; the same is true of 'The trumpet shall sound'. 'Why do the nations' has no da capo – after the middle section the chorus burst in with 'Let us break their bonds'.

The overture to *Messiah* is cast in the customary 'French' two-movement form: a slow introduction is followed by a quicker fugal movement. It is, perhaps rather oddly, in the minor key (E minor) – a strange prelude to the joyful Christmas story. The first vocal movement is not, as might be expected, an opening chorus, but instead an accompanied recitative (in E major) followed by an aria ('Comfort ye' and 'Every valley'); only then comes the first chorus 'And the glory of the Lord'.

As with many Handel works, the composer revised and modified *Messiah* for subsequent performances, re-writing parts for different singers. Watkins Shaw has edited the vocal score and his version has superseded the Victorian efforts of Ebenezer Prout. The work can be performed using only four soloists; a countertenor is sometimes engaged to sing the alto arias.

S, A, T, B: Chorus
0.2.0.2. – 0.2.0.0. – timp – cont –
  strings
Duration: 140'

Mozart made an orchestration of Messiah (K572), scoring it for 2(picc).2.2.2. – 2.2.3.0. – timp – cont – strings.

Missa Solemnis *(Beethoven)*
Beethoven* intended to write his Mass in D for the enthronement of his patron, the Archduke Rudolf of Austria, as Cardinal Archbishop of Olmütz in March 1820. The work was not in fact completed until 1823 and received its first performance in St Petersburg in 1824.

Beethoven took great pains over the composition of the work; he had the text of the mass translated into German so that he could completely grasp its meaning, and also studied Latin inflexion. He studied the music of Palestrina, Handel, Bach and C. P. E. Bach, but wanted to compose a work according to contemporary Austrian taste. Each of the movements is through-composed, and not obviously divided into choruses and arias.

The *Missa Solemnis*, like Beethoven's *Choral Symphony*, puts great demands on the chorus. However the work is a towering masterpiece and in performance is a rewarding spiritual experience.

S, A, T, B: Chorus
2.2.2.2.cbn. – 4.2.3.0. – timp – organ
  – strings
Duration: 80'

The Music Makers
The most famous setting of Arthur O'Shaughnessy's poem, *The Music Makers* is by Elgar*, although an English setting was also made by Kodály. Elgar's work dates from 1912 and is scored for mezzo-soprano soloist, chorus and orchestra. The references in the poem to makers of music gave Elgar the opportunity to quote from his own works, and also to use snatches of *Rule Britannia* and the *Marseillaise* (vocal score, p. 11). Quotations from his own works include the *Enigma Variations* (p. 3 and 44), *The Dream of Gerontius* (p. 5), *Sea Pictures* (p. 6), *Symphony No 2* (p. 44), *Violin Concerto* (p. 66, 67), and *Symphony No 1* (p. 69). At the words 'and a singer who sings no more' (p. 84) Elgar poignantly quotes from *The Dream of Gerontius* 'Novissima hora est'.

A: Chorus

2.picc.2.corA.2.bcl.2.dbn. – 4.3.3.1. –
timp – perc – 2 harps – organ –
strings
Duration: 40′

Nänie

This short work for chorus and orchestra by Brahms* was first performed in Zurich in 1881. The poem is by Schiller (*Noenia*) and Brahms wrote the work as an elegy on the death of his friend, the painter, Anselm Feuerbach.

Chorus
2.2.2.2. – 2.0.3.0. – timp – harp –
strings
Duration: 14′

Nelson Mass

Haydn's* *Nelson Mass* in D for soloists, chorus, strings, organ and three trumpets was first heard in 1798. Haydn gave it the title *Missa in angustiis* (mass in time of peril), the peril being the invading French armies under Napoleon. When news came that Nelson had destroyed Napoleon's French navy at Aboukir, Haydn added trumpet fanfares to the Benedictus of the mass. Nelson and Lady Hamilton visited Eisenstadt in 1800 and heard a performance of the mass. Haydn gave Nelson his pen and the admiral gave Haydn the gold watch he had worn at Aboukir. From that time the mass has been known as the *Nelson Mass*, although it used to be called the *Imperial Mass* in this country, and has also been known as the *Coronation Mass*.

S, A, T, B: Chorus
0.0.0.0. – 0.3.0.0. – timp – cont –
strings
Duration: 43′

Les Noces (The Wedding)

Stravinsky's* ballet *Les Noces* was first produced in Paris in 1923: the chorus sing in Russian and describe the preparations for a wedding ceremony. The work was composed between 1914 and 1917, and Stravinsky made three different versions of it: 1917, 1919 and 1923. The latter version is most frequently performed.

1917: 3.3.3.2. – 4.4.3.1.2flugelhorns. –
timp – perc – 2 harps – harmonium – cimb – hpch – piano – strings (3.0.2.2.1.)
1919: (two movements only) timp – perc – harmonium – 2 cimb – pianola (or 2 pianos)
1923: timp – perc – 4 pianos
Vocal requirements for all versions are: S, Ms, T, B: Chorus
Duration: 24′

Occasional Oratorio

Handel* wrote his *Occasional Oratorio* in a great hurry in 1745, and hence made extensive borrowings from several of his own works: *Israel in Egypt, Athalia* and the *Coronation Anthems*. The work was written to celebrate the suppression of the Jacobite rebellion, and to restore faith in the monarchy after Prince Charles Edward's march on London.

S, S, A, T, B: Chorus
0.2.0.2. – 2.3.0.0. — timp – cont –
strings
Duration: –

Ode for St Cecilia's Day

Purcell* composed four Odes for St Cecilia's Day celebrations, as well as a Te Deum and Jubilate:

Hail bright Cecilia (1692)
Treble, A, A, T, B, B: Chorus
Duration: 55′

Laudate Cecilium (1683) (hymn)
A, T, B: Chorus
Cont – strings (without violas)

Raise the voice (?1683)
S, B: Chorus
Cont – strings

Welcome to all the pleasures (1683)
S, S, A, T, B: Chorus
Cont – strings
Duration: 15'

Te Deum and Jubilate in D (1694)
S, S, A, A, T, B: Chorus
o.o.o.o. – o.2.o.o. – cont – strings

Blow composed various works for St Cecilia's Day celebrations including *Song for St Cecilia's Feast* ('Great Queen of Heaven attend'), *Begin the Song* (1684), *Song on St Cecilia's Day* (1691), and *Te Deum for St Cecilia's Day*.

Handel set Dryden's poem *Ode for St Cecilia's Day* ('From harmony, from heavenly harmony') in 1739:

S, T: Chorus
1.2.o.2. – o.2.o.o. – timp – organ – cont – lute – strings
Duration: 50'

Parry set words by Pope and gave his work the title *Ode on St Cecilia's Day*; it was written in 1889:

S, B: Chorus
2.2.2.2. – 4.2.3.0. – timp – harp – organ – strings
Duration: 40'

Oedipus Rex

Stravinsky's* opera-oratorio has variously been performed as a concert work or a staged opera. The text is by Cocteau after Sophocles's drama in the Latin translation by Danielou. At its first performance in 1927 *Oedipus Rex* was performed as an oratorio. It is scored for narrator, tenor (Oedipus), soprano (Jocasta), bass-baritone (Creon), and bass (Tiresias), who in an operatic performance would act their roles. However, even in a staged performance, the chorus (male voices only) do not act.

S, T, Bass-Bar, B: Male Chorus

3.2.corA.2.Ebcl.2.dbn. – 4.4.3.1. – timp – perc – strings
Duration: 51'

Olivet to Calvary

Olivet to Calvary is a sacred cantata by the organist and choirmaster John Maunder (1858–1920). It is obviously modelled on Stainer's *Crucifixion* and like it is scored for mixed chorus and organ with tenor and baritone soloists; congregational hymns occur throughout the work. The cantata recalls some of the incidents in the last days of the Saviour's life on earth. It was written in 1904, and is a poor piece.

T, Bar: Chorus
Organ
Duration: 60'

Paukenmesse

The mass in C by Haydn* which he composed in 1796 was called by the composer 'Missa in tempore belli', mass in time of war. The use of kettle drums at the end of the *Benedictus* has given the mass its nickname of *paukenmesse* ('pauken' is German for kettle drums, not drum roll!).

S, A, T, B: Chorus
1.2.2.2. – 2.2.o.o. – timp – cont – strings
Duration: 50'

Pavane

Fauré's* *Pavane* is usually performed by orchestra alone; its delicious flute melody is very well known. The original version, however, written in 1887, was scored for chorus and orchestra, a setting of frankly silly words by Count R. de Montesquiou, in praise of women ('C'est Lindor! c'est Tircis'). Fauré also arranged the work for chorus and piano in 1891.

Chorus
2.2.2.2. – 2.0.0.0. – strings
Duration: 6′

Perséphone

Stravinsky* collaborated with André
Gide on Perséphone, which was first
performed by Ida Rubinstein's ballet
company in 1934 at the Paris Opéra
with Stravinsky conducting. Gide
stayed away as he had not approved of
the composer's treatment of his text.
The legend tells how Persephone (Pro-
serpine), daughter of Zeus, is carried to
the Underworld by Pluto. Her mother,
Demeter, searches for her and is
allowed to bring her back, but only for
six months of the year (at the beginning of spring). The role of Persephone is written for female narrator,
and the greater portion of the work is
given to the tenor soloist (Eumolpus),
while the chorus comment on the action. In a staged performance the work
would be mimed and danced.

T, female narrator: Chorus and
   childrens' choir
3.3.3.3. – 4.3.3.1. – timp – perc – 2
harps – piano – strings
Duration: 51′

Petite Messe Solenelle

Rossini's* Petite Messe Solenelle was
first performed in 1864 when the composer was 71. He described it as the
'last mortal sin of my old age'; it was
his last major work, and the only large
scale work he had written in a number
of years (the Stabat Mater dates from
some twenty-two years before). The
Petite Messe Solenelle was first heard in a
house in Paris, and performed publicly
the following day. It is scored for two
pianos and harmonium, but it is possible (although unethical) to omit the
second piano, which merely doubles
certain bass parts.

The mass falls into various sections
(choruses and arias): Kyrie, Gloria (in
six sections), Credo (in three sections),
an instrumental Preludio Religioso (for
the Offertory), Sanctus, Benedictus,
the hymn O Salutaris, and Agnus Dei.
The four soloists must be 'opera'
singers. The chorus make a prominent
contribution to the work, including
two exciting and athletic fugues, at the
end of the Gloria and Credo movements.

Rossini orchestrated the Petite Messe
Solenelle for a performance in 1869.

S, A, T, B: Chorus
either: 2 pianos and harmonium
or: 2.picc.2.2.3. – 4.4.2cnt.3.1. – timp
– 2 harps – organ – strings
Duration: 85′

Polovtsian Dances

This suite of choral dances is an
excerpt from Borodin's opera Prince
Igor, first produced in St Petersburg in
1890. The score was left unfinished on
Borodin's death in 1887, but was completed (and orchestrated) by Rimsky-
Korsakov* and Glazunov. The Polovtsian Dances occur in Act II: the Polovt-
sians have captured the Russian prince,
but entertain him with dances. The
orchestral version of the dances is
more often performed than the original
choral version.

Chorus
2.picc.2(II corA).2.2. – 4.2.3.1. – timp
– perc – harp – strings
Duration: 14′

Prometheus

Prometheus, The Poem of Fire, is a symphonic poem by Scriabin (1872–1915)
with a chorus ad libitum. The score also
includes a part for a light machine
which would project colours onto
a screen during the performance.

Prometheus was first heard in 1911, but without the lighting effects!

Chorus (ad. lib.)
3.picc.3.corA.3.bcl.3.dbn. − 8.5.3.1. − timp − perc − cel − 2 harps − organ − piano − strings
Duration: 20′

Psalmus Hungaricus

Kodály's* *Psalmus Hungaricus* was composed in 1923. It was commissioned by the city of Buda to celebrate the fiftieth anniversary of the union of the cities of Buda and Pest. *Psalmus Hungaricus* is a setting of psalm 55 in a version by Michael Vég, written in the sixteenth century. The work should be performed in Hungarian, but there is an English translation by E. J. Dent.

T: Chorus
3.2.2.2. − 4.3.3.0. − timp − perc − harp − organ − strings
Duration: 25′

Redemption

Gounod's* oratorio *Redemption* was first performed at Birmingham in 1882 and is dedicated to Queen Victoria. The text, which was selected from the Bible by the composer, is in English. *Redemption* begins with a representation of the creation, perhaps in imitation of Haydn*. The complete work is given musical unity by the repetition of one melody, which is repeated rather too frequently.

S, A, T, B: Chorus
2.picc.2.2.2.dbn. − 4.2.3.1. − timp − perc − harp − organ − strings
Duration: 140′

Franck's* *Redemption* was performed in 1872. In its original form it had three movements: the two outer movements were choral, and the central movement was scored for orchestra alone. Franck later abandoned the choral sections and rewrote the orchestral movement.

Requiem *(Mozart)*

A gaunt stranger dressed in grey called on Mozart* to ask him to write a requiem mass. As he began work on it, Mozart, sick and poverty stricken, became convinced that he was writing his own requiem. He thought he was being poisoned, and the story of Mozart's death and Salieri's involvement in it (if any) has been fully exploited by many writers, fancifully by Pushkin (*Mozart and Salieri*) and Peter Shaffer (*Amadeus*), or more factually by numerous musicologists.

The facts are these. Count Franz Walsegg zu Stuppach was an amateur composer frequently in the habit of commissioning works from other composers and passing them off as his own. His wife had died some years before 1791 (Mozart accepted the commission in July of that year) and the requiem was to honour her memory. Mozart, however, interrupted the work on the requiem to compose the operas *La Clemenza di Tito*, and *Die Zauberflöte*. On the manuscript of the requiem Mozart wrote the date 1792, presumably the date by which he intended to finish the work.

Mozart died on December 5th 1791 and the requiem was little more than a sketch. He had completed the Introit and Kyrie, but had left only the chorus parts and a bass line with occasional remarks to indicate the orchestration for the rest of the movements up to the beginning of the Lacrymosa. He had discussed the work with his pupil Süssmayr and it is certain that Süssmayr was able to work relatively easily from Mozart's sketches, filling in the orchestration. He had, however, to complete the Lacrymosa (Mozart composed only the first eight bars) and to write his own Sanctus, Benedictus, and Agnus Dei. Süssmayr concluded with a setting of Lux aeterna and Cum sanctis tuis which uses the music of Mozart's Introit and Kyrie.

Mozart had chosen to score the first section for two basset horns, two bassoons, two trumpets, three trombones, timpani and strings; Süssmayr adheres to this orchestration for the whole work – we do not know whether Mozart would have added other woodwind instruments for later movements. Mozart indicated a trombone at the beginning of his sketch for the Tuba Mirum (the German text presents the Bible's 'last trumpet' as last trombone) but it is doubtful that he intended the whole melodic phrase now played on the trombone to be given to that instrument.

Mozart's *Requiem* was first performed in Count Walsegg's chapel in December 1793.

S, A, T, B: Chorus
0.0.0.2. bassethorns.2. – 0.2.3.0. –
timp – organ – strings
Duration: 55'

Requiem *(Verdi)*

When Rossini* died in 1868 Verdi suggested to his publisher that seven leading Italian composers should each write a movement of a requiem mass to be performed in Bologna, Rossini's birthplace. He offered to set the final movement – 'Libera me' – himself. This he completed, although the project itself came to nothing.

When his friend the statesman and author Manzoni died in 1873, Verdi was deeply moved and wanted to write a requiem mass in his memory. He decided to complete a mass from the material he had already written; the text of the 'Libera me' includes the sentences which begin 'Dies irae' and 'Requiem aeternam', both of which

appear in earlier sections of the mass text ('Requiem aeternam' at the start of the requiem, and 'Dies irae' at the beginning of the sequence). Verdi had therefore only to elaborate ideas already written for the 'Libera me' to complete the beginning of the work and the start of the second movement. The reappearance of this music in the seventh movement is dramatically and musically most effective.

The 'Manzoni' requiem was performed for the first time on 22 May 1874 at the church of St Mark in Milan with Verdi conducting a hand-picked choir and orchestra. Verdi's *Requiem* is one of the most dramatic and colourful settings of the mass for the dead; particularly operatic is the 'sequence', 'Dies irae', with its offstage trumpets representing the 'last trumpet'.

3(IIIpicc).2.2.4. – 4.4.3.1. – timp –
perc – strings and 4 offstage tpts
Duration: 90'

Rio Grande

Constant Lambert's* *Rio Grande*, which was composed in 1927, has been immensely popular since its premiere in 1928, and has recently begun to re-emerge as a regular item in choral programmes. Its crisp jazzy rhythms have always had a certain appeal. It is a setting of a poem by Sacheverell Sitwell which describes a busy South American port.

Ms: Chorus
0.0.0.0. – 0.2.2.cnt.3.1. – timp – perc
– piano
Duration: 16'

Le Roi David *(King David)*

In 1921 Honegger* was asked to provide music for a play by the Swiss poet René Morax. The performances of the play were very successful, and shortly afterwards Honegger re-arranged the music into an oratorio, which he described as a 'symphonic psalm'. The first version was scored for small orchestra, but Honegger re-orchestrated it in 1923 for full symphony orchestra. The work brought Honegger international fame. Despite the brevity of some of the sections, each of the three parts has a taut, cohesive unity. Part One is mainly concerned with the madness of Saul and the defeat of his armies, Part Two with the crowning of David, and Part Three with the reign of David, Absalom, the crowning of Solomon, and David's death.

S, A, T, Narrator: Chorus
original version:
2(II = picc).1(= corA).2(II = bcl).1. – 1.2.1.0. – timp – perc – cel – harp – piano – o.o.o.o.1.
2nd version:
2(II = picc).2(II = corA).2.(II = bcl).2(II = dbn). – 4.2.3.1. – timp – perc – cel – harp – organ – strings
Duration: 67′

Romeo and Juliet
The dramatic symphony, *Romeo and Juliet*, by Berlioz*, was first performed in 1839. Berlioz does not tell the whole story of Shakespeare's play, but instead presents a sequence of scenes which give the bare outline of the plot; some of the movements are purely orchestral. At the opening of the work the chorus sings a kind of choral recitative describing the animosity between the two Veronese houses, and telling how Romeo finds Juliet on her balcony. Queen Mab is represented by two movements: the first is a solo for tenor, the later movement is an orchestral scherzo. In the final scene Friar Lawrence takes the stage to reflect on the drama and he calls the two houses to reconciliation as they mourn the death of the two lovers.

Ms, T, Bar: Chorus

2.picc.2(IIcorA).2.4. – 4.2.2cnt.3.1. – timp – perc – 2 harp – strings
Duration: 110′

Rosamunde
A play 'Rosamunde, Princess of Cyprus' by the female writer Helmine von Chézy was performed in 1823 with incidental music by Schubert*. This music includes three choral items: a shepherd's song, a hunting chorus, and a chorus of spirits (male voices). The music was lost, but then re-discovered in 1867 by Sir George Grove and Sir Arthur Sullivan*.

Chorus
2.2.2.2. – 4.2.3.0. – timp – strings
Duration: 56′

Four Sacred Pieces (*Quattro pezzi sacri*)
Verdi's* *Four Sacred Pieces* were written before and after his last opera *Falstaff* (1893): the *Ave Maria* (1889) and the *Laudi* (1890) before it, and the *Te Deum* (1896) and *Stabat Mater* (1897) after.

1. The *Ave Maria* for unaccompanied chorus is based on a series of notes which Verdi calls an 'enigmatic scale' (the notes are C, D flat, E, F sharp, G sharp, A sharp and B, and down again). He introduces this scale four times throughout the work, once in each voice, altering the F sharp to an F natural for a downwards version of the scale. The resulting chromatic harmonies are haunting.

2. The *Stabat Mater* is scored for choir and orchestra and is a concise setting in which Verdi does not repeat a word of text. The opening unison choral phrase reappears at the very end of the work as an instrumental coda.

3. The *Laudi alla Vergine Maria*, a setting of words by Dante from his *Par-*

adiso, is scored for unaccompanied women's voices.

4. The *Te Deum* is also scored for chorus and orchestra (with soprano soloist), and is on a larger scale. It begins quietly; Verdi concentrates on the contemplative aspect of the canticle, invoking plainsong at the outset of the work.

The *Four Sacred Pieces* were performed together for the first time in Paris in 1898, and later that year in Italy.

1. *Ave Maria*
unaccompanied chorus
Duration: 6'

2. *Stabat Mater*
Chorus
3.2.2.4. – 4.3.4.0. – timp – perc – harp – strings
Duration: 12'

3. *Laudi alla Vergine Maria*
unaccompanied female chorus
Duration: 5'

4. *Te Deum*
S: Chorus
3.2.corA.2.bcl.4. – 4.3.4.0. – timp – strings
Duration: 15'

Sacred Service
Bloch composed his setting of the Jewish Sabbath morning service, known as the *Sacred Service*, in 1933, to a commission from Gerald Warburg of New York. The Hebrew title is 'Avodath Hakodesh', and the words are taken from the United States 'Reformed' rite, the Union prayer book of America. The baritone soloists sings the part of the 'cantor'. The *Sacred Service* is in five parts: the second part is called Kedushah (Sanctification), and in the third part an orchestral interlude represents 'Taking the Scroll from the Ark'. The work ends with the Benediction.

Bar: Chorus

2.picc.2.corA.2.bcl.2.dbn. – 4.3.3.1. – timp – 2 harps – celeste – piano – strings
Duration: 49'

St John Passion
Bach* composed his setting of the Passion according to St John for performance in Leipzig on Good Friday 1724. The work has arias for four soloists as well as parts for an Evangelist (tenor) and Christ, or Christus (bass). It is shorter and less tightly organised than the *St Matthew Passion*. A viola da gamba and lute are required for two short movements (although a cello and harpsichord respectively may be substituted).

Other composers who have written St John Passions include Selle (1623), Schütz (1666), and Telemann, who composed several.

S, A, T, B, (a second T & B are desirable): Chorus
2.2(2obd'a, 2obd).0.1. – 0.0.0.0. – lute (organ hpch) – 2 vla d'am soli, vla da gamba, cont – strings
Duration: 145'

St Luke Passion
This large choral piece by the Polish composer Penderecki* was inspired by the passion settings of Bach. It was composed in 1966 and is written in an unashamedly twentieth-century musical idiom. Penderecki uses many *avant-garde* devices, writing sections of aleatoric improvisation and asking for many unconventional choral sounds, including shouting. The work is in two parts, and the second part concludes with a setting of a portion of the *Stabat Mater* text. The passion is scored for soloists, childrens' choir, and a large mixed choir divided into many parts. At a number of significant points in the score, the prevailing dissonance re-

solves on to a consonant chord which brings repose.

Narrator, S, Bar, B: Chorus,
  Childrens' choir
4(I & II = picc, III = afl).o.o.bcl.2sax.
  3.dbn. – 6.4.4.1. – timp – perc – cel
  – harp – harp – organ – strings
Duration: 80'

St Matthew Passion

Bach's* *St Matthew Passion* was first performed on Good Friday 1727 at Leipzig. It is a substantial work which sets Matthew's gospel texts and poems by Picander. Four soloists perform the arias, and a tenor and bass sing the roles of the Evangelist and Christus; the words of Christ are accompanied by a 'halo' of strings. The Passion is scored for two choirs and two orchestras, with an extra choir of treble voices in the opening chorus, where they sing a chorale melody. The orchestration includes obbligato writing for viola da gamba, oboes *d'amore* and oboes *da caccia*.

Other composers who have written settings of Matthew's gospel include Davy (whose Passion is found in the Eton Choirbook) and Schütz (1666).

S, A, T, T, B, B: Chorus
Orchestra I; 2(= 2rec).2(= 2obd'a &
  2obd).o.o. – o.o.o.o. – vla da gamba
  – cont – strings
Orchestra II: 2.2(= obd'a).o.o. –
  o.o.o.o. – vla da gamba – cont –
  strings
Duration: 200'

Saint Nicolas

Britten's* cantata *Saint Nicolas* (note spelling) was written for the centenary celebrations of Lancing College, Sussex, in 1948. Although the score indicates sections for different choirs, the work can be performed by a normal mixed chorus with offstage boys' or childrens' voices for those sections so designated. *Saint Nicolas* was given its first performance at Aldeburgh in June 1948, with Peter Pears singing the title role, and the Aldeburgh Festival Chorus, conducted by Leslie Woodgate.

The work is in nine sections describing episodes in the life of the Saint. The music is somewhat eclectic and includes jaunty tunes ('Nicolas was born in answer to prayer') as well as more difficult parts for the soloist ('Persecution sprang upon the church'). Britten involves the audience by asking them to join in the singing of two hymns, one after the calming of the storm, the other at the death of Nicolas. The orchestral string parts are not particularly difficult and the work is very suitable for school performance.

4 Trebles, T: Chorus
Timp – perc – organ – piano duet –
  strings
Duration: 50'

St Paul

Mendelssohn's* first oratorio, *St Paul*, was performed in Düsseldorf in 1836. The German text, taken from the Bible, tells the story of Paul's persecution of Stephen (who is stoned to death towards the beginning of the work) and follows Paul's career from the time of his conversion to the period when he himself was persecuted. *St Paul* has been overshadowed by Mendelssohn's second oratorio, *Elijah*, which is arguably more dramatic, and more integrated. *St Paul*, however, contains some wonderful choral writing, although Mendelssohn is more concerned with fugal development than with the relevance of the chorus to the action. The overture begins with the tune 'Sleepers wake', and chorales are interspersed throughout the work.

S, A, T, B, B: Chorus
2.2.2.2.dbn. – 4.2.3.0.oph. – timp –
organ – strings
Duration: 125′

Samson

The text of Handel's* oratorio *Samson*
is based on various poems by Milton,
compiled by Hamilton. *Samson* was
first performed in 1743 and was very
popular both in Handel's day and in
Victorian England. It is not as dramatic or as stirring as some of Handel's
less frequently performed oratorios,
and it was this static quality that
recommended it to Handel's audiences.

At the beginning of the work Samson is blind and in chains. In Part Two
Harapha, a giant of Gath, taunts Samson and his God; Samson's friend
Micah proposes a contest between
Dagon, the Philistine's god, and Jehovah as manifested in Samson's power.
The chorus at the end of Part Two
takes on a dual role with each side
declaring that their god is 'of Gods the
first and last'. In Part Three Samson is
called upon to show his strength; he
brings down the temple on them all
and is himself killed. There follows a
Dead March (the Dead March from
Saul is often used here instead) and
funeral rites.

At the beginning of the work, Samson (tenor) sings the famous aria 'Total
eclipse'. One passage of text in Part
Two is bound to outrage the women of
any choral society, where the librettist
puts women firmly in their place (!):

> To man God's universal law
> Gave pow'r to keep his wife in awe
> Thus shall his life be ne'er dismay'd
> By female usurpation sway'd.

The soprano aria 'Let the bright seraphim' is sung by an Israelitish Woman
at the end of the oratorio, leading
(without da capo) into the final chorus
'Let their celestial concerts all unite'.

S, S, A, T, T, B, B: Chorus
2.2.0.2. – 2.2.0.0. – timp – organ –
strings
(trombones are also required if the
Dead March from *Saul* is
substituted)
Duration: 150′

Saul

Handel* composed his oratorio *Saul* in
1738, and it was first performed in
London the following year. His librettist Jennens took the story from the
Bible: it tells of David's victory over
Goliath and Saul's generosity to him,
of David's friendship with Saul's son
Jonathan, and of Saul's growing jea-
lousy of David's success and popularity. In a remarkable rage aria, 'A ser-
pent in my bosom warmed', Saul
breaks off singing as the second section
of the aria begins, and according to the
stage direction, 'hurls his javelin at
David'. Saul feigns friendship for
David and sends him off to war, but on
his safe return resorts to the Witch of
Endor and asks her (a part sung by a
tenor) to conjure up the spirit of
Samuel. Samuel, however, foretells
Saul's destruction and the death of
Jonathan. The famous Dead March is
played after Saul and his son are killed
in battle. The oratorio ends as David
laments their death and is proclaimed
leader by the people.

Saul is one of Handel's most com-
pelling oratorios, and includes some of
his best music; 'Envy, eldest born of
Hell' is a particularly striking chorus.
The orchestra includes a solo organ for
the overture (the third movement of
which is like an organ concerto), a harp
(which is David's instrument) and carillon.

S, S, A, T, T, T, B, B: Chorus
2.2.0.2. – 0.2.3.0. – timp – carillon –
organ – harp – strings
Duration: 110′

Sea Drift

Walt Whitman wrote a set of poems with the title 'Sea Drift'; Delius* selected verses from one of these poems, 'Out of the cradle endlessly rocking' as the text for his choral work *Sea Drift*. The poem tells how the poet as a boy watched two birds hatch their eggs by the shore, until one day the hen fails to appear. The work was first performed in 1903 in Essen, and received its British premiere in 1908, conducted by Sir Thomas Beecham.

Bar: Chorus
3.3.corA.3.bcl.3.dbn. – 6.3.3.1. – timp – perc – 2 harps – strings
Duration: 30'

A Sea Symphony

A Sea Symphony is Vaughan Williams's* Symphony No 1. It was premiered in 1910 and established Vaughan Williams's reputation as one of the foremost British composers of his generation. The work is a setting for soprano, baritone, chorus and orchestra, of poems by Walt Whitman. The striking opening is very thrilling in performance: brass instruments reiterate the chord of B♭ minor and the chorus enter in unison with the words 'Behold the sea itself', but on the word 'sea' they blossom into an unexpected D major, while the orchestra indulges in superb seascape painting. Vaughan Williams's main influence may have been the choral works of his teacher Parry, but he has left Parry far behind. Parry heard the work in rehearsal and commented, 'It's big stuff, but full of impertinence as well as noble moments'.

The first movement, 'A Song for all seas, all ships', is in sonata form, and like all four movements is choral throughout. This is followed by the slow movement, 'On the beach at night alone', which opens with a sequence of chords C minor/E major, which is a transposed version of the opening chords of the work. The third movement is a scherzo, 'The Waves', and the finale, 'The Explorers', is a rather rhapsodic movement, and is generally considered to be the weakest part of the score. The influence of Elgar is discernible, and Vaughan Williams surely has the Brahms *Requiem* in mind at the point where the choir repeat the word 'singing'.

Vaughan Williams revised the full and vocal scores in 1923.

S, Bar: Chorus
3*(III = picc).2*.corA.2.Ebcl.2.dbn. – 4.3.3.1. – timp – perc – 2*harp – (organ) – strings
Duration: 60'

* one less instrument may be used

The Seasons *(Die Jahreszeiten)*

Haydn's* oratorio *The Seasons* was first performed in Vienna in 1801. The libretto (in German) by Baron van Swieten is an adaptation of the long pastoral poem by the English poet James Thomson (1700–48). The work is in four parts, each representing one season, beginning with spring. The three soloists sing the parts of Hanne (soprano), Lucas (tenor) and Simon (bass). Simon is the farmer, Hanne his daughter, and Lucas a young countryman; these roles are not characterized, and the singers merely describe events, both physical and human, during the four seasons of the year.

There are many notable moments in the score, including the sunrise at the opening of summer, the aria for Simon where he is accompanied by the theme of the variations from Haydn's *Surprise Symphony*, the spinning chorus, and the hunting scene. Baron von Swieten translated the work back into English, but his translation is rather poor.

S, A, T, B: Chorus
2(II = picc).2.2.2.dbn. – 4.3.3.0. –
timp – perc – cont – strings
Duration: 125′

Semele

Because *Semele* was advertised by Handel* as being performed 'after the manner of an oratorio', that is, without stage action, it is nowadays usually called an oratorio, although it is really an opera. Handel composed *Semele* in 1743 and it was first performed the following year. The libretto is by Congreve after Ovid's 'Metamorphoses', and the story tells how Jupiter woos Semele, a Theban princess. The best known aria in the work is Jupiter's 'Where'er you walk'.

S, S, A, A, A, T, T, B, B, B: Chorus
0.2.0.2. – 2.2.0.0. – timp – cont –
strings
Duration: 120′

Serenade to Music

This short work by Vaughan Williams* was written to celebrate Henry Wood's jubilee as a conductor in 1938, and was dedicated to him. It is scored for sixteen solo voices and orchestra, and was written specifically for sixteen singers who were associated with Henry Wood, including the sopranos Isobel Baillie and Eva Turner, the contralto Mary Jarred, the tenor Walter Widdop and the bass Roy Henderson. Each singer is given a phrase which is particularly suited to their individual style of performance. The work can, however, be performed by four soloists and chorus, or entirely by chorus. The words are taken from Shakespeare's *The Merchant of Venice* (Act V, scene i) 'How sweet the moonlight sleeps upon this bank'.

16 soloists *or* S, A, T, B and chorus,
or chorus

2.1corA.2.2. – 4.2.3.1. – timp – perc
– harp – strings
Duration: 14′

A Sermon, a Narrative and a Prayer

This work, for mixed chorus and large orchestra with alto and tenor soloists and speaker, was written by Stravinsky* in 1961 in memory of his friend, the minister James McLane. The text of the sermon is taken from St Paul, the narrative from Acts, describing the martyrdom of Stephen, and the prayer is by Thomas Dekker. The work is written in a concentrated serial idiom.

A, T, Narrator: Chorus
1. alt fl.2.1.bcl.2. – 4.3.3.1. – perc –
harp – piano – strings
Duration: 16′

Seven Last Words of Our Saviour on the Cross

The *Seven Last Words* are Christ's last sentences spoken from the cross as recorded in the four gospels. Haydn* composed an orchestral work with this title for performance in Cadiz Cathedral in 1785; each movement was a reflection on seven texts which were recited before each section. This work was then arranged for string quartet, and also for solo piano. It was later rewritten as a cantata for soloists, chorus and orchestra, perhaps by Haydn's brother, Michael. The text of the cantata was written by Baron van Swieten.

S, A, T, B: Chorus
2.2.2.2.dbn. – 2.2.2.0. – timp –
strings
Duration: 60′
Other works setting Christ's last words from the cross include Schütz's oratorio, and a work by Gounod, *Les sept paroles du Christ sur la croix*. Another Gounod work, *Filiae Jerusalem*, published in England as

The Passion, but with the subtitle 'Seven words of our saviour from the cross', is scored for unaccompanied choir but is not in fact a setting of the seven words.

The Shepherd's Calendar

Maxwell Davies* has written many works for children to perform, and in 1965 he attended the UNESCO Conference on Music in Education, in Sydney, Australia. He was commissioned to write *The Shepherd's Calendar*, which was first performed on 20 May 1965 by members of Sydney University and boys from Sydney Church of England Grammar School, under the direction of the composer.

Treble: Chorus (SATB with a solo voice in each section)
1.6rec.1.5.1. – 0.1.1.0. – perc – piano – strings
Duration: 21'

Le Soleil des Eaux

Le Soleil des Eaux is a cantata by Boulez composed in 1948 (when he was 23) as incidental music to a play by René Char; he revised it in 1958 and 1965, and the latter version was published in 1968. Boulez set two poems by René Char, originally for three soloists, but reducing the scoring to one soprano in the revision. The work is very exacting.

1959 original version
S, T, B: Chorus
2(IIpicc).1.corA.1.bcl.2. – 3.2.1.1. – timp – perc – harp – strings

1968 revised version
S: Chorus
2.1.corA.1.bcl.2. – 3.2.1.1. – timp – perc – cel – 2 harps – strings
(12.10.8.8.6.)
Duration: 10'

Solomon

Handel's* oratorio *Solomon* was first performed in London in 1749. The story is taken from the Bible and the three parts of the oratorio tell of the piety of Solomon and his conjugal happiness, his wisdom and his riches and splendour. In Part Three, the Queen of Sheba visits the king – her famous 'Arrival' is the orchestral introduction to the act. The second part is the most dramatic of the whole work: Solomon has to decide which of two women is the mother of the child they both claim as theirs. Some of the choruses are for double choir, including the famous 'From the censer curling rise', which begins Part Two. The part of Solomon is written for an alto voice.

S, S, A, T, B: Chorus
2.2.0.2. – 2.2.0.0. – timp – cont – strings
Duration: 100'

Song of Destiny (*Schicksalslied*)

Brahms's* *Schicksalslied* was written in 1871 and is a short setting for chorus and orchestra of a poem by Hölderlin. The music of the slow orchestral introduction appears at the close as an epilogue; a quick triple metre section forms the centre of the work and is reminiscent of the choral writing in the sixth movement of Brahms's *German Requiem*.

Chorus
2.2.2.2. – 2.2.3.0. – timp – strings
Duration: 16'

Songs of Farwell

Six secular motets written by Parry* between 1916 and 1918 for unaccompanied choir are called collectively the *Songs of Farewell*. The texts are taken from the Bible, John Donne, Henry

Vaughan, and others, and include the famous 'My soul, there is a country'. The pieces can be performed as a set, and may be performed in any order. Two of the works are scored for four-part choir ('My soul, there is a country' and 'I know my soul hath power') but the others are scored for five-, six-, seven-, and eight-part choir.

Unaccompanied

Delius's* last choral work with orchestra is also called *Songs of Farewell*. It was dictated to his amanuensis, Eric Fenby, and completed in 1930. The poems are by Walt Whitman. The eight-part chorus sing mainly in block chords throughout the piece.

Chorus
2.2.corA.2.bcl.3.dbn. – 4.3.3.1. – timp – harp – strings
Duration: 19'

Spem in Alium

The motet *Spem in alium* by Thomas Tallis* is scored for 40 voices, consisting of eight choirs of five voices each. The imitative writing is a *tour de force* of contrapuntal skill on a very large canvas. The work was surely written for a special occasion, perhaps the fortieth birthday of Queen Elizabeth I.

Unaccompanied
Duration: 12'

The Spirit of England

Elgar* set three of Binyon's poems to music between 1915 and 1917, and called the three pieces *Spirit of England*. The poems are 'The Fourth of August', 'To Women' and 'For the Fallen'; the latter includes the words,

They shall not grow old, as we that are left grow old:

Age shall not weary them, nor the years condemn.
At the going down of the sun and in the morning
We will remember them.

In the first section of this movement Elgar quotes the Demon's chorus from *The Dream of Gerontius*. On the front of the score, Elgar wrote, 'My portion of this work I dedicate to the memory of our glorious men, with a special thought for the Worcesters.'

S (or T): Chorus
2.picc.2.corA.2.bcl.2.dbn. – 4.3.3.1. – timp – 2 harps – strings
Duration: 32'

Spring Symphony

Britten* originally intended setting medieval texts only for his *Spring Symphony*, completed in 1949. However, a re-reading of English poetry and a particularly lovely spring in Suffolk made him change his mind. The poems Britten chose, which are about the death of winter and the birth of spring, are by Herrick, Blake, Vaughan, Spenser and others, and include Auden's *Out on the lawn I lie in bed* which is set for alto solo. Britten arranged the poems into groups and gave the work a three movement form; the Auden poem forms part of the middle slow movement.

The chorus and soloists sing throughout the work, and there are no purely orchestral movements. In the final section Britten introduces the words and tune of *Sumer is icumen in*, which is sung by the boys' choir.

The *Spring Symphony* was first heard in Amsterdam in July 1949; the Concertgebouw Orchestra and the Dutch Radio Choir were joined by Jo Vincent (soprano), Kathleen Ferrier (alto) and Peter Pears (tenor) in a performance conducted by Eduard van Beinum.

The symphony had been written for Serge Koussevitsky and the Boston Symphony Orchestra, and was given its American premiere the following month at the Berkshire Festival, Tanglewood.

S, A, T: Chorus, boys' choir.
3(II = picc,III = afl).2.corA.2.bcl.2.dbn.
 − 4.3.3.1. − timp − perc − 2 harps − strings
Duration: 45′

Stabat Mater (Rossini)

Rossini* was commissioned to write a setting of the *Stabat Mater* in 1832. He composed the first six numbers but then handed over the work to the Italian conductor Tadolini for completion. When it was suggested that the *Stabat Mater* should be published Rossini composed the remaining pieces and the work was performed complete in Paris in 1842.

Rossini's *Stabat Mater* is written in a very operatic style, and demands solo singers of an operatic stature; the chorus writing is more straightforward and includes an unaccompanied chorus with bass solo. Another unaccompanied movement 'Quando corpus morietur' is marked to be sung by a quartet (the four soloists) but arguably works better when performed by the full choir.

S, A, T, B: Chorus
2.2.2.2. − 4.2.3.0. − timp − strings
Duration: 60′

Sumer is Icumen in

This rota (or round) is the earliest composition in six parts, and the manuscript was found at Reading Abbey. The melody itself is to be sung as a four-part round, and two further voices sing a *pes* (that is, a 'foot' or lowest part) which is also in canon. The piece is attributed to John Fornsete, who was a monk at the abbey.

Much research has been devoted to determining the date of composition and although there is still disagreement about this, it may have been written around 1250.

Symphonie Funèbre et Triomphale

In 1840 Berlioz* was commissioned by the French government to write a commemorative piece for the tenth anniversary of the July Revolution. The remains of victims of the Revolution were to be carried through the streets to the Place de la Bastille. Berlioz's first plans were to write a massive work for literally thousands of singers and an orchestra of three or four hundred, but more modest forces were mustered for the actual event. The *Symphonie* was in three sections: a march, scored for a large wind band which was to accompany the procession; an oration for performance at the Place de la Bastille, a trombone recitative accompanied by wind; and a final apotheosis ending with a choral section 'Glory and triumph for these heroes'. Berlioz added the chorus at a later stage, and also added string parts to the two outer movements.

5.4picc.5.26.5 Ebcl.8.dbn(ad lib). − 16.8.
4cnt.10.1.btmb(ad lib). 6 ophicleides.
 − perc − strings
Duration: 40′

Symphony of Psalms

Stravinsky's* *Symphony of Psalms* was composed in 1930 'for the glory of God, and dedicated to the Boston Symphony Orchestra on the occasion of the 50th anniversary of their existence'. It is a symphony in three movements, and each is a setting of verses from the Psalms (nos 38, 39 and 150) in Latin. The work is scored for choir and orchestra without violins or violas, and as in the *Mass* Stravinsky particularly specifies that there should be children's voices in the choir. Stravinsky revised the work in 1948.

Chorus (including children's voices)
5(V = picc).4.corA.o.3.dbn. – 4.4.Dtpt.
3.1. – timp – perc – harp – 2 pianos
– strings (consisting of cellos
and basses only)
Duration: 23'

Symphony of a Thousand
This rather exaggerated title is given to Mahler's* symphony no. 8 in E flat, which was completed in 1906. The work is scored for two mixed choruses, boys' choir, eight soloists and a large orchestra: not however, one thousand performers! The symphony is in two parts; the first is a setting of the Latin hymn 'Veni creator spiritus', and the second, which begins with a long orchestral introduction, is a setting of the concluding scene from Goethe's *Faust* (in German). The first movement is in sonata form and is perhaps one of the most controlled movements in Mahler's symphonic output. The second movement is necessarily more rhapsodic; the final setting of Goethe's words 'Alles Vergängliche ist nur ein Gleichnis' (All that is transient is but reflected) is one of the most powerful choruses in the entire repertoire. Mahler's symphony no. 8 is the first totally choral symphony.

S, S, S, A, A, T, Bar, B: Chorus:
Boys' chorus
5(= picc).picc.4.corA.3.2Ebcl.bcl. –
4.dbn. – 8.8.7.1. – timp – perc – cel
– 2 harp – mandolin – organ –
piano – strings
Duration: 86'

Theresa Mass
Haydn's* mass in B flat composed in 1799 is known as the *Theresa Mass*. This title is not, however, Haydn's, and cannot refer to Maria Theresa who

died in 1780. It was perhaps named after the wife of Emperor Francis II of Austria.

S, A, T, B: Chorus
0.0.2.(1). – 0.2.0.0. – timp – cont –
strings
Duration: 44'

Threni
Stravinsky's* *Threni, id est Lamentationes Jeremiae Prophetae* was composed in 1958. It is in Stravinsky's twelve-tone style, and is a very taxing work which is not often heard in the concert hall. The work is a setting of three excerpts from the Book of Lamentations of the Prophet Jeremiah, which are prescribed for matins on the Thursday, Friday and Saturday of Holy Week. It was first performed in Venice in September 1958, conducted by the composer. The choral writing includes some parlando (speech-song).

S, A, T, T, B, B: Chorus
2.2.corA.2.Ebcl.bcl.o.sarrusophone. –
4.0.flugelhorn.3.1. – timp – perc –
cel – harp – piano – strings
Duration: 35'

Der Tod Jesu *(The death of Jesus)*
The passion cantata *Der Tod Jesu* by Graun (1703–59) was composed in 1755 and was once very popular. It was performed every year in Berlin until this century. Graun was a court composer to Frederick the Great, and his music, like that of his younger contemporary C. P. E. Bach, bridges the gap between the baroque (the period of J. S. Bach*) and classical periods (the music of Haydn* for example).

S, S, T, B: Chorus
either: cont – strings
or: 2.2.0.2. – 0.0.0.0. – cont – strings
Duration: 90'

Der Tod Jesu is also the title of a cantata

by J. C. F. Bach and an oratorio by Telemann*.

The Triumphs of Oriana

The composer Thomas Morley collected together madrigals by 23 composers for the publication *The Triumphs of Oriana*. The publication bears the date 1601, but was actually issued in 1603. This collection of English madrigals was modelled on an Italian publication '*Il Trionfo di Dori*' which was published in 1592. The Italian madrigals all end with the words 'Viva le bella Dori', and in imitation of this, the English madrigals end with the lines, 'Then the shepherds and nymphs of Diana, Long live fair Oriana'. Who Oriana was has been the subject of some conjecture, but it must have been Queen Elizabeth I, who in fact died in 1601.

The original collection included 24 pieces, but others were added in later editions; of the 23 composers represented Byrd* is noticeably absent. The composers include John Milton, father of the poet. Among the finest madrigals in the collection are Bennett's *All creatures now*, Weelkes's *As Vesta was from Latmos hill*, and Wilbye's* *The Lady Oriana*.

Unaccompanied.

Via Crucis

Liszt's* *Via Crucis* (The Way of the Cross) is a contemplative meditation on the fourteen stations of the cross. It is scored for choir and keyboard, and there are a number of short solo passages which members of the choir could sing. Although it was completed in 1879, the work was not performed until 1929, over 40 years after Liszt's death. The text is drawn from the Bible and other sources, and the work is set out in a series of short movements, some of which are very brief indeed. With its strange harmonies and long pauses, *Via Crucis* is a difficult work to perform successfully, but it can be dramatic and effective.

Chorus (with small solos)
Organ, harmonium or piano
Duration: 40'

The Vision of St Augustine

Tippett's* second oratorio, *Vision of St Augustine*, is one of the most difficult choral works written this century. The choral lines are florid and make great demands on the agility of the choir and baritone soloist. (There is a short passage for soprano solo at the beginning of the second part of the work.) *The Vision of St Augustine* was written in 1965 and sets words in Latin from the Bible and the Confessions of St Augustine.

(S), Bar: Chorus
2(I&II = picc).1.corA.1.bcl.1.dbn. –
  4.2(I = Dtpt).3.1. – timp – perc – cel
  – harp – piano – strings
Duration: 35'

War Requiem

Britten* composed his *War Requiem* for the consecration of the new cathedral church of St Michael, Coventry, in 1962. This deeply moving masterpiece made a great impression on the audience. It is a very large work, written for two choirs, two orchestras and three soloists. The soprano and chorus sing the words of the requiem mass, while the tenor and baritone perform settings of war poems by Wilfred Owen. These English words are placed at relevant points throughout the work. (The tenor soloist sings one line in Latin – Dona nobis pacem – at the end of the Agnus Dei.)

At the beginning of the Introit the

interval of a tritone[1] dominates the music, and continues to do so throughout the score. There are many other musical cross-references, including a quotation of the 'Te decet hymnus' (sung by the boys choir) in the first Owen poem at the words 'Not in the hands of boys' (v.s. page 17). There is also a reference to another Britten score, the canticle *Abraham and Isaac*, when the two male soloists sing Owen's grim poem about Abram (as spelt by Owen) slaying his son 'and half the seed of Europe one by one'. Three of the six movements end with the same music: hushed chords for unaccompanied chorus presenting the ever present tritone dissolve into a sublime F major.

The soloists in the first performance were Heather Harper, Peter Pears and Dietrich Fischer-Dieskau, with the Coventry Festival Chorus, the City of Birmingham Symphony Orchestra, the Melos Ensemble, and the boys of Holy Trinity Leamington and Holy Trinity Stratford, conducted by Meredith Davies and the composer (who conducted the chamber orchestra).

S, T, B: Chorus and Boys choir
3(III picc).2.corA.3(III Eb&bcl).2.dbn. − 6.4.3.1. − timp − perc − piano − organ (ad lib) − chamber organ (to accompany boys) − strings − chamber orchestra: 1(picc).1(corA).
1.1. − 1.0.0.0. − timp − perc − harp − 1.1.1.1.1.
Duration: 85′
[1] a tritone consists of notes three whole tones apart (in this case C−F♯)

The Whale
John Tavener* composed his dramatic cantata *The Whale* in 1966; a disc was issued in 1970 on the Beatles' Apple label. The music itself is brash and extrovert, combining aleatoric sections with passages in conventional notation. The text was selected from Colins's Encyclopaedia and the Vulgate (the Latin version of the Bible).

MS, B, speaker: Chorus
Tape
2(I = picc,II = bfl).2.2C(II = bcl).2(II = dbn). − 4.3.3.1. − timp − perc − harp −
organ − piano − strings (without violins)
Duration: 31′

Zadok the Priest
Zadok the Priest was the first of the anthems written by Handel* for the coronation of George II in 1727, and has remained in the order of service for the crowning of British monarchs. The orchestral introduction is one of the most striking passages in Handel's output, as are the grand chords which the chorus sing to the words 'Zadok the priest and Nathan the prophet anointed Solomon king'. The other sections of this short anthem are rather more straightforward and functional. (See Coronation Anthems)

Chorus
0.2.0.2. − 0.3.0.0. − timp − cont − strings
Duration: 7′

Terms

A Cappella (It. 'chapel')
This term means unaccompanied, in the chapel or church style.

Agnus Dei (Lat. 'Lamb of God')
The *Agnus Dei* is the final portion of the Ordinary of the mass – 'O Lamb of God that takest away the sins of the world'. The three-fold petition ends with the words *dona nobis pacem* – 'grant us thy peace'. In the requiem mass the *Agnus Dei* ends with the words *dona eis requiem sempiternam* – 'grant them rest eternal'; the *Lux aeterna* follows.

Aleatoric Music
Aleatory (from the Latin 'alea'-dice) is a term applied to music in which an element of chance is introduced. This arises because the composer has left certain options open to the performers. One of the most straightforward examples is the device whereby a musical phrase is sung (or played) by a performer in his/her own time – and not in synchronization with the other performers.

Alleluia (Lat.)
The Hebrew exclamation *Hallelujah* means 'praise Jehovah'. The word has been added to various responses, and music of a joyful nature written for it. Many composers have set the word as a conclusion to works with sacred texts or themes; Handel's famous *Hallelujah* chorus comes at the end of Part Two of the oratorio *Messiah*; Bach's motet

Lobet dem Herrn ends with an *Alleluia* movement, as does Beethoven's oratorio *Christ on the Mount of Olives*.

Alto (It. 'high')
The alto is the lowest female voice, but the word also describes a male singer who has cultivated a strong falsetto range as well as a boy's unbroken voice. Some male singers prefer the term countertenor, but despite attempts to define alto and countertenor as two distinct types, the terms are interchangeable.

Female altos have a vocal range of , and until a few years ago were expected to make a full-voiced masculine sound, rather like that of Dame Clara Butt. Kathleen Ferrier's voice was arguably more masculine than that of most present day altos. Some altos prefer to use the term mezzo-soprano, partly because many of the roles in oratorio and opera require a higher tessitura. The Victorian oratorios on the other hand included alto parts with a lower range well suited to the deep rich altos of the period. For example, Mendelssohn's *Elijah* includes alto arias which have a low tessitura. The alto part of the Angel in Elgar's *The Dream of Gerontius*, originally written with Dame Clara Butt in mind, has today become the province of warm-voiced mezzo-sopranos who are able to sing the alternative high a'' of the climactic

'Alleluia' (Vocal score p. 158; see also Mezzo-Soprano).

The term contralto, specifically used to describe a female alto, has almost dropped out of use. It was in vogue in Victorian times. The alto solo in Bernstein's *Chichester Psalms* was specifically written for a boy. The alto parts in works by Bach, Handel and Purcell were written for male singers, but those in Vivaldi for women.

Anglican chant

In the Anglican church the psalms are sung to a harmonized tune in regular phrases; the irregular length of the text is accommodated in the chant by reciting many words to one chord as required. Composers of the sixteenth century harmonized plainsong melodies and these are precursors of the Anglican chant, but after the Reformation new chants were composed. The nineteenth-century Oxford Movement encouraged choral services and the chanting of psalms became increasingly popular. In 1837 a system of 'pointing' was adopted and during the Victorian era psalters were published for use in churches throughout the country.

Anthem

The word anthem is derived from 'antiphon' and has come to refer to the settings of non-liturgical texts in Anglican services; since the publication of the 1662 Prayer Book the anthem has traditionally been placed after the third collect. The English anthem was inevitably indebted to the Roman Catholic motet, but since the Reformation it has had an independent history. In the late sixteenth century, composers began to write 'verse anthems' with solo sections, the whole piece being accompanied by organ or strings (viols); the 'full' anthem was for choir with no solos, and accompaniment is not necessary or desirable. The verse anthems of Purcell include *Rejoice in the Lord alway*, the so-called *Bell Anthem*; these should be accompanied by strings and organ continuo. The anthems of Handel are a development of this English genre, and are grand affairs for soloists, chorus and orchestra; examples include the *Chandos Anthems* written for the Duke of Chandos in 1717–1718.

More modest anthems have been written for cathedral performance through successive generations from Tudor times, and include outstanding examples by S. S. Wesley, Stanford, and many composers of this century. Nowadays the anthem is most often a choral piece accompanied by organ and sung in church services; choruses from oratorios and motets written for the Catholic church are also used as church anthems.

Antiphon

An antiphon is a plainsong setting of words sung before and after a psalm or canticle in the Latin church; it was originally a refrain to be sung after each verse of a psalm, and to be sung antiphonally – one choir answering another, or alternating with a soloist, possibly the priest. The Introit and Communion sections of the mass were originally antiphons. The word is also used to describe processional melodies and four hymns to the Virgin; settings of these are also called antiphons, and later, anthems. These four antiphons are *Alma Redemptoris Mater* ('Sweet mother of the Redeemer'), *Ave regine coelorum* ('Hail, Queen of Heaven'), *Regina coeli laetare* ('Queen of Heaven, rejoice') and *Salve Regina* ('Hail, Queen'); they are referred to as Marian antiphons. (See BVM).

Aria

An aria is a solo song, and the term is particularly used to describe a song in an opera; arias became distinct from recitative (the narrative sections) during the seventeenth century. They became established in opera to such an extent that eighteenth-century operas consisted of a succession of arias designed primarily to show off the expertise of the performers. The recitative and aria arrangement found in opera was adopted as the regular pattern for solo voice cantatas from the 1600s to the days of Haydn and beyond, and was also carried into the English oratorio by Handel.

Arias in eighteenth-century opera follow a regular symmetrical pattern in which the first part is repeated, usually ornamented by the soloist, after a central contrasting episode; these arias are called 'da capo' arias because when the performers reach the end of the middle section they are required to go 'from the top' (da capo) and to repeat the first section. Da capo arias are common in Handel oratorios, although the middle section is sometimes omitted (both 'The trumpet shall sound' and 'He was despised' are obvious examples from *Messiah*). The habit of performing the first and middle sections of a da capo aria and then only repeating the opening orchestral ritornello of the first part (instead of the whole of part one) is to be deplored.

The da capo ABA musical form is not always relevant to the sense of the text, and Gluck (1714–1787) in his efforts to reform opera, composed arias in one section only (although there was still some repetition of musical material through the course of the aria). Arias of this kind are found in the operas of Mozart, Haydn and the Italian composers of the early romantic era – Bellini, Donizetti and Rossini.

With Verdi and his contemporaries the aria became divided into two halves: a slow section properly termed aria, and after an interruption, a faster section called a cabaletta. (Violetta's 'Ah fors' è lui ... Sempre libera' from *La Traviata* is a good example). Gradually under the influence of Wagner the operatic aria ceased to be so clear cut; it was no longer a set piece easily extractable from its context. Wagner himself abandoned arias altogether in his later works, but many composers, while adhering to Wagnerian principles, still retained sections in their operas which can be called arias. Verdi's *Otello* has few arias as such, but Iago's 'Credo' is an obvious one. Debussy's *Pélleas and Mélisande* has no real arias at all, yet Puccini continued to rely on arias for his greatest melodic impact, for example, 'Vissi d'arte' from *Tosca*.

Aria is also used to describe song-like instrumental pieces; 'air' is the English term for aria.

Arioso *(It. – 'like an aria')*

The word arioso describes music which is not recitative and not aria. It usually refers to a short lyrical section in a regulated tempo appearing in a passage of recitative. Handel occasionally used it to describe a short aria, and Mendelssohn in *Elijah* uses the word arioso to describe the alto solo 'Woe unto him who forsake him'.

Ave Maria *(Lat. 'Hail Mary')*

Ave Maria is the prayer to the Virgin Mary as used in the Roman Catholic church since the fifteenth century. It has been set to music by many composers – Josquin, Willaert (*c.* 1490–1562), Victoria, etc. Other works with the title *Ave Maria* include the Schubert song to words by Scott (Ellen's Song) and the 'meditation' which Gounod wrote as an extra melody to the first of Bach's preludes from the Well-tempered Clavier; the words of the prayer were added to the melody, giving us the Bach/Gounod *Ave Maria*.

BVM
Abbreviation for Blessed Virgin Mary. Two settings of the litany by Mozart incorporate this abbreviation – Litaniae Lauretanae BVM. See also Antiphon.

Barber shop
The barber shop was a popular meeting place in the sixteenth and seventeenth centuries; while the customers waited to be shaved or to have their teeth pulled, they made music, accompanying themselves on various instruments. Morley mentions such barber shop music in his *Plain and Easy Introduction to Practical Music*, published in 1597. A change in fashion brought about the decline of barbers in the early eighteenth century – barbers turned into wig makers!

Today the term barber shop implies a male voice unaccompanied choir singing popular music in close harmony; many examples of this sort of composition are to be found in the Yale Song Book, a publication of music performed at Yale University and collected at the beginning of this century. Barber shop quartets flourish still in America, where the competitive element encourages a high standard of performance.

Baritone
A baritone is a male voice with a range between that of tenor and bass . True basses are in fact quite rare, so most low voice male singers are baritones. Baritone roles in opera exploit the upper range, for example in Verdi's *Rigoletto* and many roles in operas by Donizetti and Bellini. In oratorio, baritones appear as soloists in Brahms's *German Requiem*, Fauré's *Requiem*, Mendelssohn's *St Paul* and *Elijah*, but their lighter quality makes them unsuitable for works such as Verdi's *Requiem* and Rossini's *Stabat Mater*.

Bass
A real bass, as distinct from a baritone, should be able to reach notes down to a bottom D with a range extending upwards beyond d' above the stave: a range of at least two octaves . In Mozart's opera *Die Entführung aus dem Serail* the character Osmin is expected to sing bottom D as well as top e', all in the same aria . Mozart also writes a bottom D for the bass soloist in his *Litaniae Lauretanae* K195.

Other notable parts written for bass soloists include the Angel of the Agony in Elgar's *The Dream of Gerontius* (the part lies rather high yet requires a dark bass tone), and the bass part in Rossini's *Stabat Mater*, which also demands secure and resonant bottom notes (down to a bottom F). The bass in Verdi's *Requiem* also needs weight at the bottom of the register (down to a bottom F) despite the generally high tessitura.

The word bass is usually used when advertising a quartet of soloists (soprano, alto, tenor and bass) even when the singer's actual range may adhere more to that of a baritone.

Bel canto (It.)
The term bel canto means 'beautiful singing' and has been used to describe the music of the Italian school of singing, particularly in the nineteenth century when opera composers such as Bellini and Donizetti provided perfected vehicles for bel canto artists.

Benedictus (Lat.)
The *Benedictus* is the second part of the *Sanctus*, a portion of the Ordinary of the mass – 'Blessed is he that cometh in the name of the Lord, Hosanna in the

highest'. The Benedictus Dominum Israel – 'Blessed be the Lord God of Israel' is an alternative to the Jubilate in the Anglican Morning Service.

Benedicite *(Lat. 'Bless ye')*

The *Benedicite* is the canticle 'The song of the Three Holy Children' (Shadrach, Meschach and Abednego) and is used as an alternative to the *Te Deum* in the Anglican Morning Service. Vaughan Williams's *Benedicite* was composed in 1930; it is scored for chorus and orchestra, and sets the canticle as well as a poem by J. Austin (1613–69).

Bocca Chiusa *(It.)*

Bocca Chiusa is singing with closed lips (humming).

Cadenza

A cadenza is a passage of virtuoso writing in which the soloist can demonstrate his abilities. In baroque choral works a cadenza may be improvised at the final cadence of an aria. Most Handel arias have a final cadence point in a slower tempo which allows the singer time to embellish the written notes. The singers in baroque opera and oratorio were famous for their improvisations. In the early nineteenth century composers began to write out exactly what they wanted performed, giving singers little chance of improvising.

Canon

A canon is a contrapuntal composition in which each voice enters in turn with the same melody. A round such as 'Three Blind Mice' is an obvious example of a canon. (See Round). Tallis's Canon (a hymn-like melody composed by Thomas Tallis) can be performed as a round with one voice following each other, but it is actually published as a hymn (in *The English Hymnal*) with only the tenor and soprano parts in

canon, the alto and bass being free.

'Three Blind Mice' is a canon at the octave or unison, but canons can be written with voices entering on different degrees of the scale, while retaining the exact contours of the original melody. In Brahms's *Geistliches Lied* op. 30 (1856) there is a double canon between the voices: a canon at the ninth between soprano and tenor, and a second canon between alto and bass. In the second *Agnus Dei* of Palestrina's *Missa Brevis*, the two soprano parts are in canon throughout, while the other parts are free.

Cantata *(It.; Fr. 'cantate', Ger. 'Kantate')*

A cantata is a composition to be sung (cantare) as opposed to played (sonore – sonata). In the early seventeenth century a cantata was an extended secular composition for one or two voices with accompaniment in clearly divided sections: recitatives and arias. These pieces were intended for concert performance and were very popular; many of them could be performed to the accompaniment of keyboard and bass instruments alone. In the baroque era cantatas were more often accompanied by a small orchestra, and in France, Germany and England they might include settings of religious texts also. In Lutheran Germany the cantata found a place in the church as a comment on the sermon: Bach and his contemporaries composed dozens of cantatas for church services Sunday by Sunday. Bach's secular cantatas were written for specific court events.

Haydn uses the term to describe a work for solo voice and orchestra, such as *Arianna a Naxos*, a monologue in which the deserted Arianna expresses her varying emotions. Beethoven's *Ah! Perfido* is another solo voice cantata in all but name, as is

Mendelssohn's *Infelice*. All of these have recitatives accompanied by the full orchestra.

But already in Haydn's day the term cantata had been used to identify pieces for chorus, soloists, and orchestra which were not grand enough or serious enough to be called oratorios. Beethoven wrote cantatas early in his career for the death of Emperor Joseph II and the accession of Emperor Leopold II. Cantatas were written throughout the nineteenth century, and include Sterndale Bennett's *The May Queen* (1858), and a number of works by Parry and Stanford as well as early choral pieces by Elgar (*The Black Knight, Caractacus*), and Coleridge-Taylor's *Hiawatha*.

Canticle *(Lat. canticulum – 'little song')*

A canticle is strictly speaking a Biblical text other than a psalm, used in the liturgy. The Benedicite is called a canticle in the Book of Common Prayer. In common usage the word canticle also embraces the Magnificat and Nunc Dimittis as well as the hymn *Te Deum* (although this text is not drawn from the Bible), and is also confusingly used to describe the psalms *Venite, Cantate Domino*, and *Deus Miseratur*. The canticles are defined as 'greater' or 'lesser' depending on the source of their text – the 'greater' canticles have texts from the Old Testament, the 'lesser' from the New Testament. Britten used the term canticle to describe five works for solo voices and instruments to a variety of texts.

Cantilena *(It.)*

The word *cantilena* has been used at various times to describe songs; in medieval music *cantilena* referred to two-part songs and also described English music of that period which was notable for its writing in parallel thirds. The word has variously been used to describe a single line of melody in a sacred composition and has further been used to describe any long flowing melody or an exercise in singing.

Cantus firmus *(Lat. 'fixed melody')*

A cantus firmus is a melody in long notes used as the basis of a polyphonic composition for voices or instruments. Most often the cantus firmus was taken from plainsong, and was heard in the tenor voice of a composition with the other parts written in smaller value notes above it. But a cantus firmus could be any existing tune, sometimes secular such as the popular *L'homme armé* or the *Western Wind*, or it could be a formula of notes bearing no resemblance to existing melodies. The plainsong cantus firmus is usually repeated throughout a movement or throughout a complete work – a mass, for example. Many Elizabethan keyboard works were also based on a cantus firmus. The chorale preludes of J. S. Bach rely on a similar method of composition, as do some more recent organ pieces based on established hymn tunes (e.g. *Three Preludes on Welsh hymn tunes* by Vaughan Williams and the fourteen Chorale Preludes (two sets) by Parry.

Carol

A carol is not strictly definable, but now refers almost exclusively to hymn-like pieces sung at Christmas time, and to other compositions written for Christmas. However, there are carols for almost every season of the year – new year carols, Easter carols, spring carols etc. In medieval times the carol implied dancing, and pieces were written in a form with repeated verses and refrains. The oldest printed examples are from the press of Wynken de Worde (1521) and include the *Boar's*

Head Carol as well as other carols in English which are still sung today. Before that publication, many carols had already been composed in England including examples by Fayrfax and Henry VIII.

In Victorian times there was a resurgence of interest in church music of all types, including Christmas carols, and in this century many composers have written works for various carol books. *The Oxford Book of Carols* was published in 1928, and a popular collection of volumes with the title *Carols for Choirs* has appeared since 1961. The joint editor of all but Volume One, John Rutter (b.1943), has written many carols and arrangements in a lighter style which have proved immensely popular.

Castrato

A castrato was an adult male singer with a soprano or alto range, produced by operating on the genital organs before puberty. The operation ensured that the voice did not 'break', but did take on the power of an adult voice. Castrati were employed in the Sistine Chapel from the sixteenth century; they sang in the very first operas such as Peri's *Euridice* (1600) and Monteverdi's *Orfeo* (1607) and their popularity increased to such an extent that in Handel's day they were amongst the most sought-after performers. The title role in Handel's *Julius Caesar* was written for a castrato, but is nowadays sung by a countertenor or mezzo soprano. Composers continued to write for castrati in the opera house, and famous castrato parts include the title role in Gluck's *Orfeo* (1762), the role of Idamante in Mozart's *Idomeneo* (1781), and the role of Sextus in Mozart's *La Clemenza di Tito* (1791). The last important opera to include a castrato was Meyerbeer's *Il Crociato in Egitto* (1824).

Catch

A catch is a round or canon for three or four voices. The earliest examples were printed in Ravenscroft's *Pammelia: Musicke's Miscellanie of Pleasant Roundelayes and delightful Catches* (1609). Catches continued to be published during the Commonwealth and were popular in the Restoration, when they became coarse and bawdy. A clever device is the overlapping of words as each voice enters, so that the ear hears a juxtaposition of sounds which suggest other words. Purcell wrote over fifty catches, many of which are frankly obscene. By the eighteenth century the texts of these catches were more concerned with literary word-play and puns. It has been suggested that the word catch derives from the Italian *caccia* – a term used to describe hunting songs.

Cecilian movement

This nineteenth-century movement advocated the reform of Roman Catholic church music, making it more readily intelligible to the general public. It set out to restore Gregorian chant in the liturgy, and suggested that the music of sixteenth-century Italy should be regarded as a model for sacred compositions, considering Mozart's Viennese compositions unsuitable. The movement encouraged the specific study of Palestrina and the imitation of his style, although most of his imitators used their own nineteenth-century language (Liszt in his *Missa Choralis*, for example). Dr Carl Proske (1794–1861), a canon and choirmaster of Ratisbon Cathedral, issued pamphlets and music, and encouraged the movement first in Germany, and then abroad; eventually he was responsible for the founding of the General German Society of St Cecilia. Despite the vigour of the enthusiasts, their knowledge of early music (Palestrina and his contemporaries) was often scanty, and their editions are unreliable and often grossly incorrect.

Chanson *(Fr.)*
Today the word implies a song for solo voice with piano accompaniment (although French solo song should more correctly be referred to as *mélodie*), and also refers to the lighter type of French cabaret song.

Chapel Royal
The Chapel Royal consists of the singers of the English court chapel; its records go back to 1135. In early times, singers followed their monarch, travelling with King John to York in 1200, and with Henry VIII at the Field of the Cloth of Gold in 1520. In Henry VII's time, 79 people were employed in the Chapel Royal and this was augmented to 114 in the reign of Edward IV. During Queen Elizabeth I's reign a number of famous composers were attached to the Chapel – Tye, Tallis, Gibbons, Morley, Tomkins and John Bull. The Chapel Royal was disbanded at the execution of Charles I and restored in 1660 when Charles II became king. Pelham Humfrey and Purcell were members at this time, and Captain Cooke was master of the boys. Later composers who were associated with the Chapel Royal include Sir Arthur Sullivan, who was a boy chorister there. Today the Chapel Royal sing at the Chapel of St James's Palace, Kensington, and consists of a choir of ten boys, six gentlemen and an organist.

Choir, chorus
Both words describe a body of singers, but a distinction can be made between a chorus, which implies a very large body of amateur singers, and a choir, which implies a smaller group, not necessarily amateur. The choruses attached to various orchestral bodies (such as the London Symphony Orchestra) are examples of the first type, and chamber choirs are examples of the latter. From the earliest times, choirs have been employed in church services to sing the mass and motets. It is obvious from the works of Lassus, Gabrieli, Monteverdi and many English Tudor composers that they were written for a highly organised and proficient body of singers.

Choral Symphony
Beethoven's ninth symphony, often referred to as the *Choral Symphony*, was one of the first symphonies to add voices, and many more were written throughout the nineteenth century. The next composer to write one was Berlioz; he called his *Romeo and Juliet* a 'symphony' although it bears no relation to the classical four-movement form. The natural successor to Beethoven in this field was Mendelssohn, whose symphony no. 2 in B flat is called *Lobgesang*, or *Hymn of Praise*. The work begins with three orchestral movements and ends with a cantata; but whereas Beethoven's finale grows out of what has been heard before it, Mendelssohn's cantata is merely appended to the three orchestral movements. Liszt composed two symphonies which call for voices in their final movements: the 'Faust' and 'Dante' symphonies. In the first of these, a tenor soloist and male chorus provide a choral finale, and in the second, women's voices represent Dante's vision of Paradise by singing the Magnificat.

The choral symphony found its greatest exponent in Mahler. In his symphony no. 2 'Resurrection', he sets Klopstock's *Resurrection Ode* as the grand finale to a very long symphony; the third symphony is scored for women's and boys' voices, who add colour to a poem from *Des Knaben Wunderhorn*.[1] Mahler's eighth symphony is the so-called 'Symphony of a Thousand', and the first completely choral symphony. It has two massive movements; the first a setting of the Latin hymn 'Veni creator spiritus', and the second a setting of the closing scene from Goethe's *Faust*.

The English composer Havergal Brian demands even larger forces than Mahler in his *Gothic Symphony*. The work consists of three orchestral movements and a choral finale, which is a Latin setting of the *Te Deum*. Scriabin's *First Symphony* has a choral finale (1900), and Busoni composed the first choral piano concerto (1904), which uses a male chorus in the finale. Holst's *Choral Symphony*, which has no purely orchestral movements, appeared in 1924, and is a setting of several poems by Keats. Other choral symphonies include: Vaughan Williams's *Sea Symphony*, Sibelius's *Kullervo Symphony*, Britten's *Spring Symphony*, Shostakovich's symphonies nos. 2, 3 and 13, Milner's symphony no. 2, and Rubbra's Symphony no. 9, *Sinfonia Sacra*.

The term choral symphony may also describe unaccompanied choral works, sometimes on a grand scale, and by implication, symphonic. Some examples are Bantock's *Atalanta in Calydon* (1912), and *Vanity of Vanities* (1913), and Malcolm Williamson's *Symphony for voices* (1962). These works invoke the real meaning of the word symphony – sounding together.

[1] *Des Knaben Wunderhorn* was a collection of poems published in Germany in the early years of the nineteenth century.

Chorale

A chorale is a German metrical hymn tune for congregational singing, the equivalent of our hymn. The early chorales which pre-date Bach do not fall into regular musical phrases, but Bach, who re-harmonized many of the melodies already in use, gave them a symmetrical form. Early chorales had the melody in the tenor voice, but by the seventeenth century the melody line was always the top part. Bach used chorales in his cantatas, oratorios, and passions to involve the congregation in these works; his church cantatas usually end with a chorale.

Compass

The compass of an instrument is the range between its highest and lowest notes. In choral terms the word range is more often used. The use of capital letters and vertical lines after the letter indicates the notes in their various octaves as shown below:

c''' to c''''

c'' to b''

c' to b'

c to b

C to B

C, to B,

Continuo

This Italian term is an abbreviation for *basso continuo*, and describes the continuous bass line of a baroque work. The continuo instruments consist of a bass instrument (cello, double bass or bassoon) and a keyboard instrument (harpsichord or organ), and there was great flexibility in the combination and number of instruments used. Figures were placed under the bass line to indicate to the keyboard player the chords which were to be played above it – he could therefore accompany an ensemble by reading the bass line alone. The figured bass was developed throughout the seventeenth century, but by the eighteenth century was generally only retained in church music. Mozart and Haydn still wrote figured bass lines for the organ continuo.

Contralto – see Alto

Counterpoint (from Lat. punctus contra punctum – 'note against note')

When two or more independent lines of music make harmony then they are in counterpoint; canons and fugues inevitably provide examples of counterpoint in the interaction of independent lines. Pieces such as madrigals use counterpoint between voices for only some of the time, whereas the works of Palestrina and Byrd are composed mainly of counterpoint. Counterpoint can be strict or free; invertible counterpoint exists if the upper and lower parts could change places and still make harmonic sense.

Counterpoint originated in the thirteenth century in pieces known as motets, which were based on three independent lines of music. The lowest part consisted of plainsong in long notes, with two separate parts in counterpoint above. By the fifteenth century the parts above the plainsong had become interrelated, and this sometimes extended to the plainsong, by imitation.

Countertenor – see Alto

Creed (Lat. Credo – I believe)

The prayer of affirmation of belief called the Creed exists in at least three different textual versions in use in the Anglican and Roman church. The priest intones the opening words 'Credo in unum deum' to plainsong, and the choir or congregation continue the text 'Patrem omnipotentem'. Settings of the Creed in some of Mozart's Masses, as well as those of Haydn and Bruckner, begin with these latter words, and therefore need the plainsong intonation in concert performance. Bach's B Minor Mass also requires the opening intonation, because the tenor chorus line gives the musical 'answer' to it. Since the text of the Creed is rather long it is often telescoped in musical settings; one of the most extreme examples is the one in Haydn's Little Organ Mass which lasts under three minutes, because the different lines of text are sung simultaneously against each other.

Crucifixus

The words 'Crucifixus etiam pro nobis' ('He was crucified for us') are taken from the Creed. The seventeenth-century composer Lotti made a number of chromatic and dissonant settings of these words; the setting for eight-part choir is the one most frequently heard. There is also a setting of the same text by Caldara (c. 1670–1736).

Descant

A descant is an additional part above a melody, particularly a part written above the melody of a carol or hymn. Originally the term referred to a part written above the plainsong melody.

Dies Irae

The Dies Irae is a poem by Thomas of Celano (d. c. 1250) describing the day of judgement, and is written in rhyming Latin in a form known as the 'sequence'. It forms part of the requiem mass. Its dramatic images, 'Day of anger,' etc. have inspired composers to use spectacular effects in this section of the mass – Verdi adds a large bass drum and four off-stage trumpets in his *Requiem Mass*, and Berlioz (*Grande Messe des Morts*) augments an already large orchestra with four off-stage brass bands!

The traditional plainsong melody associated with the Dies Irae has been used in a number of orchestral works by nineteenth and twentieth-century composers: for example, the finale of Berlioz's *Symphonie Fantastique*; Rachmaninov's *Rhapsody on a theme of Paganini* and *Symphonic Dances*; and even Sondheim's *Sweeney Todd*!

Equal voices

Equal voices are either voices of the same range, or of the same kind – all male or all female.

Eton Choirbook

The Eton Choirbook was compiled around 1500, and consists of polyphonic music for use in Eton College chapel; the manuscript is still housed in the college library. It originally contained 92 compositions, comprising 67 antiphons, 24 magnificats, a St Matthew Passion, and a setting of the Apostle's Creed in the form of a round, but only 64 pieces still exist, 21 of which are incomplete – including a setting of the passion by Davy. Other composers represented in the collection include Browne, Cornysh, Fayrfax, Dunstable and Lambe.

Falsetto

When an adult male singer is required to sing notes above his normal range, this is described as singing falsetto. The effect is achieved by vibrating only the edges of the vocal chords, and is much cultivated by countertenors (male altos). Examples of choral works which require soloists singing falsetto

are Stravinsky's *Les Noces*, and Orff's *Carmina Burana*.

Fauxbourdon

This word has had a number of confusing meanings. Originally it meant two-part writing in medieval music, but it soon came to apply to parallel melodies written above plainsong. Today it is used in the context of hymn singing when the tune is in the tenor, or when the descant is the top line. A bourdon is a drone bass, and a burden is a refrain, particularly in a carol.

Festivals

Music festivals in Britain usually embrace other branches of art; festivals of this kind are held in Bath, Edinburgh, Cheltenham, Aldeburgh, London and elsewhere. Festivals with a choral tradition began with the Sons of the Clergy, whose annual service held in St Paul's Cathedral included a charity sermon; from the beginning music played an important part and from 1698 the musical aspect of the service had begun to predominate. Elgar's Psalm 29 *Give unto the Lord* was written for such a service in 1914.

The Three Choirs Festival was founded before 1724 and is held in turn in Gloucester, Worcester and Hereford. It raises money for charity. The combined choirs have a long tradition of performing new and commissioned works including pieces by Parry, Bantock, Vaughan Williams, Holst, Elgar, Bax, Berkeley, Howells, Richard Rodney Bennett, Crosse, Maxwell Davies, Hoddinott, Joubert, McCabe, Williamson and many more.

Other festivals of this type include: the Birmingham Festival which took place sporadically from 1768 to 1912 (Mendelssohn's *Elijah* was written for Birmingham in 1846); the Norwich Festival held from 1770, but irregularly; the Manchester Festival, held occasionally, and the Leeds Festival held from the mid nineteenth century to the present day (it takes place triennially).

Handel Festivals have been held in this country since the first celebrations in 1784 to mark the 25th anniversary of his death. That festival was held in Westminster Abbey, and the festivals continued regularly until 1791. The Crystal Palace became the home of the Handel Festivals from 1857 to 1926 and during the nineteenth century these were large-scale affairs with thousands of performers.

A number of festivals have been started by composers themselves – the Aldeburgh Festival by Benjamin Britten, the Montepulciano Festival by Hans Werner Henze, and the Orkney Festival by Peter Maxwell Davies. Some festivals concentrate on particular areas of music making – opera at Bayreuth, Glyndebourne, Vienna and Wexford, and contemporary music at Cheltenham, Warsaw, Venice and others.

The most significant international festivals are the Edinburgh Festival, Lucerne Festival, Holland Festival and the Maggio Musicale Fiorentino, as well as festivals in Munich, Zurich, Salzburg and Aix-en-Provence.

(*see also* **St Cecilia**)

Folk songs

Folk songs are indigenous strophic melodies whose composers are not identifiable; they have been handed down through successive generations in a continuous oral tradition, and often betray their antiquity by their modal or pentatonic[1] patterns. These unharmonized melodies have been modified over the years as they have been passed down. In the late nineteenth and early twentieth centuries a number of composers collected folk music in their respective countries and found inspiration in it. Bartók and Kodály collected folk music in Hungary, Percy Grainger made collections in Britain and Scandinavia, and British folk songs were systematically collected by Vaughan Williams, Cecil Sharp and Mrs Kennedy-Fraser (who collected folk melodies from the Hebrides). In 1898 the English Folk Music Society was founded and a separate Folk Dance Society was formed in 1911; the two societies combined in 1932.

Folk music has been used by composers for many centuries: eighteenth-century 'ballad opera' borrowed serious works from contemporary composers as well as using popular folk melodies (for example, *The Beggar's Opera*); Beethoven, Haydn and Weber published arrangements of Scottish songs, and Beethoven also arranged Irish and Welsh songs, mainly for voice and piano trio. Other composers who utilised folk material include Grieg, Dvořák, Smetana, Rimsky-Korsakov, Stanford, and many of the early-twentieth-century Spanish composers. Dvořák was inspired by American Indian music while teaching in New York (the *New World Symphony* comes nearest to actual quotation). In this country, apart from collecting folk music, some composers such as Vaughan Williams, Grainger, Holst and Britten have taken folk tunes and harmonized them, fashioning them into pieces of their own. Tippett's *Four songs of the British Isles* are a further example.

[1] Based on a five-note scale made up completely of tones

Glee

A glee is a short and simple unaccompanied choral piece in various sections for male voices, written mainly in a homophonic style. The word is per-haps derived from the Anglo-Saxon *gliw* or *gleo* meaning entertainment or music, and was first used in Playford's publication *Select Musicall Ayres and Dialogues* of 1652. The glee flourished in England between 1750 and 1830, and special glee clubs were formed to encourage the composition and perfor-mance of glees. One of the most famous of these clubs was the Noble-men and Gentlemen's Catch Club, founded in 1761, which still exists today. Composers of glees include Bat-tishill, Attwood, Dibdin, Storace, Spofforth (*Hail, smiling morn*), Walmis-ley, Beale, Goss, Pearsall, and Webbe (whose *Glorious Apollo* is still used to open all meetings of the Noblemen and Gentlemen's Catch Club). The so-called Glee Clubs which continue today at American universities are male voice choirs where glees form only part of the repertoire.

Gloria

Gloria in excelsis Deo – Glory be to.God on high. This 'Greater Doxology' is an amplification of the words sung by the angels at the birth of Christ. It is the second portion of the Ordinary of the Mass in the Roman church. The priest intones the opening words to plain-song and the congregation or choir continue the text from *Et in terra pax*. Some masses by Mozart, Haydn and Bruckner, for example, omit the open-ing words, and it is necessary in con-cert performance to insert them, intoned to the plainsong melody. Vivaldi and other composers (for ex-ample, Poulenc and Walton) have set the Gloria as an isolated movement, and not as part of a complete mass setting. The Lesser Doxology is the *Gloria Patri* (Glory be to the Father) which is used at the end of psalms.

Gradual – *See* Responses

Harmony

When various lines of music are sounded together harmony results. Harmony is the relationship between chords. Music is propelled forward by moving from discords (chords with dissonant notes) to concords (chords without dissonant notes); the juxtapo-sition of chords also offers the possibi-lity of modulating from one key to another. Nineteenth-century harmony became very complex as composers accepted more and more chromatic chords (chords with notes altered by sharpening or flattening them) and began to disregard the rules and guide-lines which dictated acceptable chord progressions.

The final break with traditional har-mony came when Schoenberg, feeling he had exhausted romantic harmony, devised the twelve-tone system in which any note of the chromatic scale (any black or white on the piano) could be equal to another. All sense of key and traditional harmony were now des-troyed. Although many composers were influenced by the twelve-tone technique, traditional harmonic writ-ing has never been superseded.

Homophony (Greek, *'same-sounding'*)

Homophonic music is music in which all the parts move together; the top line is the melody and the other parts mere-ly accompany, as in an English hymn tune.

Hymn

The word 'hymn' originally referred to plainsong melodies and the words associated with them, as used in the early Roman church. St Augustine des-cribed as 'songs of praise to God'. In contrast to psalms, the words of hymns are not taken directly from the scriptures but are specially written, although both are composed in verses which repeat the same music. In the Lutheran Church, hymns were called chorales.

The Wesley family were responsible for a new impetus in hymn writing and singing in the early part of the nineteenth century, and a number of important and popular hymn books have appeared since then. The best known of these are: *Hymns Ancient and Modern* (1861) which reflected Victorian taste; *The English Hymnal* (1906) which added much folk music to the hymn repertory, and avoided the excesses of Victorian hymnody; and *Songs of Praise* (1925). The first two are now being revised in an attempt to reflect contemporary taste.

See **Metrical Psalter**

Kyrie *(Greek)*

The Kyrie is the first part of the Ordinary of the mass. It consists of three sentences, each repeated three times: 'Kyrie eleison, Christe eleison, Kyrie eleison'. The original Greek was retained for this portion of the mass. The earliest Kyrie settings were in plainsong but from the thirteenth century composers wrote polyphonic settings: one of the first is the Kyrie of Machaut's *Messe de Notre Dame*.

Continental composers always began their mass compositions with the Kyrie, but in England it was traditionally sung to plainsong, so the polyphonic masses of Taverner, Tye and their contemporaries all begin with the Gloria. Byrd's three masses are, however, exceptions to this tradition: each has a Kyrie, although the Kyrie of the three part mass is very short and simple. At the Reformation (1549) the words were translated as 'Lord have mercy, Christ have mercy, Lord have mercy'.

Lamentations

At Matins (Tenebrae) on the Thursday, Friday and Saturday of Holy Week, the first three lessons of the Lamentations of Jeremiah are chanted, including the Hebrew letters with which the verses begin. The first polyphonic setting of these words date from the middle of the fifteenth century; later settings include those by Tallis, Byrd, White and Palestrina, whose setting has been sung every year since 1588 at the Sistine Chapel.

Lauda *(Lat. praise)*

Laude (plural of *lauda*) were devotional songs dating from the twelfth century. By the fourteenth century they were specifically associated with flagellants who roamed the North of Italy, and sang *Laude Spirituale* while in procession. It was the dramatic representation of *Laude Spirituale* in the sixteenth century at the oratory of Filippo Neri that gave birth to the Italian oratorio. *Lauda Sion* is one of the five 'sequences' and is appointed for use at Corpus Christi; the words are by St Thomas Aquinas. Mendelssohn set the *Lauda Sion* as a cantata for a church festival at Liège in 1846, including the original plainsong. Rubbra has also made a setting of the *Lauda Sion*.

L'homme armé *(Fr. 'the armed man')*

The melody of the fifteenth-century chanson which begins with the words *L'homme armé* was frequently used by composers as a cantus firmus for their polyphonic compositions. It was used mainly in long notes, often in the tenor voice of a choral or instrumental composition. Composers who used the tune as the basis for their mass settings include Dufay, Busnois, Ockeghem, Tinctoris, Obrecht, Josquin, Brumel, Pierre de la Rue, Morales, Palestrina and Carissimi.

Litany

A litany is a supplication and most often consists of a list of prayers with a refrain such as *ora pro nobis* – 'pray for us'. There are settings of litanies by Palestrina and his contemporaries. Mozart's four litanies are multi-movement works: K.109 and K.195, both called *Litaniae Lauretanae*, are settings of the thirteenth-century litany of Loreto to the Virgin Mary; K.125 and K.243 are both called *Litaniae de venerabili altaris sacramento*. Modern settings of a litany include Poulenc's *Litanies à la Vierge Noire* for female voice and organ, and Szymanowski's *Litany to the Virgin Mary*, also for women's voices.

Liturgy

The term 'liturgy' is used specifically to describe the Christian Eucharist, but may be applied to any organised service in the Christian church. The Rome Liturgy consists of the mass, the Office, and the Sacramental (Burial and Wedding services, etc.).

Madrigal

The word madrigal may either be derived from the Italian words for mother tongue (matricale) or for a pastoral poem (madriale). In fourteenth-century Italy the term was used to describe compositions in two (or three) parts to secular texts by Landini (*c.* 1325–1397) and his contemporaries; its main characteristic was the repetition of music in a kind of rondo form. The madrigal then disapeared and re-emerged in Italy in the sixteenth century as a development of the 'frottola' (a type of secular song). In this period, such composers as Verdelot (d. *c.* 1552), Festa (*c.* 1480–1545), Arcadelt (*c.* 1500–1545), Willaert (*c.* 1490–1562) and Rore (1516–65) wrote madrigals. The frottola which preceded it had been a homophonic composition, but gradually the madrigal became more polyphonic in style. The polyphonic madrigals of Gabrieli and Palestrina, Lassus and Monte (1521–1603) are full of musical effects and emotional climaxes which express the text. Chromaticism and word-painting became characteristic of later works by Marenzio (*c.* 1553–99), Gesualdo, and Monteverdi – who published unaccompanied works and also madrigals for voices and instruments.

The great flowering of the English madrigal in Elizabethan England was a direct result of the publication by Nicholas Yonge in 1588 of *Musica Transalpina*, a collection of Italian madrigals translated into English. Between 1589 and 1627 forty collections of madrigals were published by over thirty English composers. The first to publish and to use the word madrigal in England was Thomas Morley in 1594. The English madrigal imitated the Italian in its use of homophonic and polyphonic writing, and in its word-painting. English madrigals are further characterized by their word-play: for example, in Weelkes's madrigal 'As Vesta was from Latmos hill descending', the words 'first two by two, then three by three' and 'all alone' are directly imitated in the music by the use of a pair of voices, then three voices, and finally, a solo voice for 'all alone'.

The term madrigal was revived in England in the early nineteenth century by Pearsall (1795–1856), who wrote in a romantic style but imitated the Elizabethan madrigals and even occasionally set the same texts; for example, *No, No, Nigella*, previously set by Morley. In the twentieth century composers such as Hindemith and Rubbra have used the title madrigal to indicate the polyphonic and secular nature of their compositions.

Magnificat

St Luke gives the text of this canticle of

the Virgin Mary – 'My soul doth magnify the Lord'; it is used in the Roman Catholic service of Vespers, and the Anglican Evening Service as a companion to the *Nunc Dimittis*. Many composers have set the *Magnificat* including Dunstable, Dufay, Lassus, Palestrina, Monteverdi, Bach and Schütz. Vaughan Williams's *Magnificat* includes words to represent Mary's Annunciation; it is scored for soprano soloist, female chorus and orchestra, and was first performed at the Three Choirs Festival in 1932. Settings of the *Magnificat* and *Nunc Dimittis* for the Anglican church include famous and popular examples by S. S. Wesley, Dyson, Stanford and Charles Wood.

Masque

A masque is a particular type of English court entertainment which flourished at the beginning of the seventeenth century. It combined speech and music, dance and spectacular stage effects; thus a typical masque would consist of songs, spoken dialogue and dances, and the subject was almost always taken from mythology. Court writer Ben Jonson and the stage architect Inigo Jones were famous exponents of such works.

There are elements of the masque in a number of Shakespeare's plays; and many works of poetry (such as Milton's *Comus*, with music by Henry Lawes, 1634), and of music (such as the semi-operas of Purcell) are embraced by the term masque. Purcell's *The Fairy Queen* was performed in 1692, and has spoken dialogue interspersed with songs and instrumental music. Blow's *Venus and Adonis* (1685) is sometimes referred to as a masque, but should properly be called an opera since it does not contain spoken dialogue. On the other hand, a work such as Shirley's *Cupid and Death* (1653) with music by Locke (*c.* 1630–77) and Christopher

Gibbons (1615–76) is typical of the genre. Arne's *Alfred* (1740), which includes the song 'Rule Britannia', is a particularly late example of the English masque.

Mass

The Ordinary of the mass (or eucharist) consists of the Kyrie, Gloria, Credo, Sanctus with the Benedictus and Agnus Dei. These portions of the text are designated to be recited at each mass, although the Gloria and Creed are sometimes reserved for special feasts.

The first musical settings of the mass are to plainsong melodies, but by the fourteenth century composers had begun to set parts of the mass in polyphonic writing. The first complete setting by one composer of all of the movements, plus a final sentence 'Ita missa est' – 'the mass is ended, let us depart in peace' – is by Machaut, his *Messe de Notre Dame*. Earlier complete settings of the mass, including the *Tournai Mass* (dating from the early fourteenth century) are compilations by different composers.

Composers after Machaut, such as Dufay, Ockeghem, Obrecht, Josquin and Palestrina, wrote many masses; the mass to a renaissance composer had a similar status as the symphony to a classical or romantic composer. Contrapuntal settings of the mass were given musical unity by the use of plainsong throughout the movements, woven into the fabric of the polyphony, or by quoting recognizable material from another work, by the same composer or by someone else.

During the early baroque period (around 1600) composers were grappling with harmonized bass lines (continuo) and with newly developed key schemes. During the period, composition of polyphonic church music ceased, and there is a considerable gap before composers felt able to write large scale settings of the mass in the new style. Some composers continued to write short masses in an archaic style (there are two examples by Monteverdi) while other composers wrote 'organ masses' – settings of portions of the text interspersed with movements from organ only. It is not until we come to J. S. Bach that we find a composer equal to the task of writing a grand mass; his *Mass in B minor* (1733) is certainly the finest example of the baroque mass.

In the classical period there was a renewed interest in mass composition, most particularly for court use on special occasions, or for cathedrals and churches to which composers were attached as employees. Mozart wrote his masses for the Archbishop at Salzburg, Haydn for Prince Esterházy. Schubert also wrote for local performance; Beethoven provided his first mass (the *Mass in C*) for the Esterházy family. When Beethoven composed his second mass – the *Missa Solemnis* – he took the mass from the church and into the concert hall. From this time onwards composers wrote mass settings more often as an expression of their own feelings and beliefs than to order. The masses of Hummel, Weber, and Cherubini are not frequently heard today, but many mass settings from the later nineteenth century are among the most performed choral works in the repertory. Most notably the mass for the dead (the requiem) has appealed to composers and audiences alike.

Modern settings of the mass include Kodály's *Missa Brevis* (1945), and Stravinsky's *Mass* for voices and wind instruments (1948), and more recently Williamson's *Mass of Christ the King* (1977).

See **Missa**

Messa di voce *(It. 'placing of the voice')*

Messa di voce is an eighteenth-century term meaning to place the voice, and to crescendo and diminuendo on a single note. *Filar la voce* is a similar term, meaning drawing out the voice.

Metrical psalter

The reformed churches in various countries replaced plainsong psalm singing with settings of metrical translations of the psalms; sometimes these were written in a polyphonic style (for example, by Goudimel in 1564), but more usually in a homophonic style, very much like our own hymn tunes. Metrical psalm publications were issued during the sixteenth century in the Netherlands, England, Scotland and Switzerland. English psalters were published by Day (the psalter of Sternhold and Hopkins) in 1563, East (1592), Ravenscroft (1621) and Playford (1677); they were all in a homophonic style, with the tune either in the treble or tenor voice. Many of the psalm tunes from the Genevan and French psalters are still sung in churches today (for example, *All people that on earth do dwell*, taken from the Genevan Psalter of 1551).

Metronome

The first metronome was made by Loulié in 1696, but it is Maelzel's metronome, patented in 1814, which is generally known. It is an apparatus for sounding beats in an adjustable pattern of beats per minute. Maelzel, a friend of Beethoven's, stole the idea from D. N. Winkel. The pocket metronome was issued in 1945.

The metronome mark at the beginning of a piece, either given by the composer or the editor, should only be taken as a guide: composers who have conducted or played their own music have often been at odds with their own markings. A composition by Villa Lobos (1887–1959) actually calls for three metronomes as part of the orchestra.

Mezzo-soprano

A mezzo-soprano is a female voice with a range ♩ ; that is below that of a soprano. Mezzo-sopranos are expected to have a wide range which is particularly exploited in opera; the dramatic role of Amneris in Verdi's *Aida* exploits both ends of a mezzo's range; the title role in Rossini's *Cenerentola* requires a lighter agile voice able to sing coloratura, while the fiery role of Carmen in Bizet's opera of that name makes great demands on the middle and lower ends of the voice. Inevitably, these very different roles call for different voices and techniques. The mezzo-soprano repertory also overlaps with that of the soprano (more particularly the dramatic soprano) and with the alto (or contralto). Many mezzo-sopranos sing roles originally ascribed by the composer for soprano or alto. They will usually be advertised as 'alto' when they form one a quartet of soloists: soprano, alto, tenor and bass.

Verdi in his *Requiem* asks his alto to sing a top A♮ and a bottom B♭ ; this part is often sung by mezzo-sopranos. Elgar writes a top A for the contralto role of the Angel in his *Dream of Gerontius* a role created by Dame Clara Butt, although he gives it as an alternative. ♩ *Al - le - lu - ia*

Miserere

The most famous setting of psalm 50 (No. 51 in the English Bible), the *Miserere*, was written by Allegri (1582–1652) for the Sistine Chapel. (Both Mozart and Mendelssohn wrote out Allegri's *Miserere* from memory after one hearing!) Other settings of this psalm have been made by Josquin, Palestrina, Anerio and Lully. The so-called *Miserere* in Verdi's *Il Trovatore* opens Act IV, where Leonora's aria is punctuated by a chorus of monks singing 'miserere' – have mercy.

Missa

'Missa' means 'mass'; hence a 'Missa Brevis' is a short mass, or in the German Lutheran church, a setting of the Kyrie and Gloria only (such as those by Bach and Buxtehude, etc.). In Italy a setting of these two portions only is called a 'Messa di Gloria', and there are examples by Rossini and Bellini. A 'Missa Solemnis' is a solemn mass, or a large-scale setting such as Schubert's setting in A flat or Beethoven's in D. Mozart's Mass in C K.337 is sometimes referred to as a Missa Solemnis.

Masses with names were common from before the fifteenth century, and many took their nickname from the melodies on which they were based. A Missa 'Alma redemptoris mater' is based on the plainsong melody associated with those words, or on another composition which sets that text; a Missa 'L'homme armé' is a setting using the secular tune 'L'homme armé' as if it were a plainsong melody. The secular tune 'Western Wind' was used by at least three English composers as the basis of their mass settings, and provides an example of a 'parody' mass. Here the term 'parody' is not used in the modern sense, but means the use of an existing melody in the fabric of a new composition.

'Missa sine nomine' describes a mass without a name, and is usually reserved for compositions which are not based on existing material. Palestrina's *Missa Papae Marcelli* is named after the Pope Marcellus, who banned all elaborate church music because he maintained that the words were not intelligible in polyphonic compositions. Palestrina composed a mass to prove that composers could write polyphonic settings in which the words were distinct.

see **Mass**

Modes

The 'Church Modes' developed from the earliest times, and were an attempt to use ancient Greek musical terms to codify the growing body of Western church music. The modes are best understood by thinking of the scales made up of the white notes of the piano from one octave to the next – for example, the Dorian mode is from D to D on the white notes. Each mode is unique because it has its own set of intervals, unlike the key system, in which every major scale has the same set of intervals.

Early theorists recognized four modes: on D (Dorian), E (Phrygian), F (Lydian) and G (Mixolydian). Two more, on A (Aeolian) and C (Ionian), were later added, and together these six are known as the 'authentic' modes. 'Plagal' modes (identified by the preface 'Hypo-') use the six distinctive scales of the 'authentic' modes, but allow a different range of notes – for example, the Hypodorian corresponds to the intervals of the Dorian mode, but has a range from A to A.

Until scales and the instruments which played them (particularly keyboard instruments) were 'tempered' to give the same-sounding scale in each key, all music was based on modes. Folk music was originally modal, but many tunes have been modified over the centuries to suit the tempered scale. The works of Palestrina and his contemporaries are particularly interesting, as the hitherto predominantly model flavour gradually gives way to an awakening sense of key.

Motet

The motet is the Roman Catholic equivalent of the Anglican anthem; it is a choral piece, usually unaccompanied, with a text taken from the scriptures. In the thirteenth century a motet was a composition for three voices: the lowest part had a plainsong melody in long notes, and the upper two voices sang independent lines of melody above the plainsong with their own words. This type of motet flourished throughout the thirteenth century. In the hands of such composers as Machaut, Dunstable and Dufay the motet developed into a complicated rhythmically organised musical form with sacred or secular texts.

From the fifteenth century the word motet was used to describe a sacred work with Latin text, but all the voices now have the same words; one or more of the parts may still be based on plainsong or quote plainsong melodies. The motets of Palestrina, Victoria, Lassus and Byrd include some of the greatest single compositions of any age. Later motets could include instrumental accompaniment. From the baroque era onwards the term motet describes any vocal piece with sacred text whether for solo voices and instruments or for full choir without accompaniment. Bach's motets appear to be unaccompanied, but Bach would have expected a continuo to be used. Romantic composers such as Mendelssohn and Brahms wrote motets both with and without accompaniment, but the term was not frequently used in the nineteenth century. Modern composers who have used the term include Joubert who composed a motet sequence, *Pro Pace*.

Nunc Dimittis

The words 'Lord now lettest thou thy servant depart in peace' (spoken by Simeon as quoted in St Luke's gospel) have been incorporated into the Roman Catholic service of Compline and the Anglican Evening Service, as a companion to the *Magnificat*. Many settings of the *Magnificat* and *Nunc Dimittis* have been written for the Anglican church (for example, those by Purcell, Wesley, Stanford, Dyson, Tippett, and Leighton).

Ode

An ode is a poetic form, and famous literary odes date from the days of the earliest Greek writers. Roman poets also adopted the form, and the Odes of Horace are among the greatest examples in Latin. In musical terms an ode is a vocal composition written in honour of some person or event. Purcell's odes for St Cecilia's Day and his Birthday and Welcome odes are some of the finest. Later composers such as Blow and Handel (*Alexander's Feast*) composed similar pieces. Other works of a less specific nature bearing the title ode include Parry's *Ode to Music* and Holst's *Ode to Death*. Elgar's *The Music Makers* is also an ode.

Old Hundredth

The Old Hundredth is a metrical psalm tune. It takes its name from the fact that it was numbered 100 in the publication of metrical psalms by Sternhold and Hopkins, published by John Day in London in 1562; this publication was later superseded by a 'new' volume produced by Tate and Brady. When the tune appeared in Sternhold and Hopkins it was set to the words 'All people that on earth do dwell', but it has also appeared in other metrical psalm publications (for example, in the Genevan psalter) with other words. An arrangement of the tune for congregation, organ and orchestra with trumpets was made by Vaughan Williams for the Coronation of Elizabeth II in 1953.

Old Hall manuscript

The manuscript of early-fifteenth-century polyphonic music sung in the Royal Household is now in the library of St Edmund's College, Old Hall near Ware. The manuscript was probably compiled during the reign of Henry IV (1399–1413) and the pieces by 'Roy Henry' may well have been composed by the monarch himself. The manuscript contains 147 pieces, including single mass movements, motets and antiphons. At least 24 composers are represented, including Dunstable, Damett, Power, Pycard and Byttering, but many pieces are anonymous.

Office

In the Roman Catholic church the 'Office' is the term used for the services of the Hours as distinct from the mass. These consist of eight services appointed throughout the day: Matins, Lauds, Prime, Terce, Sext, None, Vespers and Compline. Each service consist of a sequence of psalms with their antiphons, hymns, prayers and lessons. All of these were originally sung to plainsong, but composers soon began setting the texts to polyphonic music. The service of Vespers attracted most composers, and particularly the Magnificat, which featured in this service.

Opus

Opus is the Latin word for work. The plural is opera, a word which has been used since 1600 to describe the particular art form which combines music and drama. Opus numbering is a device by which works can be identified and put in chronological order. Composers in the seventeenth century often used a single opus number for a volume of published works, most commonly a set of concertos or sonatas. Some opus numbers have been added by the publishers without reference to the composer, and some composers have been unsystematic in their numbering (notably Dvořák) which leads to confusion. The term Opus Posthumus refers to pieces which were not numbered by the composer but were published after his death. Some composers' works have been catalogued subsequently by scholars whose initials precede the number. Hence the 'K' numbers of Mozart's works refer to the chronological order given them by Ludwig Köchel (1809–77) – although this order has since been revised. The 'D' numbers of Schubert's works refer to the cataloguing by Otto Deutsch (1883–1967).

Bach's works were catalogued by the German music librarian Wolfgang Schmieder (b.1901). His catalogue published in 1950 has the title *Thematisch-Systematisches Verzeichnis der musikalischen Werke von Johann Sebastian Bach*; this is usually abbreviated to BWV – Bach-Werke-Verzeichnis. Bach's works appear with either an 'S' (for Schmieder) or BWV number.

Oratorio

The oratorio developed in Italy in the early part of the seventeenth century, and took its name from the Oratory of the church in Vallicella where St Philip Neri performed sacred plays in the mid sixteenth century (see 'laude'). The first oratorio was Cavalieri's *La Rappresentatione di anima di corpo*, performed in 1600, but actually staged like an opera. The composer who took up the oratorio and made it very much his own was Carissimi whose *Jephtha* is typical of his output; it lasts about 25′ and is in one extended section, consisting of narrative and solos with chorus, accompanied by strings and continuo, and written in Latin. In common with operas of this period the music hardly falls into distinct arias and recitatives, but is almost best described as arioso.

Carissimi's pupil, Charpentier, took the oratorio to France. In Germany,

Schütz composed a number of works of the oratorio kind, *Seven Last Words* (1645), and *Christmas Oratorio* (1664); they were extensions of the Lutheran musical representations of biblical stories. This tradition was continued by Buxtehude and J. S. Bach, who wrote Christmas and Easter oratorios (Bach's Christmas Oratorio is a compilation of six church cantatas). J. S. Bach's son, C. P. E. Bach, wrote two oratorios of note. Later Italian composers of oratorio, such as Alessandro Scarlatti and Caldara (d. 1736), were also opera composers, and so oratorio, like opera, began to fall into distinct recitatives and arias.

The oratorio in the form we most readily recognize it was 'invented' by Handel. Turning away from opera, which was rapidly losing him vast sums of money, he mounted a sacred work in a concert performance. (*Haman and Mordecai* (1720)). When Handel revised this work in 1732 he was prevented from staging it by the Bishop of London as the performance fell during Lent, so another concert performance was given. Thus with this work, now re-named *Esther*, the English oratorio was born. In a succession of works including *Saul* (1739), *Israel in Egypt* (1739), *Messiah* (1742) and *Samson* (1743), Handel established a form for the oratorio – a sacred drama with important choral sections. It should be noted that they are not all on sacred texts (for example, *Athalia* (1733)), nor all dramatic (for example, *Messiah*).

The English oratorio inspired Haydn when he visited this country and *The Creation* (1800) and *The Seasons* (1802) were both performed here soon after their premieres in Vienna. Mendelssohn was also familiar with Handel's works, and although *St Paul* (1836) was written in German, *Elijah* was first performed in English in Birmingham in 1846.

The oratorio flourished in England from Handel's day onward, and the oratorios written during the nineteenth century include Spohr's *The Last Judgement* (performed here in 1830), Costa's *Eli* (1855) and *Naaman* (1864), Sullivan's *The Prodigal Son* (1869), Benedict's *St Peter* (1870), Macfarren's *Joseph* (1866), Stainer's *The daughter of Jairus* (1878), Gounod's *Redemption* (performed in 1882 in Birmingham), Mackenzie's *Rose of Sharon* (1884), Cowen's *Ruth* (1887), and the works of Stanford, Parry and Elgar. All of the above named works have fallen from the repertory.

On the continent during the nineteenth century, oratorios were composed by Beethoven (*Christ on the Mount of Olives* (1803)), Schubert (*Lazarus* (1820)), Wagner (*The Lovefeast of the Apostles* (1843)), Berlioz (*The Childhood of Christ* (1854)), Massenet (*Eve* (1875)), Saint-Saëns (*Deluge* (1876)), Franck (*The Béatitudes* (1879)) and Dvořák (*St Ludmilla* (1886)). Modern composers of oratorios include Tippett, whose *A Child of our Time* was first heard in 1941, and most recently, Michael Berkeley (b. 1948) has written *Or shall we die?* (1983).

Ordinary *(of the Mass)*

The Ordinary of the mass refers to those portions of text which do not vary, that is Kyrie, Gloria, Credo, Sanctus, Benedictus and Agnus Dei. The Propers of the mass are those portions which pertain to specific festivals, saints' days, etc. The portions of text used for a requiem mass (mass for the dead) may vary.

Organ mass

Organ masses were composed from the fifteenth century onwards and consisted of sections of plainsong sung by the choir alternating with organ elaborations of the plainsong. Composers such as Cavazzoni (b. c. 1520) and de Grigny (1672–1703), who were primarily organists, composed organ masses, as did Frescobaldi (1683–1743) and François Couperin (1668–1733).

Various masses have been given the nickname 'organ' mass because of the prominent part played by the organ; for example, Haydn's mass in E♭ is known as the 'Great organ mass', and the *Missa Brevis* in B♭ as the 'little organ mass'. There is also an 'organ solo mass' by Mozart, K259 in C.

Organum *(Latin from Greek 'organa', meaning tool, instrument)*

In medieval music organum indicates a method of composition in which an extra voice is added to plainsong, usually in parallel fifths, although the parts may converge onto a final unison note. It is probable that this writing in fifths reflects the relative voice ranges of an average congregation. In the earliest organum the added part was written beneath the plainsong but in later examples it was added above. Gradually the upper voice part became more florid with the lower voice still moving in longer value notes. Composers of this sort of organum include Léonin and Pérotin, who flourished at Notre Dame in the twelfth century. Later composers added new words to the upper voice part and created the medieval motet.

Part-song

The term part-song is all-embracing and can be used to describe any secular unaccompanied choral work written for a number of voices; therefore a glee or a catch can be described as a partsong. In the early part of the nineteenth century the popularity in England of the part-song led to the founding of various societies for the composition and promulgation of the repertory.

But towards the end of the century

composers gave particular care to their choral compositions, and Parry, Stanford and Elgar each wrote a number of very fine part-songs. Some of these are miniature masterpieces and include Stanford's setting of *The Blue Bird*; Parry's *Music, when soft voices die* and Elgar's *O' wild west wind* are both exceptional settings of poems by Shelley. This century the term part-song has rather slipped out of use, partly because the genre is identified so strongly with the late nineteenth century that it implies something rather dated.

Passion

From medieval times the gospel accounts of Christ's betrayal and crucifixion appointed for Palm Sunday and the days of Holy week have been sung by three singers who portray Christ (bass), the Evangelist (tenor) and the other characters including the crowd (turba) originally in plainsong. By the fifteenth century a choir was used to portray the crowd, but the other parts remained as before. Victoria and Palestrina both made settings of the passion texts with solo lines in plainsong recitation, and four-part, mainly homophonic, choral settings of the words of the crowd; these settings are unaccompanied.

During the sixteenth century the whole passion was sung by a choir, even the parts of Christ and the Evangelist. However, the tradition of solo singers persisted, and from 1640 in Lutheran Germany passion settings used recitative, arias and choruses. The recitative carries the narration, whilst the arias and choruses are settings of contemplative texts reflecting on the action. German passion settings include those by Selle (1643), Sebastiani (1663), Theile (1673), and the greatest of all, J. S. Bach, whose two surviving passions use texts according to St John

(1724) and St Matthew (1727). There are also passions by Telemann and over twenty by C. P. E. Bach.

There are very few settings of the passion after this period, although Graun's *Der Tod Jesu* (1755) was very popular. There are a few Victorian works including Stainer's meditation *The Crucifixion* (1887) and Somervelle's *Passion of Christ* (1914), which are in the same tradition. Penderecki's *St Luke Passion* (1965) is a great modern setting of the passion story.

Plainsong

Plainsong is the single line of melody associated with the Latin texts of the early Western church. These melodies were codified in the sixth century by Pope Gregory and have since been called Gregorian chant. Their origins go back to Greek and Jewish services and the music associated with them. The chanting could be antiphonal (performed alternately by one side and then the other) or responsorial (an intonation from the priest and a reply by the congregation). All propers, ordinaries, antiphons, hymns and psalm tones had their own plainsong melodies.

As the art of composition developed so plainsong began to decline, although it was the source of all religious music for many hundreds of years. In fact plainsong still permeates the music of even the most contemporary composers (Maxwell Davies for example, *Missa super l'homme armé*). The monks of Solesmes in France have made a study of the chant and have put forward theories as to how plainsong may have been performed. Various scholars suggest that the music may have been interpreted rhythmically, while others suggest that all notes are more or less equal and follow verbal stress.

In England plainsong was ousted by the Reformation, although Merbecke set plainsong to English words for use in Anglican services, and composers such as Tallis harmonized this plainsong. At various times there has been a revival of interest in plainsong; the Oxford Movement encouraged the re-use of plainsong in the nineteenth century.

Polyphony (Gk. polyphonia – 'many sounds')

Polyphony is church music in two or more parts, in which the voices follow independent lines of music, in independent rhythms.

Proper (see Ordinary)

Recitative

The narrative section of an opera or oratorio is called recitative. In the very first operas the recitative is hardly distinguishable from arioso (arioso is a style half-way between recitative and aria), but by the seventeenth century clear divisions were made between the recitatives and arias. The latter were accompanied by the orchestra and encapsulated the emotions of the characters at a given moment. By Handel's time, opera seria (serious or tragic opera) had become a succession of recitatives and arias; the recitatives were accompanied by continuo only, although particularly expressive recitatives were sometimes accompanied by full orchestra.

Handel transferred all of these operatic conventions to the oratorio; in *Messiah*, 'Comfort ye' is an example of accompanied recitative, or more accurately arioso, whereas 'Behold a Virgin shall conceive' is a recitative accompanied by continuo only. This latter recitative with chordal accompaniment is described as 'secco' (dry) and is a common feature of opera until the time of Haydn, Mozart and Rossini. Haydn's oratorio *The Creation* calls for continuo instruments (perhaps a forte-piano is

more apt than a harpsichord at this period) as does *The Seasons*. Once the harpsichord had been superseded by the piano, 'secco' recitative disappeared. The piano has, however, been used to accompany recitative in twentieth-century scores such as Stravinsky's opera *The Rake's Progress* and Britten's *The Rape of Lucretia* (also in Britten's *Cantata Accademica*).

Requiem

The mass for the dead, *Missa pro defunctis*, in the Roman Catholic church is properly to be celebrated on All Soul's Day, 2nd November. The opening words are 'Requiem aeternam dona eis domine' – 'Rest eternal grant unto them O Lord'. A requiem consists of the following sections: Introit – Requiem; Kyrie; Sequence – Dies Irae; Offertorium – Domine Jesu Christe; Sanctus; Benedictus; Agnus Dei; Communion – Lux aeterna. To these may be added the Responsory, Libera me, on solemn occasions. Fauré ended his *Requiem* with a setting of the words 'In Paradisum'.

In the late fifteenth century composers often wrote single movements from the requiem mass; Ockeghem's complete setting, dating from just before 1500, is the oldest extant setting, since Dufay's *requiem* was lost. Ockeghem set the Introit, Kyrie, Gradual (Si ambulem) and Tract (Sicut cervus), but the latter two movements were abolished by the Council of Trent (1543–63). Other settings of the requiem from this period are by Brumel (flourished 1500) and Pierre de la Rue (d. 1518).

Sixteenth-century settings of the requiem include those by the Spanish composer Morales (c. 1500–53), the Italian, Clemens non Papa (d. c. 1588), Anerio (1560–1614), two settings by Lassus, a four-part setting by Palestrina, and two by Victoria. After 1660

there were many settings which included instrumental parts; notable
amongst them are those by Cavalli
(1602–76) and Viadana (1564–1645).
Settings continued to expand in style
and size throughout the 1700s, with
works by J. C. Bach (1642–1705), Fux
(1660–1741), Hasse (1699–1783) and
Pergolesi, culminating in Mozart's
Requiem of 1791. During the nineteenth
century large scale requiem settings
were no longer written for liturgical
performances, but for concert halls,
and include works by Cherubini (two
settings), Berlioz, Verdi, Bruckner,
Liszt, Saint-Saëns, Fauré and Dvořák.
Twentieth-century settings include
works by Duruflé (1947), Ligeti (1965),
Wilfred Josephs (1963) and Geoffrey
Burgon (1976).

Responses and graduals

Responses are the replies of the congregation to the Preces or Versicles
intoned by the Priest, and in the Anglican church are most frequently sung to
the music of Merbecke. There are harmonized versions by Byrd, Tomkins,
Morley and Tallis; the most familiar
are those sung at Evensong. The Responsory consists of music for Matins
and Vespers – the responses after the
reading of lessons.

A gradual is a response chanted
between the reading of lessons in the
Roman mass, and may take its name
from the fact that the clergy move
from one place to another to read the
different lessons ('gradus', Latin for
step). Or, alternatively, it may take its
name from the steps at which the lesson was read (that is, the steps of the
altar). The Gradual is also the name of
the book which contains the choir
chants of the mass.

Round

A round is a perpetual canon for three
or more voices. The canon is at the

unison – in other words all the voices
sing the same notes one after another.
The term 'rota' was used in medieval
times. (See 'Sumer is icumen in'.)

St Cecilia

St Cecilia was a martyr of the early
church who was executed in Sicily
under Marcus Aurelius. She was
adopted as patroness of music in the
late fifteenth century, perhaps for the
following reason: the fanciful Acts of
St Cecilia, written around 500 A.D.,
mentions her praying in her heart to
God to the accompaniment of musical
instruments on the day of her wedding.
The Vesper antiphon for St Cecilia's
day mentions the musical instruments,
but implies that the Saint played them
herself, thus making her a worthy candidate as patroness of music.

The first musical celebration of St
Cecilia's Day (November 22) was held
in France in 1571; the first 'Feast' in
this country was held in 1653, and
Purcell composed an ode for the occasion. Purcell also wrote an ode for the
festivities in 1692 and a Te Deum and
Jubilate for the 1694 celebrations.
Other composers who wrote odes for
St Cecilia include Blow (1684, 1691,
1695 and 1700) and Handel (*Alexander's Feast*). The Musical Society
were responsible for the annual St
Cecilia's Day concerts, and throughout
the eighteenth century they were a
prominent feature of London musical
life. Since 1905 the concerts have again
been given annually, and now the pro-
ceeds are donated to the Musician's
Benevolent Fund. Other cities which
have been host to St Cecilia celebrations include Edinburgh and
Oxford. In France, the tradition has
also continued, with a celebration of
mass at St Eustache, Paris; it was for
this occasion in 1855 that Gounod
wrote his *St Cecilia Mass*.

See **Cecilian movement**

Sanctus *(Latin, 'Holy')*

The Sanctus is a portion of the Ordinary of the mass and communion service – Holy, holy, holy, Lord God of Hosts.

Schola Cantorum *(Latin, 'school of singers')*

St Gregory founded a Schola Cantorum (school of singing) in Rome in the sixth century. The term can also describe a choir school attached to a church, such as that established at York in 627. The title Schola Cantorum has now been taken up by various singing groups, for example, the Schola Cantorum of Oxford, which is an undergraduate choir.

Sequence

The sequence (from sequor, Latin, 'to follow') is a form of Latin liturgical poetry which flourished in the Middle Ages. When singing plainsong with many notes and few words, the monks added texts to fill the gap between words; this device of filling out the melody with new texts developed to such an extent that independent poems were incorporated into the plainsong. The first important writer of sequences was Notker Balbulus of St Gall (*cd.* 912) who described writing sequences as adding words to the long musical coda (the jubilus) of an alleluia. The sequence relies on the repetition of the musical line to coincide with the rhyming couplets. Four sequences were retained for church use after the Council of Trent (1545–63) exluded the majority – Dies irae (from the requiem mass), Lauda Sion Salvatorem (Corpus Christi), Veni Sancte Spiritu (Whitsun), and Victimae paschali (Easter).

A sequence is also a musical repetition of a phrase, and usually refers to a sequence of notes repeated more than once, often at different pitches to facilitate a change of key.

Service

In the Anglican church a service is a setting of the canticles for morning or evening prayer, or a setting of the communion service. The morning service consists of Te Deum and Benedicite or Jubilate; the evening service of Magnificat (or Cantate Domino) and Nunc dimittis (or Deus miseratur); the communion service consists of Kyrie, Gloria, Sanctus, Benedictus and Agnus Dei. All of these are sung in English.

A service can be described as 'short' or 'great'; basically the difference between a simple setting or an elaborate polyphonic setting. Complete services were composed by Tallis, Byrd and Tomkins. Byrd's *Second Service* has verses with organ accompaniment like a verse anthem. Later examples include works by Purcell (*Te Deum and Jubilate in D*, and the full service in B♭) and numerous nineteenth-century examples by S. S. Wesley (1810–76), Walmisley (1814–56), Stanford, and a host of lesser composers. Modern settings include those by Rawsthorne, Tippett, Howells, Rubbra and Leighton.

Soprano

A soprano is the highest female voice, and has an average range of 🎼.

A number of professional sopranos have rejoiced in exceptionally high notes, but they have usually pursued a career in opera (Mado Robin (1918–60) could sing notes upwards to c ′′′′). The role of the Queen of the Night in Mozart's opera *The Magic Flute* calls for a top f′′′ 🎼 while Strauss in his opera *Salome* exploits the lowest notes, writing a bottom g♭ 🎼 for Salome.

Most oratorios rely on a more modest vocal range, but there are top c′′′s [musical notation] in Verdi's *Requiem*, Rossini's *Stabat Mater*, Haydn's *The Creation*, Dvořák's *Spectre's Bride* and Tippett's *A Child of Our Time*. The soprano soloist in Verdi's *Requiem* is also required to sing down to a middle c [musical notation], while in Mozart's *C Minor Mass* the two soprano soloists leap from the top of their range to the bottom – a total range of [musical notation].

Stabat Mater dolorosa *(Latin, 'sorrowfully stood his mother')*

The sequence Stabat Mater, a Latin poem in rhyming couplets ascribed to Jacopone da Todi (*c.* 1306), was admitted to the Roman Missal in 1727 for use on the Feast of the Seven Dolours (15th September), but is nowadays appointed to be sung on the Friday of Passion week. Originally sung to plainsong, the earliest polyphonic settings are English and date from the late fifteenth century; there are examples by Browne, Cornyshe and Davy. There are also settings by Josquin and later by Lassus and a famous one by Palestrina.

Stabat Mater settings from the eighteenth century onwards include those by Caldara, Pergolesi (for womens' voices), Haydn, Schubert, Rossini, Verdi, Dvořák, Stanford and Liszt (as part of the oratorio *Christus*, where Liszt quotes the original plainsong melody). Penderecki's unaccompanied *Stabat Mater* for three choirs does not include all the text; it was later incorporated into his *St Luke Passion*. Other modern settings of the Stabat Mater include those by Szymanowski and Poulenc.

Street cries

The calls of street vendors have at various times been incorporated into musical compositions. In England street cries were written by Gibbons, Weelkes and Deering (*c.* 1580–1630), and arrangements of cries were published in Ravenscroft's *Pammelia* (1609) and *Melsimata* (1611). In France Jannequin composed chansons incorporating street cries (*Les cris de Paris*, 1550). Handel uses street cries in Act 2, scene i of his opera *Serse* (1738); Vaughan Williams brings in the lavender seller's cry in his *London Symphony*, and more recently, Lionel Bart's musical *Oliver* quoted London street cries.

Te Deum

According to legend, the Te Deum was improvised and sung antiphonally by St Ambrose at the baptism of St Augustine. This Latin hymn has been translated into English as 'We praise thee O Lord', and is used in the Roman Catholic service of Matins, and the Church of England Morning Service. In the context of a service the Te Deum is sung to traditional plainsong or to a specially composed setting.

A number of large-scale pieces have been composed to the Te Deum text, including Purcell's setting for St Cecilia's Day (1694), Handel's for the Peace of Utrecht (1713) and for the victory at Dettingen (1743), and also by Berlioz (1855), Bruckner (1884), Dvořák (1896), Verdi (1898), Stanford (1898), Kodály (1936) and Walton for the Coronation (1953). There are also short settings by Britten, Stanford and Vaughan Williams.

Tenor *(Lat. tenere – 'to hold')*

The tenor voice takes its name from the tenor part of a polyphonic composition in medieval music. The tenor part sustained the plainsong melody on which the work was based, that is, he 'held' the plainsong. The other voices took their names from their relationship with the tenor: the countertenor above it; the duplex, the second voice above; and the triple, that is, the treble, the third voice above.

In the early romantic period the operatic tenor sang his upper notes in a falsetto voice; Rossini, Donizetti and their contemporaries wrote for tenors with a range extending to top db'' and above (for example, the tenor aria 'Cujus animam' in Rossini's *Stabat Mater* has a written db'' in the cadenza).

The average tenor soloist has a range of but the average choral tenor will rarely be asked to sing above an a' although Brahms writes two bb's in his *German Requiem*, and Bach's *B minor mass* (if performed at modern pitch) carries the tenors up to a top b'. Tenors may be required to sing down to a c or even bb .

Modern tenor soloists sing in full voice voice throughout their range even up to a top c'' ; inevitably, however, most tenors are not agile enough nowadays to sing the florid roles of early Italian opera in full voice. A Heldentenor is a tenor who specializes in the heavy and demanding roles in German opera, particularly those by Wagner, which require stamina and volume.

In oratorio tenors have taken the main roles in works by Handel (for example, *Samson, Belshazzar*) but in comparatively few subsequently: the main roles in many romantic works have been written for baritones. Two of the most celebrated tenor solos in the choral repertory are 'operatic' in style: Rossini's *Stabat Mater* and Verdi's *Requiem*. The tenor soloist in Haydn's *The Creation* has to be very agile indeed: his solo part includes florid scales which take him up to a top b' (in the chorus 'The Lord is great'). The part of Gerontius in Elgar's ora-

torio *The Dream of Gerontius* is a heroic part which requires great strength and stamina, while the tenor solos in many works by Britten (originally written for Peter Pears) require a dramatic vocal interpretation over a wide range of notes.

The treble clef is used for writing tenor parts; a small 8 indicates that the music is to be sung an octave lower.

Tessitura *(It. 'texture')*

Tessitura is a term used to describe the average range of a piece of music in relation to the voice for which it is written. The Priest Angel of the Agony in Elgar's *The Dream of Gerontius* is written for a bass or baritone, but the role has a high tessitura.

Tonic Sol-fa

Tonic Sol-fa is a method of teaching sight singing invented by John Curwen in the nineteenth century. Each note in a major scale is given a syllable so that whatever the key, the key note is always doh; then follow ray, me, fah, soh, lah, te and doh' (the ' indicating an octave above the original doh). Chromatic notes are accommodated by substituting 'e' (pronounced 'ee') for sharpened notes and 'a' (pronounced 'aw') for flattened notes. Any change of key is accomplished by moving 'doh' to the key note of the new key. Minor scales begin on lah. A variety of other signs define rhythm, so that a complete piece could be printed without musical notes – a cheap method of music printing.

Curwen also devised a system of hand signals to aid the memory of the Tonic Sol-fa syllables, and Kodály adopted and modified these. In the late nineteenth century Tonic Sol-fa was taught in schools and was in use by many choral societies (some Welsh choirs still use it). Although tonic sol-fah has dropped out of fashion this century, a New Curwen Method has now been published (1980) and the value of this method of teaching has again been recognized in schools.

Treble

A treble is the highest male voice, a boy soprano. In Tudor music the highest voice part was called the 'triple', meaning the third voice above the tenor, and this has given us the derivative, the treble. The treble clef fixes the note g' on the stave.

A number of choral works include parts for trebles, usually in addition to the full choir. Treble soloists figure in Britten's *St Nicolas* and a number of other twentieth-century scores.

Tutti (Italian, plural of 'tutto')

Tutti means all, and refers to the full choir, as opposed to soli, or semi-chorus.

Twelve-tone music

Schoenberg developed a system of composition in which all twelve notes of the octave (the black and white notes on a piano) are equal one to another. This was a natural development for him, as his music had become increasingly 'atonal', that is, without a key centre. Schoenberg's method relied on a series (the technique is sometimes referred to as 'serial') of twelve notes forming a melody in which each note is sounded only once, and is therefore equal to its neighbours; this 'note row' forms the basis of the composition. Strictly 'serial' compositions are inevitably dissonant, but some composers have used twelve-tone rows in the context of conventional harmony, for example Frank Martin, and Britten in his opera *The Turn of the Screw*.

Verse anthem

A verse anthem is an anthem with solo sections accompanied by organ.

Vespers

Vespers is the service immediately preceding Compline in the Roman Catholic Rite. It includes a series of psalms with their antiphons, and a hymn and the magnificat. One of the most elaborate settings is by Monteverdi (1610). Other composers have set Vespers texts – Mozart made two settings (K321 and K339) and Rachmaninov set the Vespers service in Russian for unaccompanied choir.

Voice

The human voice is set into action by wind from the lungs passing through the voice box – the Adam's apple – and out through the mouth. Two vibrating strips of cartilage form the vocal cords, and these are situated in the voice box; they can be varied in length to give flexibility of pitch. The lungs are responsible for the intensity of breath, and they are supported by the diaphragm, which is a thick muscular membrane.

The mouth and throat provide the resonating cavities, although many other facial cavities come into play. The placing of the voice – that is the 'head' or 'chest' voice – really refers to the pitch of the notes. Falsetto notes can be produced by male singers, and it is probable that only the edges of the vocal cords are set in vibration to form this high pitch. A boy soprano has a naturally high voice which 'breaks' during puberty and settles an octave lower.

Texts

The Mass

Kyrie

Kyrie eleison	Lord, have mercy
Christe eleison	Christ, have mercy
Kyrie eleison	Lord, have mercy

Gloria

Gloria in excelsis Deo; et in terra pax hominibus bonae voluntatis. Laudamus te; benedicimus te; adoramus te; glorificamus te. Gratias agimus tibi propter magnam gloriam tuam, Domine Deus, Rex coelestis, Deus Pater omnipotens.

Glory be to God on high, and on earth peace, goodwill towards men. We praise thee, we bless thee, we worship thee, we glorify thee, we give thanks to thee for thy great glory, O Lord God, heavenly King, God the Father Almighty.

Domine Fili unigenite Jesu Christe; Domine Deus, Agnus Dei, Filius Patris, qui tollis peccata mundi, miserere nobis; qui tollis peccata mundi, suscipe deprecationem nostram: qui sedes ad dexteram Patris, miserere nobis.

O Lord, the only-begotten Son Jesu Christ; O Lord God, Lamb of God, Son of the Father, that takest away the sins of the world, have mercy upon us. Thou that takest away the sins of the world, receive our prayer. Thou that sittest at the right hand of God the Father, have mercy upon us.

Quoniam tu solus sanctus: tu solus Dominus: tu solus altissimus, Jesu Christe, cum Sancto Spiritu, in gloria Dei Patris. Amen.

For thou only art holy; thou only art the Lord; thou only, O Christ, with the Holy Ghost, art most high in the glory of God the Father. Amen.

Credo (*The Nicene Creed*)

Credo in unum Deum, Patrem omnipotentem, Factorem coeli et terrae, visibilium omnium et invisibilium.

I believe in one God the Father Almighty, Maker of heaven and earth, And of all things visible and invisible.

Et in unum Dominum Jesum Christum, Filium Dei unigentum, et ex Patre natum ante omnia saecula. Deum de Deo; Lumen de Lumine;

And in one Lord Jesus Christ, the only-begotten Son of God, Begotten of his Father before all worlds, God of God, Light of Light, Very God of

Deum verum de Deo vero; genitum non factum; Consubstantialem Patri, per quem omina facta sunt. Qui propter nos homines, et propter nostram salutem, descendit de coelis, et incarnatus est de Spiritu Sancto, ex Maria Virgine: et homo factus est. Crucifixus etiam pro nobis: sub Pontio Pilato passus et sepultus est. Et resurrexit tertia die secundum Scripturas; et ascendit in coelum, sedet ad dexteram Patris: et iterum venturus est cum gloria judicare vivos et mortuos: cujus regni non erit finis.

Very God, Begotten, not made, Being of one substances with the Father, By whom all things were made: Who for us men, and for our salvation came down from heaven, And was incarnate by the Holy Ghost of the Virgin Mary, And was made man, And was crucified also for us under Pontius Pilate. He suffered and was buried, And the third day he rose again according to the Scriptures, And ascended into heaven, And sitteth on the right hand of the Father. And he shall come again with glory to judge both the quick and the dead: Whose kingdom shall have no end.

Et in spiritum Sanctum Dominum et vivificantem, qui ex patre filioque procedit. Qui cum patre et Filio simul adoratur et conglorificatur; qui locutus est per Prophetas; et in unam sanctam catholicam et apostolicam Ecclesiam. Confiteor unum baptisma in remissionem peccatorum. Et exspecto resurrectionem mortuorum; et vitam venturi saeculi. Amen.

And I believe in the Holy Ghost, The Lord and giver of life, Who proceedeth from the Father and the Son. Who with the Father and the Son together is worshipped and glorified, Who spake by the Prophets. And I believe in one Holy Catholic and Apostolic Church. I acknowledge one Baptism for the remission of sins. And I look for the Resurrection of the dead, And the life of the world to come. Amen.

Sanctus and Benedictus

Sanctus, sanctus, sanctus, Dominus Deus Sabaoth. Pleni sunt coeli et terra gloria tua. Hosanna in excelsis. Benedictus qui venit in nomine Domini. Hosanna in excelsis.

Holy, holy, holy, Lord God of Sabaoth. Heaven and earth are full of thy glory. Hosanna in the highest. Blessed is he that cometh in the name of the Lord. Hosanna in the highest.

Agnus Dei

Agnus Dei, qui tollis peccata mundi, miserere nobis. Agnus Dei, qui tollis peccata mundi, miserere nobis. Agnus Dei, qui tollis peccata mundi, dona nobis pacem.

Lamb of God, who takest away the sins of the world, have mercy upon us. Lamb of God, who takest away the sins of the world, have mercy upon us. Lamb of God, who takest away the sins of the world, grant us thy peace.

Mass for the Dead (Requiem Mass)

The text of the Requiem mass is not fixed, but these portions are most often set.

Introit

Requiem aeternam dona eis Domine: et lux perpetua luceat eis. Te decet hymnus Deus in Sion; et tibi reddetur votum in Jerusalem: exaudi orationem meam; ad te omnis caro veniet. Requiem aeternam dona eis Domine; et lux perpetua luceat eis.

Eternal rest give unto them, O Lord: and let perpetual light shine upon them. A hymn, O God, becometh Thee in Sion; and a vow shall be paid to Thee in Jerusalem: hear my prayer: all flesh shall come to Thee. Eternal rest give unto them, O Lord: and let perpetual light shine upon them.

Kyrie

Kyrie eleison
Christe eleison
Kyrie eleison

Lord, have mercy
Christ, have mercy
Lord, have mercy

Sequence

Dies irae, dies illa
Solvet saeclum in favilla,
Teste David cum Sibylla.

Quantus tremor est futurus,
Quando Judex est venturus;
Cuncta stricte discussurus!

Tuba mirum spargens sonum
Per sepulchra regionum,
Coget omnes ante thronum.

Mors supebit et natura,
Cum resurget creatura,
Judicanti responsura.

Liber scriptus proferetur,
In quo totum continetur,
Unde mundus judicetur.

Judex ergo cum sedebit,
Quidquid latet apparebit:
Nil inultum remanebit.

Quid sum miser tunc dicturus?
Quem patronum rogaturus,
Cum vix justus sit securus?

Day of wrath! O day of mourning,
See fulfilled the prophets' warning;
Heaven and earth in ashes burning.

Oh, what fear man's bosom rendeth
When from heaven the Judge descendeth,
On the sentence all dependeth!

Wondrous sound the trumpet flingeth,
Through earth's sepulchres it ringeth,
All before the throne it bringeth.

Death is struck, and nature quaking
All creation is awaking
To its Judge an answer making.

Lo! the book exactly worded,
Wherein all hath been recorded;
Thence shall judgment be awarded.

When the Judge His seat attaineth
And each hidden deed arraigneth,
Nothing unavenged remaineth.

When shall I, frail man, be pleading,
Who for me be interceding,
When the just are mercy needing?

Rex tremendae majestatis,
Qui salvandos salvas gratis,
Salva me fons pietatis.

King of majesty tremendous,
Who dost free salvation send us,
Fount of pity, then befriend us!

Recordare Jesu pie,
Quod sum cause tuae viae,
Ne me perdas illa die.

Think, good Jesu, my salvation
Caused Thy wondrous Incarnation
Leave me not to reprobation.

Quaerens me sedisti lassus,
Redemisti crucem passus;
Tantus labor non sit cassus.

Faint and weary Thou hast sought me,
On the cross of suffering bought me;
Shall such grave be vainly brought me?

Juste Judex ultionis,
Donum fac remissionis
Ante diem rationis.

Righteous Judge! for sin's pollution
Grant Thy gift of absolution,
Ere that day of retribution.

Ingemisco tanquam reus,
Culpa rubet vultus meus,
Supplicanti parce Deus.

Guilty, now I pour my moaning,
All my shame with anguish owning:
Spare, O God, Thy suppliant groaning.

Qui Mariam absolvisti,
Et latronem exaudisti,
Mihi quoque spem dedisti.

Thou the sinful woman savedst;
Thou the dying thief forgavest;
And to me a hope vouchsafest.

Preces meae non sunt dignae:
Sed tu bonus fac benigne,
Ne perenni cremer igne.

Worthless are my prayers, and sighing;
Yet, good Lord, in grace complying,
Rescue me from fires undying.

Inter oves locum praesta,
Et ab hoedis me sequestra,
Statuens in parte dextra.

With thy favoured sheep, O place me,
Nor among the goats abase me,
But to Thy right hand upraise me.

Confutatis maledictis,
Flammis acribus addictis,
Voca me cum benedictis.

While the wicked are confounded,
Doomed to flames of woe unbounded,
Call me with Thy saints surrounded.

Oro supplex et acclinis,
Cor contritum quasi cinis:
Gere curam mei finis.

Low I kneel, with heart-submission;
See, like ashes, my contrition;
Help me in my last condition.

Lacrymosa dies illa,
Qua resurget ex favilla
Judicandus homo reus.
Huic ergo parce Deus.

Ah! that day of tears and mourning!
From the dust of earth returning
Man for judgement must prepare him.
Spare, O God, in mercy spare hm!

Pie Jesu Domine
Dona eis requiem.

Lord all pitying, Jesu blest,
Grant them Thine eternal rest.

Sanctus

Sanctus, sanctus, sanctus, Dominus
Deus Sabaoth. Pleni sunt coeli et
terra gloria tua. Hosanna in excelsis.
[1]Benedictus qui venit in nomine
Domini. Hosanna in excelsis.

Holy, holy, holy, Lord God of
Hosts. Heaven and earth are full of
Thy Glory: Hosanna in the highest.
Blessed is He that cometh in the
name of the Lord. Hosanna in the
highest.

Offertory

Domine Jesu Christie, Rex gloriae,
libera animas omnium fidelium
defunctorum de peonis inferni, et de
profundo lacu: libera eas de ore
leonis, ne absorbeat eas tartarus, ne
cadant in obscurum; sed signifer
sanctus Michael repraesentet eas in
lucem sanctam, quam olim Abrahae
promisisti, et semini eius.

O Lord Jesus Christ, King of Glory,
deliver the souls of all the faithful
departed from the pains of hell and
from the deep pit: deliver them from
the lion's mouth, that hell may not
swallow them up, and may they not
fall into darkness; may Thy holy
standard-bearer Michael lead them
into the holy light; which Thou didst
promise to Abraham and to his seed.

Hostias et preces tibi Domine, laudis
offerimus; tu suscipe pro animabus
illis, quarem hodie memoriam
facimus: fac eas Domine transire ad
vitam. Quam olim Abrahae promisisti
et semini eius.

We offer to Thee, O Lord, sacrifices
and prayers: do Thou receive them in
behalf of those souls whom we
commemorate this day. Grant them,
O Lord, to pass from death unto life;
which Thou didst promise to
Abraham and to his seed.

Agnus Dei

Agnus Dei, qui tollis peccata mundi,
dona eis requiem. Agnus Dei, qui
tollis peccata mundi, dona eis
requiem. Agnus Dei, qui tollis peccati
mundi, dona eis requiem
sempiternam.

Lamb of God, who takest away the
sins of the world, grant them rest.
Lamb of God, who takest away the
sins of the world, grant them rest.
Lamb of God, who takest away the
sins of the world, grant them rest
eternal.

Communion

Lux aeterna luceat eis Domine. Cum
sanctis tuis in aeternum, quia pius es.
Requiem aeternam dona eis Domine;
et lux perpetua luceat eis.

May light eternal shine upon them, O
Lord. With Thy saints for ever, for
Thou are merciful. Eternal rest grant
them, O Lord; and let perpetual light
shine upon them.

---

[1] Not set by Fauré. (A surprising
omission.)

Mozart's setting ends here

Responsory

Libera me, Domine, de morte aeterna in die illa tremenda, quando coeli movendi sunt et terra, dum veneris judicare saeculum per ignem. Tremens factus sum ego et timeo, dum discussio venerit atque ventura ira. Quando coeli movendi sunt et terra. Dies illa, dies irae, calamitatis et miseriae, dies magna et amara valde. Dum veneris judicare saeculum per ignem.

Deliver me, O Lord, from eternal death in that awful day, when the heavens and the earth shall be moved: When Thou shalt come to judge the world by fire. Dread and trembling have laid hold on me, and I fear exceedingly because of the judgement and the wrath to come. When the heavens, and the earth shall be shaken. O that day, that day of wrath, of sore distress and of all wretchedness, that great and exceeding bitter day. When Thou will come to judge the world by fire.

Requiem aeternam dona eis Domine; et lux perpetua luceat eis.

Eternal rest grant to them, Lord, and let perpetual light shine upon them.

Verdi's setting ends here.

Faure and Duruflé omit the Sequence and end their settings with:

Antiphon

In paradisum deducant te Angeli: in tuo adventu suscipiant te Martyres, et perducant te in civitatem sanctam Jerusalem. Chorus Angelorum te suscipiat, et cum Lazaro quondam paupere aeternam habeas requiem.

May the angels lead thee into paradise: may the martyrs receive thee at thy coming, and lead thee into the holy city of Jerusalem. May the choir of angels receive thee, and mayest thou have eternal rest with Lazarus, who once was poor.

Apostle's Creed

This version of the Creed is used in the Church of England at Morning Prayers (Matins) and Evening Prayer (Evensong).

I believe in God the Father Almighty, Maker of heaven and earth: And in Jesus Christ his only Son our Lord, Who was conceived by the Holy Ghost, Born of the Virgin Mary, suffered under Pontius Pilate, was crucified, dead, and buried, He descended into hell; the third day he rose again from the dead, He ascended into Heaven, and sitteth on the right hand of God the Father Almighty; from thence he shall come to judge the quick and the dead.

I believe in the Holy Ghost; the
holy Catholic Church; the Communion
of Saints; the Forgiveness of sins;
the Resurrection of the body, and the
life everlasting. Amen.

Te Deum Laudamus

Te deum laudamus: te Dominum
confitemur.

We praise thee, O God: we
acknowledge thee to be the Lord.

Te aeternum Patrem: omnis terra
veneratur.

All the earth doth worship thee:
the Father everlasting.

Tibi omnes angeli: tibi caeli et
universae potestates:

To thee all Angels cry aloud: the
Heavens, and all the Powers therein.

Tibi cherubim et seraphim:
incessabili voce proclamant:

To thee, Cherubin, and Seraphin:
dontinually do cry,

Sanctus sanctus sanctus: Dominus
Deus Sabaoth.

Holy, Holy, Holy: Lord God of
Sabaoth;

Pleni sunt caeli et terra:
majestatis gloriae tuae.

Heaven and earth are full of the
Majesty: of thy Glory.

Te gloriosus apostolorum chorus:

The glorious company of the Apostles:
praise thee.

te prophetarum laudabilis numerus:

The goodly fellowship of the Prophets:
praise thee.

Te martyrum candidatus: laudat
exercitus.

The noble army of Martyrs: praise thee

Te per orbem terrarum: sancta
confitetur ecclesia:

The holy Church throughout all the
world: doth acknowledge thee:

Patrem immensae majestatis.

The Father: of an infinite majesty;

Venerandum tuum verum: et unicum
Filium:

Thine honourable, true: and only
Son;

sanctum quoque paraclitum Spiritum.

Also the Holy Ghost: the Comforter.

Tu rex gloriae Christe.

Thou art the King of Glory, O Christ.

Tu Patris sempiternus es Filius.

Thou art the everlasting Son: of
the Father.

Tu ad liberandum suscepturus
hominem: non horruisit virginis
uterum.

When thou tookest upon thee to deliver
man: thou didst not abhor the Virgin's
womb.

Tu devicto mortis aculeo: aperuisti
credentibus regna caelorum.

When thou hadst overcome the
sharpness of death: thou didst open
the Kingdom of Heaven to all believers.

Tu ad dexteram Dei sedes: in gloria Patris.

Thou sittest at the right hand of God: in the Glory of the Father.

Judex crederis esse venturus.

We believe that thou shalt come: to be our Judge.

Te ergo quaesumus famulis tuis subveni: quos pretioso sanguine redemisti.

We therefore pray thee, help thy servants: whom thou hast redeemed with thy precious blood.

Aeterna fac cum sanctis tuis: in gloria numerari.

Make them to be numbered with thy Saints: in glory everlasting.

Salvum fac populum tuum Domine: et benedic haereditati tuae.

O Lord, save thy people: and bless thine heritage.

Et rege eos: et extolle illos usque in aeternum.

Govern them: and lift them up for ever.

Per singulos dies: benedicimus te.

Day by day: we magnify thee.

Et laudamus nomen tuum in saeculum: et in saeculum saeculi.

And we worship thy Name: ever world without end.

Dignare Domine die isto: sine peccato nos custodire.

Vouchsafe, O Lord: to keep us this day without sin.

Miserere nostri Domine: miserere nostri.

O Lord, have mercy upon us: have mercy upon us.

Fiat misericordia tua Domine super nos: quemadmodum speravimus in' te.

O Lord, let thy mercy lighten upon us: as our trust is in thee.

In te Domine speravi: non confundar in aeternum.

O Lord, in thee have I trusted: let me never be confounded.

Jubilate Deo (Psalm 100)

Jubilate Deo omnis terra: servite Domino in laetitia. Introite in conspectu ejus, in exsultatione.

O be joyful in the Lord, all ye lands: serve the Lord with gladness, and come before his presence with a song.

Scitote quoniam Dominus ipse est Deus: ipse fecit nos, et non ipsi nos. Populus ejus, et oves pascuae ejus:

Be ye sure that the Lord he is God: it is he that made us, and not we ourselves; we are his people, and the sheep of his pasture.

introite portas ejus in confessione, atria ejus in hymnis: confitemini illi. Laudate nomen ejus:

O go your way into his gates with thanksgiving, and into his courts with praise: be thankful unto him, and speak good of his Name.

quoniam suavis est Dominus, in aeternum misericordia ejus, et usque in generationem et generationem veritas ejus.

For the Lord is gracious, his mercy is everlasting: and his truth endureth from generation to generation.

Gloria Patri et Filio et Spiritui Sancto.	Glory be to the Father, and to the Son: and to the Holy Ghost;
Sicut erat in principio et nunc et semper et in saecula saeculorum. Amen.	As it was in the beginning, is now, and ever shall be: world without end. Amen.

Magnificat (St Luke 1)

Magnificat anima mea Dominum, et exultavit spiritus meus in Deo salutari meo.	My soul doth magnify the Lord: and my spirit hath rejoiced in God my Saviour.
quia respexit humilitatem ancillae suae;	For he hath regarded: the lowliness of his hand-maiden.
ecce enim ex hoc beatam me dicent omnes generationes,	For behold, from henceforth: all generations shall call me blessed.
quia fecit mihi magna qui potens est et sanctum nomen ejus;	For he that is mighty hath magnified me: and holy is his Name.
et misericordia ejus a progenie in progenies timentibus eum.	And his mercy is on them that fear him: throughout all generations.
Fecit potentiam in brachio suo; dispersit superbos mente cordis sui.	He hath shewed strength with his arm: he hath scattered the proud in the imagination of their hearts.
Deposuit potentes de sede et exaltavit humiles.	He hath put down the mighty from their seat: and hath exalted the humble and meek.
Esurientes implevit bonis, et divites dimisit inanes.	He hath filled the hungry with good things: and the rich he hath sent empty away.
Suscepit Israel puerum suum, recordatus misericordiae suae, sicut locutus est ad patres nostros, Abraham, et semini ejus in saecula.	He remembering his mercy hath holpen his servant Israel: as he promised to our forefathers, Abraham and his seed, for ever.
Gloria Patri et Filio et Spiritui Sancto.	Glory be to the Father, and to the Son: and to the Holy Ghost;
Sicut erat in principio et nunc et semper et in saecula saeculorum. Amen.	As it was in the beginning, is now, and ever shall be: world without end. Amen.

Nunc Dimittis (St Luke 2.29)

Nunc dimittis servum tuum, Domine, secundum verbum tuum in pace.	Lord, now lettest thou thy servant depart in peace: according to thy word.
Quia viderunt oculi mei salutem tuam,	For mine eyes have seen: thy salvation,

Quam parasti ante faciem omnium populorum,	Which thou hast prepared: before the face of all people;
Lumen ad revelationem gentium et gloriam plebis tuae Israel.	To be a light to lighten the Gentiles: and to be the glory of thy people Israel.
Gloria Patri et Filio et Spiritui Sancto.	Glory be to the Father, and to the Son: and to the Holy Ghost;
Sicut erat in principio et nunc et semper et in saecula saeculorum. Amen.	As it was in the beginning, is now, and ever shall be: world without end. Amen.

The Lord's Prayer

English

Our Father, which art in heaven, Hallowed by thy Name. Thy Kingdon come. Thy will be done, in earth as it is in heaven. Give us this day our daily bread. And forgive us our trespasses, As we forgive them that trespass against us. And lead us not into temptation; But deliver us from evil. Amen.

Latin

Pater noster, qui est in caelis: sanctificetur nomen tuum; adveniat regnum tuum; fiat voluntas tua, sicut in caelo, et in terra. Panem nostrum cotidianum da nobis hodie; et dimitte nobis debita nostra, sicut et nos dimittimus debitoribus nostris; sed libera nos a malo. Amen.

French

Notre Père qui es aux cieux, que Ton Nom soit sanctifié, que Ton règne vienne, que Ta volonté soit faite sur la terre comme au ciel. Donne-nous aujourd'hui notre pain quotidien, pardonne-nous nos offenses, comme nous pardonnons à ceux qui nous ont offensés. Ne nous induis point en tentation, mais délivre-nous du mal. Amen.

German

Unser Vater in dem Himmel, Dein Name werde geheiliget, Dein Reich komme, Dein Wille geschehe auf Erden wie im Himmel. Unser täglich Brot gib uns heute, und vergib uns unsere Schuld, wie wir unsern Schuldigern vergeben. Und führe uns nicht in Versuchung, sondern erlöse uns von dem Übel. Amen.

Stabat Mater

Stabat mater dolorosa Juxta crucem lacrimosa Dum pendebat Filius	The grieving mother stood by the cross weeping while her son hung there
Cujus animan gementem, Contristatam et dolentem, Pertransivit gladius	Through her weeping soul sad and sorrowful a sword passed

O quam tristis et afflicta Fuit illa benedicta Mater Unigentiti	O how sad and afflicted was the blessed mother of the only-begotten one
Quae moerebat et dolebat Pia mater cum videbat Natie peonas inclyti	There remained and wept the loving mother while she watched the agonies of her glorious Son
Quis est homo qui non fleret, Christi matrem si videret In tanto supplicio?	Who is he who would not weep if he saw Christ's own mother in such torment?
Quis non posset contristari Piam matrem contemplari Dolentem cum filio?	Who could not be sorrowful to see Christ's mother grieving with her Son?
Pro peccatis suae gentis Vidit Jesum in tormentis Et flagellis subditum	For the sins of the people she sees Jesus in agony having undergone scourges
Vidit suum dulcem natum Morientem desolatum Dum emisit spiritum	she sees her own sweet son forsaken in death while he gives up the spirit
Eja mater, fons amoris Me sentire vim doloris Fac ut tecum lugeam	Mother, spring of love, let me feel the strength of thy grief that I may weep with thee
Fac ut ardeat cor meum In amando Christum Deum Ut sibi complaceam	Let my heart burn with love of Christ the Lord to please Him
Sancta mater, istud agas: Crucifixi fige plagas Cordi meo valide	Holy mother, do this: fix the wounds of the Crucified firmly in my heart
Tui nati vulnerati Tam dignati pro me pati Poenas mecum divide	Share with me the pains of thy wounded son that deigned to suffer for me
Fac me vere tecum flere Crucifixo condolere Donec ego vixero	Let me weep with you and lament the Crucified as long as I live
Juxta crucem tecum stare Te libenter sociare In planctu desidero	I desire to stand by the cross with you and to share in your grief
Virgo virginum praeclara Mihi jam non sis amara Fac me tecum plangere	most famous virgin of virgins be not now bitter with me but let me weep with you
Fac ut portem Christi mortem Passionis ejus sortem et plagas recolere	Make a gate of Christ's death; make me a sharer of the Passion and let me remember His wounds

Fac me plagis vulnerari	Make me to be wounded with
Cruce hac inebriari	His wounds and to drink
Ob amorem Filii	deep of the cross for love of Thy Son
Inflammatus et accensus	On fire and burning, may I
Per te Virgo, sim defensus	be defended by thee, o
In die judicii	virgin, on the day of Judgement
Fac me cruce custodiri	Grant that I may be
Morte Christi praemuniri	protected by the cross,
Confoveri gratia	saved by Christ's death and
	supported by His grace
Quando corpus morietur	When my body dies, let my
Fac ut animae donetur	soul be granted the glory
Paradisi gloria. Amen.	of paradise. Amen.

Pergolesi, Rossini and Dvořák all set the text (with slight variants) as above, but Poulenc sets a different version whereby the verse beginning 'Fac me cruce custodire' becomes:

Christe, cum sit hunc exire	Christ, when I go from hence
Da per matrem me venire	grant through thy mother
Ad palman victoriae	that I may gain the palm of victory

There are many versions of the complete poem; the version set by Palestrina, for example, is substantially different from the above text.

Ave Maria

Ave Maria, gratia plena; Dominus tecum: benedicta tu in mulieribus, et benedictus fructus ventris tui, Jesus. Sancta Maria, mater Dei, Ora pro nobis peccatoribus, nunc et in hora mortis nostrae. Amen.

Hail Mary, full of grace, the Lord is with thee: blessed art thou amongst women, and blessed is the fruit of thy womb, Jesus. Holy Mary, Mother of God, pray for us sinners, now and at the hour of our death. Amen.

Ave Verum

Ave verum corpus, natum	Jesu, Word of God Incarnate,
Ex Maria Virgine,[1]	Of the Virgin Mary born,
Vere passum, immolatum	On the Cross Thy sacred body
In cruce pro homine.	For us men with nails was torn.
Cujus latus perforatum,	Cleanse us, by the blood and water
Vero fluxit sanguine;	Streaming from Thy pierced Side;
Esto nobis praegustatum,	Feed us with Thy Body broken,
Mortis in examine.	Now, and in death's agony.
O clemens, O dulcis Jesu, Fili Mariae.[2]	O Jesu, O Jesu hear us, Son of Mary.

[1] Or De Maria Virgine.
[2] This additional line was set by Elgar, but not by Mozart.

Lists

Twentieth-century choral works by British composers

The following is a list of works by composers not otherwise listed in the book. They all require orchestral accompaniment unless otherwise stated:

Malcom Arnold (b. 1921)	*The Return of Odysseus*	30'
Richard Rodney Bennett (b. 1936)	*Spells*	35'
	Epithalamion	23'
Michael Berkeley (b. 1948)	*Or shall we die?*	50'
David Blake (b. 1936)	*Lumina*	60'
Christopher Brown (b. 1943)	*David*	45'
Geoffrey Burgon (b. 1941)	*Requiem*	45'
	Revelations	60'
Geoffrey Bush (b. 1920)	*A Christmas Cantata*	35'
Philip Cannon (b. 1929)	*Lord of Light*	35'
Brian Chapple (b. 1945)	*Cantica*	20'
Edward Cowie (b. 1943)	*Choral Symphony*	30'
David Cox (b. 1916)	*Of Beasts* (unaccompanied)	16'
Gordon Crosse (b. 1937)	*Changes*	51'
Harold Darke (b. 1888)	*An Hymne of Heavenly Beauty*	30'
Stephen Dodgson (b. 1924)	*Magnificat*	28'
	Te Deum	34'
Paul Drayton (b. 1944)	*Templa quam dilecta* (piano duet, perc and strings only)	20'
John Gardner (b. 1917)	*The Noble Heart*	40'
	The Ballad of the White Horse	43'
Alexander Goehr (b. 1932)	*Babylon the Great is fallen*	50'
Iain Hamilton (b. 1922)	*The Bermudas*	32'
	The Passion of Our Lord According to St Mark	120'
Jonathan Harvey (b. 1939)	*Ludus Amoris*	36'
Michael Head (1900–1976)	*Daphne and Apollo*	25'
Alan Hoddinott (b. 1929)	*The Tree of Life*	55'
Robin Holloway (b. 1943)	*Sea-surface of Clouds*	35'
Gordon Jacob (b. 1895)	*The New-born King*	32'
	The Nun's Priest's Tale	90'
Daniel Jones (b. 1912)	*St Peter*	60'
Wilfred Josephs (b. 1927)	*A Child of the Universe*	90'
	Requiem	50'

Bryan Kelly (b. 1934)	*At the round Earth's imagin'd*	
	Corners (strings)	18'
Kenneth Leighton (b. 1929)	*The Light Invisible*	35'
Andrew Lloyd Webber (b. 1948)	*Requiem*	44'
John McCabe (b. 1939)	*Voyage*	42'
	Stabat Mater	15'
Elizabeth Maconchy (b. 1907)	*Heloise and Abelard*	75'
William Mathias (b. 1934)	*This Worldes Joie*	50'
	St Teilo	58'
	Lux aeterna	58'
Wilfred Mellers (b. 1914)	*The Song of Ruth*	45'
Anthony Milner (b. 1925)	*Roman Spring*	20'
	St Francis	21'
	Symphony no. 2	35'
Thea Musgrave (b. 1928)	*The Five Ages of Man*	27'
Bernard Naylor (b. 1907)	*King Solomon's Prayer*	11'
Robin Orr (b. 1909)	*Spring Cantata*	25'
Paul Patterson (b. 1947)	*Requiem*	46'
	Voices of Sleep	42'
John Rutter (b. 1945)	*The Falcon*	22'
	Requiem	40'
Gerard Schurmann (b. 1928)	*Piers Ploughman*	60'
Phyllis Tate (b. 1912)	*Serenade to Christmas*	22'
	St Martha and the Dragon	42'
Eric Thiman (b. 1900)	*Songs of England*	20'
Gilbert Vintner (1909–69)	*The Trumpets* (brass)	38'

Secular choral works

The majority of works performed by choral societies throughout the country are
sacred. Settings of the mass, the requiem, and various other Latin canticles,
hymns and services make up the bulk of the choral repertory. Choir members
invariably ask for the chance to sing something secular; here is a list of the most
important secular works with orchestra:

Bach *Peasant Cantata*
Bartók *Cantata Profana*
Beethoven *Choral Fantasia, Choral Symphony* (Symphony no. 9)
Berlioz *Damnation of Faust, Romeo and Juliet*
Bliss *Pastorale*
Brahms *Alto Rhapsody, Song of Destiny* (Schicksalslied)
Britten *Cantata Academica, Spring Symphony*
Coleridge-Taylor *Hiawatha's Wedding Feast*
Delius *Songs of Farewell*
Dvořák *The Spectre's Bride*
Dyson *The Canterbury Pilgrims*
Elgar *Caractacus, The Music Makers*
Handel *Acis and Galatea, L'Allegro and Il Penseroso, Semele*
Haydn *The Seasons*
Holst *Choral Fantasia, Choral Symphony*

Lambert *Rio Grande*
Mahler *Das klagende Lied*
Mendelssohn *Die erste Walpurgisnacht*
Orff *Carmina Burana*
Parry *Blest Pair of Sirens*
Purcell *Come ye sons of art, Hail Bright Cecilia, Welcome to all the pleasures*
Rachmaninov *The Bells*
Schumann *Scenes from Goethe's Faust*
Stanford *Songs of the Fleet, Songs of the Sea*
Stravinsky *Les Noces*
Vaughan Williams *Five Tudor Portraits, A Sea Symphony*
Walton *Belshazzar's Feast, In honour of the city of London*

Choir and strings

The following list includes some works for choir (perhaps with soloists) accompanied by string orchestra. In some cases the string parts may consist of two violins and a bass part only, but in others a full complement of strings will be required. Baroque works for string orchestra will always include a keyboard continuo part, to be played on the organ or harpsichord. Composers of the classical period (including Mozart and Haydn) wrote a figured bass line for a keyboard player.

Albinoni *Magnificat*
Bach *Cantata no. 61, Cantata no. 165, Cantata no. 196*
Berkeley *Signs in the Dark*
Blow *Ode to St Cecilia 'Begin the song'*
Bononcini *Stabat Mater*
Bush G. *A Christmas Cantata* (with oboe)
Buxtehude *Das neugeborne Kindelein, Magnificat*
Carissimi *Jephtha*
Donizetti *Ave Maria*
Dyson *Hierusalem*
Finzi *In terra pax* (with harp)
Handel *Dixit Dominus*
Hasse *Miserere* (SSAA)
Haydn *Jugendmesse, Kleine orgelmess mass* ('Little organ mass'), *Salve Regina*
Holst *Two Psalms*
Mozart *Ave Verum* K618, *Inter natos mulierum* K72, *Litany* K109, *Misericordias Domini* K222, *Sancta Maria* K273, *Te Deum* K141
Pergolesi *Magnificat, Stabat Mater* (SSA)
Purcell *Welcome to all the pleasures*
Rubbra *Inscape* (with harp)
Saint-Saëns *Christmas Oratario* (*Oratorio de Nöel*, op. 12) (harp and organ)
Scarlatti A. *St Cecilia Mass*
Scarlatti D. *Dixit Dominus, Salve Regina*
Schubert *Mass no. 2 in G, Mass no. 4 in C*
Schütz *Easter Oratorio, Seven Last Words*
Steffani *Stabat Mater*
Vivaldi *Credo*

Works without strings

A few choral works are scored for an orchestra excluding strings. These include the following:

Bach *Cantata no. 118* (1st version)
Bernstein *Chichester Psalms* (version for harp, organ and perc)
Bliss *The world is charged with the grandeur of God* (brass)
Bruckner *Mass no. 2 in E minor*
Dallapiccola *Canti di prigonia*
Hindemith *Apparabet repentina dies* (brass)
Holst *A Dirge for Two Veterans* (male voices and brass)
Horovitz *Samson* (brass band)
Orff *Catulli Carmina* (four pianos and perc)
Paynter *God's Grandeur* (brass and organ or organ only)
Respighi *Lauda per la natività*
Rutter *Gloria* (brass and percussion)
Stravinsky *Mass*, *Les Noces* (four pianos and perc)
Vinter *The Trumpets* (brass)

Choir and organ

The following list includes works written for choir (with or without soloists) and organ:

Arne *Libera me*
Berkeley *A Festival Anthem*
Bernstein *Chichester Psalms* (with harp and perc)
Bliss *Shield of Faith*
Britten *Rejoice in the Lamb*
Davies *Solstice of Light*
Duruflé *Requiem*
Dvořák *Mass in D*
Elgar *Psalm 29 'Give unto the Lord'*, *Psalm 48 'Great is the Lord'*
Fauré *Cantique de Jean Racine*
Finzi *Lo, the full final sacrifice*, *Magnificat*
Janáček *Otčenáš* ('Our Father') (with harp)
Jackson *A Time of Fire*
Kelly *Surrexit Hodie*
Kodály *Pange Lingua*, *Missa Brevis*, *Laudes organi*
Leighton *Crucifixus pro nobis*
Liszt *Via Crucis*, *Missa Choralis*
Mathias *Ave Rex*
Rorem *Miracles of Christmas*
Stainer *Crucifixion*
Vaughan Williams *A Vision of Aeroplanes*
Wesley *The Wilderness*, *Ascribe unto the Lord* and other anthems

There are also mass settings by Langlais, Widor and others.

Choir and piano

Arnold *A John Clare Cantata* (piano duet)
Bartók *Four Slovak folk songs*
Brahms *Liebeslieder Waltzer, Neues Liebeslieder Waltzer*
Britten *Ballad of Lady Barnard and Little Musgrave* (male voices)
Elgar *From the Bavarian Highlands*
Fauré *Cantique de Jean Racine* (or organ)
Gardner *A Shakespeare Sequence* (SSAA and piano duet)
Hold (Trevor) *A Cantata of St Crispin* (piano duet)
Hoddinot *The Lady and the Unicorn*
Holst *Choral Hymns from the Rig Veda*, group 3 (SSAA) (or harp)
Joubert *The Holy Mountain* (two pianos), *Leaves of Life*
Orff *Carmina Burana* (version for two pianos and perc), *Catulli Carmina* (four pianos and perc)
Patterson *Gloria, Kyrie* (piano duet)
Rossini *Petite Messe Solenelle* (two pianos and harmonium)
Schubert *Song of Miriam* (etc.)
Stravinsky *Les Noces* (four pianos and perc)
Williamson *In Place of Belief* (piano duet)

Works with harp

Although a harp is needed for some of the largest orchestrally accompanied choral works (such as Elgar's *The Music Makers*), there are a few works for smaller orchestra or ensemble which include a harp part. The following list gives a few examples, one or two of which are Christmas works:

Bax *Of a rose I sing a song* (chorus, harp, cello and bass)
Bernstein *Chichester Psalms* (boy alto, chorus, perc, harp and organ)
Britten *Cantata Misericordium* (T, B, chorus, timp, harp, piano and strings)
Finzi *In terra pax* (Baritone, chorus, harp and strings)
Janáček *Otčenáš* ('Our Father') (T, chorus, harp and organ)
Rubbra *Inscape* (harp and strings)

Works for choir and harp alone include:

Britten *A Ceremony of Carols* (SSA or SATB)
Holst *Choral Hymns from the Rig Veda*, group 3 (SSAA)
Rawsthorne *Lament for a sparrow* (SATB)
Rutter *Dancing Day* (SSA)

Christmas music

Bach *Christmas Oratorio*
Berlioz *The Childhood of Christ* (*L'enfance du Christ*)
Britten *St Nicolas, A boy was Born*

Finzi *In terra pax*
Gardner *Cantata for Christmas*
Haydn *St Nicolai Mass*
Holst *Christmas Day* (choral fantasy on carols)
Honegger *A Christmas Cantata (Une Cantate de Noël)*
Parry *Ode on the Nativity*
Poulenc *Four motets pour Le temps de la Nöel*
Resphigi *Lauda per la natività del Signore*
Rheinberger *Der Stern von Bethlehem*
Rootham *Ode on the Morning of Christ's Nativity*
Saint Saëns *Oratorio de Noel*
Schütz *Christmas Story*
Tate *Serenade to Christmas*
Vaughan Williams *Fantasia on Christmas Carols, Hodie*

There are of course many Christmas motets, including settings of the words '*Hodie Christus natus est*' by Sweelinck, Palestrina, Byrd and others.

Easter music

Bach *Easter Oratorio, St John Passion, St Matthew Passion*
Bononcini *Stabat Mater*
Caldara *Stabat Mater*
Dvořák *Stabat Mater*
Gounod *Sept Paroles*
Graun *Der Tod Jesu*
Haydn *Seven Last Words, Stabat Mater*
Liszt *Via crucis*
Maunder *Olivet to Calvary*
Pergolesi *Stabat Mater*
Poulenc *Stabat Mater, Four motets pour un temps de pénitence*
Rossini *Stabat Mater*
Schubert *Stabat Mater*
Schütz *Easter Oratorio, Seven Last Words, Passions*
Somervell *Passion of Christ*
Stainer *Crucifixion*
Stanford *Stabat Mater*
Telemann *Passion according to St Mark, Passion according to St Matthew*
Verdi *Stabat Mater*
Vivaldi *Stabat Mater*

Stage works for concert performance

Many works intended for the stage may be performed in the concert hall. Some works have been rewritten specifically for concert performances; the operettas of German, for example, were rewritten to include choral numbers not in the original stage work, and omitting some of the slighter and less relevant solo numbers of the original score. Inevitably some arrangements have wrecked the outlines of the original – for example, the concert version of Bizet's opera *Carmen* ends with a rousing chorus of the Toreador's Song.

Balfe *The Bohemian Girl*
Benedict *The Lily of Killarney*
Berlioz *Benvenuto Cellini* (choral suite)
Bizet *Carmen*
Borodin *Prince Igor* (Polovtsian Dances)
Flotow *Martha*
German *Merrie England, Tom Jones*
Gilbert and Sullivan (various)
Gluck *Orpheus* (Orfeo)
Gounod *Faust*
Holst *The Perfect Fool*

Monteverdi *Orfeo*
Offenbach *The Tales of Hoffmann*
Phillips *The Rebel Maid*
Purcell *Dido and Aeneas, The Fairy Queen, King Arthur*
Rimsky-Korsakov *Sadko* (Choral suite, arr. Foster)
Smetana *The Bartered Bride*
Stravinsky *Oedipus Rex*
Verdi *Aida* (arr. Sargent), *Il Trovatore*
Wagner *Tannhäuser*

Works for female voices

Bantock part-songs
Bartók *Village Scenes*
Bennett R. R. *Two Lullabies*
Berlioz *La mort d'Ophélia*
Bliss *Two Ballads*
Brahms *Lieder und Romanzen* op. 44, part-songs (*Gesänge für frauenchor* op. 17)
Britten *A Ceremony of Carols, Missa Brevis, The Oxen*
Busoni *Turandot Suite*
Caplet *Mass*
Carter E. *The harmony of morning*
Chabrier *À la musique*
Coleridge-Taylor part-songs
Crosse *Two Christmas Songs*
Davies *Five Carols*
Debussy *La damoiselle élue, Nocturnes* (Sirènes)
Elgar part-songs
Fauré *Messe basse*
Goehr A. *Psalm 4*
Hadley *I sing of a maiden*
Hasse *Miserere*
Hindemith *A Song of Music*
Hoddinott *The Wondrous Night*
Holst *Lullay my lyking, The Princess, The Planets, Seven songs of Bridges*
Janáček *Říkadla* (Nursery Rhymes), *The Diary of one who disappeared*
Kodály part-songs
Krenek *Five Prayers*
Lassus (various)

Liszt *Dante Symphony*
Lutoslawski *Children's songs*
Maconchy *Fly-by-nights*
Mahler *Symphony no. 3*
Martinů part-songs
Mendelssohn *A Midsummer Night's Dream*
Messiaen *Trois Petits Liturgies*
Milhaud *Cantata from Proverbs*
Monteverdi various
Morley madrigals
Mozart *Alleluia* K553, *Ave Maria* K554
Palestrina (various)
Parry part-songs
Pergolesi *Stabat Mater*
Persichetti *Spring Cantata*
Poulenc *Litanies à la Vierge Noire*
Quilter part-songs
Rachmaninov *Six songs for female voices* op. 15
Roberton part-songs
Roussel *Madrigal aux Muses*
Rubbra *The Beatitudes*
Schubert part-songs, including *Coronach* and *The Lord is my Shepherd*
Schumann part-songs
Smetana part-songs
Stanford part-songs
Stravinsky *Peasant Songs Cantata*
Szymanowski *Litany to the Virgin Mary*
Tippett *The Crown of the Year*
Vaughan Williams part-songs
Victoria (various)

Warlock part-songs
Weelkes madrigals

Wilbye madrigals
Williamson *The Brilliant and the Dark*

Works for male voices

Bantock part-songs
Barber *A stopwatch and an ordnance map*
Bartók *Four Old Hungarian Folk Songs, Five Slovak Folk Songs*
Bax *The Boar's Head, Now is the time of Christymas*
Berkeley *Three Songs*
Berlioz *Le chant des Bretons, Le temple universal*
Boughton part-songs
Brahms *Alto Rhapsody, Rinaldo*
Bridge part-songs
Britten *The Ballad of Little Musgrave and Lady Barnard*
Bruckner *Helgoland*, part-songs
Busoni *Piano concerto*
Cherubini *Requiem in D minor*
Copland *Song of the Guerrillas*
Walford Davies part-songs
Dunhill part-songs
Dvořák *Six Choruses for male voices, Five choruses op. 27, Three Slovak Folk Songs op. 43*
Elgar *The Reveille, The Herald* and other part-songs
Finzi *Thou didst delight mine eyes*
Fricker *Ave Mais Stella*
Gibbs part-songs
Grainger (various songs with orchestra)
Greig *Landkjening*
Gounod two mass settings
Hatton part-songs and glees
Hindemith part-songs
Holst *A Dirge for Two Veterans, Six choruses, Choral Hymns from the Rig Veda op. 26*
Jacob part-songs
Janáček *Three part Songs, Four Folk Choruses, Kantor Halfar*, etc.
Kodály (various male choruses)
Liszt *A Faust Symphony, Requiem* and other religious pieces
Lotti mass settings

Martinů *Field Mass, Prophecy of Isaiah*
Mathias *Gloria op. 52*
Massenet *Villanelle* and other part-songs
Mendelssohn *Antigone, Oedipus at Colonnus,* part-songs
Milhaud *Psalm 121*
Moeran part-songs
Monteverdi psalms and madrigals
Morley madrigals
Mozart *Cantata K 623* and other works
Mussorgsky *Four Russian Folk Songs*
Orff *Concento di voce: 111 Sunt lacrimae rerum*
Palestrina motets
Penabroki *Ecloga VIII*
Pearsall part-songs
Persichetti *Song of Peace*
Pfitzner *Das Schifflein*
Pizzetti *Canzoni Corali*
Poston *The Passion*
Poulenc *Chanson à boire, Laudes de St Antoine de Padoue, Quatre petites prières de St François d'Assise*
Purcell songs and catches
Quilter part-songs
Reger part-songs op. 38 and 83
Roberton part-songs
Rimsky-Korsakov *Song of Oleg the Wise*
Rossini *Preghiera, Chant Funèbre*
Saint-Saëns *Les Soldats de Gedeon, Two Choruses op. 71*
Schoenberg *A Survivor from Warsaw, Stücke für Männerchor op. 35*
Schubert *Gesang der Geister über den Wassern* (and others)
Schumann *Sechs Lieder op. 33, Gesänge op. 62,* etc.
Shostakovich *Symphony no. 13 'Babi Yar', Faithfulness*
Sibelius part-songs, *Kullervo Symphony, The Origin of Fire*
Smetana part-songs
Stanford part-songs

Strauss *Drei Männerchörè op. 45*
Stravinsky *Babel, Oedipus Rex*
Sullivan *The Long Day Closes*
Tallis motets

Vaughan Williams part-songs
Wagner *Das Liebesmahl der Apostel*
Warlock part-songs
Wood part-songs

The majority of compositions written before 1600 were intended for male voices only, but would usually require male altos as well as tenors and basses. The majority of the works listed above are specifically for tenor and basses.

Children's voices

A number of works include chorus parts for a children's choir, sometimes implying boys' voices:

Bach *St Matthew Passion*
Berlioz *The Damnation of Faust, Te Deum*
Bernstein *Kaddish Symphony*
Britten *A Boy was born, St Nicolas, Spring Symphony, War Requiem*
Dallapiccola *Requiescat*
Davies *The Shepherd's Calendar*
Hindemith *Wir bauen eine Stadt* (play)
Honegger *A Christmas Cantata, Nicolas de Flue*
Kabalevsky *Requiem*
Kodály *Psalms Hungaricus*
Mahler *Symphony no. 3, Symphony no. 8*
Martin *Psaumes*
Martinů *Kytice*
Mathias *St Teilo*
Mellers *Mortales*
Mendelssohn *A Midsummer Night's Dream* (or female voices)
Milhaud *Cantate de croix de charité*
Monteverdi *Vespers*
Nielsen *Hymnus Amoris, Springtime in Funen* (Fynsk Forar)

Orff *Carmina Burana, Comoedia de Christi Resurrectione*
Penderecki *St Luke Passion*
Pierné *Les enfants à de Bethleém, La Croisade der enfants*
Poulenc *Petites voix, Sept réponds de ténèbres*
Prokofiev *On Guard of Peace, Winter Bonfire*
Rubbra *Cantata op. 97*
Rutter *The Falcon*
Shostakovitch *Song of the Forests*
Sibelius *Song of the Athenians*
Strauss *An dem Baum Daphne*
Stravinsky *Perséphone*
Tate *St Martha and the Dragon*
Vaughan Williams *Thanksgiving for Victory, Hodie*
Villa Lobos *Mass in Honour of St Sebastian*
Weill *Recordare*

A number of works written specifically for children's choir (unbroken voices) include:

Bartók part-songs (various)
Bennett R. R. *The Insect World, The Aviary*
Britten *A Ceremony of Carols, Children's Crusade, The Golden Vanity, Missa Brevis*

Crosse *Dream of Adachigahara, History of the Flood*
Davies *Five Carols, Seven Songs Home, Songs of Hoy*
Kodály part-songs (various)
Leighton *An Easter Sequence*

Lutoslawski *Children's Songs*
Maconchy *Fly-by-nights*
Maw *Nonsense Songs*

Mellers *Life Cycle*
Rutter *Dancing Day*
Williamson *Ode to music*

The masses of Haydn

Haydn's masses have acquired many different nicknames over the years. The scholar Anthony van Hoboken (1887–1983) has catalogued Haydn's works and in the following list the Hoboken number is given after the title.

Caecilienmesse	XXII: 5
Coronation mass	XXII:11
Creation mass	XXII:13
Grosse Orgelsolo Messe	XXII: 4
Harmoniemesse	XXII:14
Heiligmesse	XXII:10
Imperial mass	XXII:11
Jugendmesse	XXII: 1
Kleine Orgelmess	XXII: 7
Little organ mass	XXII: 7
Mariazeller Messe	XXII: 8
Mass in time of war	XXII: 9
Missa brevis	XXII: 1
Missa brevis alla cappella	XXII: 3
Missa brevis Sancti Johannis de Deo	XXII: 7
Missa cellensis	XXII: 5, or 8
Missa in angustiis	XXII:11
Missa in honorem beatissimae virginis Mariae	XXII: 4
Missa in tempore belli	XXII: 9
Missa Sanctae Caeciliae	XXII: 5
Missa Sancti Bernardi von Offida	XXII:10
Missa Sancti Josephi	XXII: 6
Missa Sancti Nicolai	XXII: 6
Nelsonmesse	XXII:11
Nicolaimesse	XXII: 6
Orgel-Solo-Messe	XXII: 4
Paukenmesse	XXII: 9
Rorati coeli desuper	XXII: 3
Saint Cecilia mass	XXII: 5
Schöpfungsmesse	XXII:13
Theresienmesse	XXII:12

Two further numbering sequences are given below; the first is generally used in library and gramophone catalogues, while the second and more satisfactory numbering acknowledges a total of fifteen masses.

No. 1 in F Missa Brevis (1750)
No. 2 in E♭ Great Organ Mass (*c*. 1768)
No. 3 in C Missa Cellensis (St Cecilia Mass) (1766)

No. 3a in G Mass 'Rorate coeli desuper'
No. 4 in G Missa Sancti Nicolai (1772)
No. 5 in B♭ Little organ Mass (c. 1775)
No. 6 in C Missa Cellensis (Mariazellar Mass) (1782)
No. 7 in C Paukenmesse (1796)
No. 8 in B♭ Heiligmesse (1796)
No. 9 in D minor Nelson Mass (1798)
No. 10 in B♭ Theresa Mass (1799)
No. 11 in B♭ Creation Mass (1801)
No. 12 in B♭ Harmoniemesse (1802)

No. 1a Mass 'Rorate coeli desuper'
No. 1b Mass in G
No. 2 Missa brevis in F
No. 3 Missa Cellensis (St Cecilia mass)
No. 4 Missa 'Sunt bona mixta malis' (a cappella)
No. 5 Great Organ Mass
No. 6 Missa Sancti Nicolai
No. 7 Little Organ Mass
No. 8 Missa Cellensis (Mariazeller Mass)
No. 9 Heiligmesse
No. 10 Paukenmesse
No. 11 Nelson Mass
No. 12 Theresa Mass
No. 13 Creation Mass
No. 14 Harmoniemesse

Concert programmes

Here is a list of concerts given by the BBC Club Choir over the first ten years of its existence. The programmes with an asterisk were accompanied by organ only. The choir began with a membership of roughly 40, but has now grown to about 150. These programmes may help suggest ideas for programme planning. Brackets indicate works performed in a single concert.

1975   Handel *Messiah*
        Carols*
1976   Stainer *Crucifixion*
        ⎰ Purcell *Funeral Sentences* ⎱
        ⎱ Mozart *Requiem* ⎰
        Carols*
1977   ⎰ Vivaldi *Gloria* ⎱
        ⎱ Britten *St Nicolas* ⎰
        Stainer *Crucifixion*
        ⎧ Buxtehude *Alles was ihr tut* ⎫
        ⎨ Handel *Concerto for organ* op. 7 no. 4 ⎬
        ⎩ Fauré *Requiem* ⎭
        Carols*

1978   { Beethoven *Symphony no. 8*
        { Beethoven *Mass in C*
        Handel *Messiah* (Parts Two and Three)*
        { Mozart *Vesperae de confessore* K339
        { Haydn *Nelson Mass*
        Handel *Saul*
        Carols*

1979   Bach *St John Passion*
        { Wesley *The Wilderness*
        { Wesley *Cast me not away*
        { Wesley *Lead me Lord*
        { Wesley *Ascribe unto the Lord*
        { Dvořák *Mass in D*
        Handel *Belshazzar*
        Carols*

1980   Brahms *A German Requiem*
        { Vivaldi *Gloria*
        { Charpentier *Te Deum*
        { Purcell *Come ye sons of art*
        { Janáček *Otčenáš*
        { Kodály *Missa Brevis*
        { Bernstein *Chichester Psalms*
        Carols*

1981   Mendelssohn *Elijah*
        { Handel *Zadok the Priest*
        { Handel *Alexander's Feast*
        { Stravinsky *Mass*
        { Hindemith *Apparebit repentina dies*
        { Bruckner *Mass no. 2*
        Carols*

1982   Verdi *Requiem*
        { Mozart *Litaniae Lauretanae* K195
        { Mozart *Mass in C Minor* K427
        { Elgar *Give unto the Lord* (Psalm 29)
        { Britten *Rejoice in the Lamb**
        { Duruflé *Requiem*
        Carols*

1983   Bach *Mass in B Minor*
        { Vaughan Williams *Five Mystical Songs*
        { Tippett *A Child of our Time*
        { Vivaldi *Beatus Vir*
        { Corelli *Concerto Grosso*
        { Vivaldi *Magnificat*
        { Handel *Dixit Dominus*
        { Parry *The Soul's Ransom* (first London performance)
        { Vaughan Williams *Dona nobis pacem*
        Carols*

1984   Handel *Israel in Egypt*
{ Poulenc *Gloria* }
{ Rossini *Stabat Mater* }
{ Bach *Magnificat* }
{ Mozart *Requiem* }
Haydn *The Creation*
Carols*

1985   Dvořák *Stabat Mater*
{ Brahms *Academic Festival Overture* }
{   *Alto Rhapsody* }
{   *Song of Destiny* }
{ Elgar *The Music Makers* }
{ Mozart *Ave Verum* }
{   *Litany* K 125 }
{ Haydn *Paukenmesse* }
Handel *Messiah*
Carols*

Orchestration of various works

This list includes a selection of works with their orchestrations which are otherwise not detailed in the book.

Beethoven *Mass in C*   Duration 40$'$
S, A, T, B; Chorus
2.2.2.2. – 2.2.0.0. – timp – strings

Berlioz *Te Deum*   Duration 55$'$
T; Chorus
4.picc.4.corA.4.bcl.4. – 4.2.2cnt. B♭sxhn.6.2. – timp – perc – organ
12 Harp (doubling one part) – strings

Bruckner *Mass no 3 in F minor*   Duration 60$'$
S, A, T, B; Chorus
2.2.2.2. – 2.2.3.0. – timp. – strings

Bruckner *Te Deum*   Duration 22$'$
S, A, T, B; Chorus
2.2.2.2. – 4.3.3.1. – timp – strings

Charpentier *Messe de minuit*   Duration 25$'$
S, S, A, T, B; Chorus
2.2.corA.0.1. – 0.0.0.0. – cont – strings

Charpentier *Te Deum*   Duration 25$'$
S, S, A, T, B; Chorus
2.2.corA.0.1. – 0.0.0. – timp – cont – strings

Duruflé *Requiem*   Duration 38′
S (or mezzo soprano), B; Chorus
3.2picc.2(corA). CorA.2.bcl.2. – 4.3.3.1. – timp – perc – cel – harp – organ –
strings.
reduced orchestration:
o.o.o.o. – o.3.o.o. – timp – harp – organ – strings

Dvořák *Requiem*   Duration 95′
S, A, T, B; Chorus
2.picc.2.corA.2.bcl.2.dbn. – 4.3.3.1. – timp – perc – harp – organ –
strings

Dvořák *Stabat Mater*   Duration 85′
S, A, T, B; chorus
2.2corA.2.2. – 4.2.3.1. – timp – perc – strings

Dvořák *Te Deum*   Duration 22′
S, B; Chorus
2.2.corA.2.2. – 4.2.3.1. – timp – perc – strings

Fauré *Requiem*   Duration 40′
S,B; Chorus
2.0.2.2. – 4.2.3.0. – timp – organ – harp – strings

Gounod *St Cecilia Mass*   Duration 41′
S, T, B; Chorus
3.2.2.4. – 4.4.3.0. – timp – perc – harp – organ – strings

Kodály *Missa Brevis*   Duration 32′
small solos for 3S, A, T, B; Chorus
3.picc.2.2.2. – 4.3.3.1. – timp – opt. organ – strings

Monteverdi *Vespers*   Duration 90′
(full title *Vespro della beata vergine*)
There are various editions of the Vespers with differing orchestrations, but the
basic requirements are:
2 recorders, one bassoon, 3 cornetti, 3 sackbuts (trombones),
continuo (including lute) and strings

Mozart *Mass in C minor K 427*   Duration 80′
S, S, T, B; Chorus
1.2.0.2. – 2.2.3.0. – timp – cont – strings

Mozart *Vesperae solennes de confessore K 339*   Duration 26′
S, A, T, B; Chorus
o.o.o.1. – o.2.3.0. – con – strings (no violas)

Poulenc *Gloria*   Duration 28′
S; Chorus
2.picc.2.corA.2.bcl.2.dbn. – 4.3.3.1. – timp – harp – strings

Schubert *Mass in A flat*   Duration 50′
S, A, T, B; Chorus
1.2.2.2. – 2.2.3.0. – timp – organ – strings

Schubert *Mass in E flat*   Duration 60′
S, A, T, B; Chorus
0.2.2.2. – 2.2.3.0. – timp – organ – strings

Schumann *Scenes from Goethe's Faust*   Duration 120′
S, S, A, T, Bar, B; Chorus
2.picc.2.2.2. – 4.2.3.1. – timp – harp – strings

Vaughan Williams *Dona nobis pacem*   Duration 40′
S, B; Chorus
3.picc.2.2.2.dbn. – 4.4(= 2).5(= 3).1. – timp – perc – harp (organ) – strings

Vaughan Williams *Five Tudor Portraits*   Duration 45′
A, B; Chorus
3.picc.2.corA.2.2.dbn. – 4.2.3.1. – timp – perc – harp – strings
or 2.1.2.2. – 2.2.3.0. – timp – perc – harp (piano) – strings

Vivaldi *Gloria*   Duration 32′
S, S, A; Chorus
0.1.0.0. – 0.1.0.0. – cont – strings

Addresses

General

AMERICAN SOCIETY OF COMPOSERS,
 AUTHORS & PUBLISHERS (ASCAP)
Suite 9
52 Haymarket
London SW1Y 4RP
United Kingdom
01-930 1121

One Lincoln Plaza
New York NY 10023
United States
(212) 595-3050

INTERNATIONAL ASSOCIATION OF
 MUSIC LIBRARIES (IAML)
The Library
Royal Northern College of Music
124 Oxford Road
Manchester M13 9RD
United Kingdom
061-273 6283 ext. 244

Northwestern University Music
 Library
Evanston IL 60201
United States
(312) 492-3434

UK addresses

AMATEUR MUSIC ASSOCIATION
c/o The Music Department
Manchester Education Committee
Medlock Junior School
Wadeson Road
Manchester M13 9UR
061–273–3094

MUSIC PUBLISHERS' ASSOCIATION
 (MPA)
103 Kingsway London WC2B 6QX
01-831 7591

NATIONAL ASSOCIATION OF CHOIRS
48 Crossefield Road
Cheadle
Hulme
Cheshire SK8 5PE
061-485 3535

NATIONAL FEDERATION OF MUSIC
 SOCIETIES (NFMS)
Francis House
Francis Street
London SW1P 1DE
01-828 7320

NATIONAL MUSIC COUNCIL OF GREAT
 BRITAIN
10 Stratford Place
London W1N 9AE
01-499 4795

PERFORMING RIGHTS SOCIETY (PRS)
29–33 Berners Street
London WC2B 6QX
01-580 5544

US addresses

ASSOCIATION OF CHORAL
 CONDUCTORS
130 West 56th Street
New York NY 10019
(212) 246-3361

NATIONAL CHORAL
 COUNCIL/NATIONAL CHORALE
20 West 40th Street
New York NY 10018
(212) 869-0970

Select Bibliography

ANDERSON, KENNETH H. (*comp.*) *Music for Choirs: Sets of choral works in the Public Libraries of Cambridgeshire, Derbyshire, Leicestershire, Lincolnshire, Norfolk, Northamptonshire, Nottinghamshire and Suffolk: Catalogue* Nottingham, East Midlands Regional Library System, 1984

ANDERSON, KENNETH H. (*comp.*) *Sets of vocal music available for loan in the public libraries of Greater London and the Counties of Bedfordshire, Berkshire, East Sussex, Essex, Hertfordshire, Kent, West Sussex: Catalogue* London, London and South Eastern Library Region (Laser), 1979

British Music Yearbook: 1972/3– (annual publication) from 1985– London, Rhinegold Publishing

COMPTON, SHEILA (*comp.*) *British Union Catalogue of Orchestral Music* ed. Maureen Simmons London, IAML (UK)/Polytechnic of North London, 1982

DUTTON, PHYL *Music Clubs, Festivals and Concerts: How to organise them* Henley-on-Thames, Gresham Books, 1981

FLINT, MICHAEL F. *A User's Guide to Copyright* London, Butterworths, 2/1985

HOOD, ALAN & THOMPSON, MARGARET (*comp. & ed.*) *Vocal Scores in the Northern Region: a Union Catalogue of Sets of Vocal Music available for loan in the Libraries of the Northern Regional Library System* Newcastle upon Tyne, Northern Regional Library (NRLS), 1983

JACOBS, ARTHUR (*ed.*) *Choral Music: A Symposium* Harmondsworth, Penguin Books, 1963

The *Music Industry Directory*: (annual publication) formerly: *The Musician's Guide: The Directory of the World of Music* from 1980– Chicago, Marquis Academic Media

Musical America: International Directory of the Performing Arts: 1965– (annual publication) New York, ABC Leisure Magazines

NARDONE, THOMAS R., NYE, JAMES H. & RESNICK, MARK ed. *Choral Music in Print: (Music in Print* series) *1. Sacred Choral Music, 2 1985 2. Secular Choral Music 1974*

NARDONE, THOMAS R. (*ed.*) *Choral Music in Print: 1976 Supplement*

NARDONE, NANCY K. (*ed.*) *Secular Choral Music in Print: 1982 Supplement* Philadelphia, Musicdata, 1974–

PENNY, BARBARA (*comp. & ed.*) *Music in British Libraries: A Directory of Resources* London, Library Association Publishing, 3/1981

WILLIAMSON, JULIAN & LEGGE, HARRY (*ed.*) *National Federation of Music Societies: Catalogue of Choral Works* London, National Federation of Music Societies (NFMS), 5/1985

Copyright

Copyright is the exclusive right of ownership and protection from unauthorized exploitation given to a composer (or author, playwright, artist etc.) by law. It protects his work for a specified number of years. The period of protection varies from one art form to another, and from one country to another.

In the United Kingdom the Copyright Act of 1956 particularly refers to publishing, reproducing, performing in public, broadcasting and adapting a composer's work. The length of copyright runs for 50 years after the composer's death, expiring on the last day of December of the 50th year. If a work is not published in the composer's lifetime, its copyright runs for 50 years after its first performance or publication, whichever is the sooner.

The owner of the copyright is initially the composer, who usually transfers copyright to a publisher in exchange for royalties. Texts and translations may also be copyright, and editions of works are copyright if they have been registered with the Performing Rights Society (PRS), provided the composer whose work is edited is out of copyright. Arrangements are also copyright.

Photocopying or writing out by hand is illegal, although a small extract may be photocopied or reproduced for private study purposes.

1. *The Performing Right.*   Broadcast and public performances are administered by the PRS who usually issue a blanket licence to premises used for public performances. Charges are waived in the case of music performed in school lessons (but not public occasions such as speech days) and for church services; that is, acts of worship. If performers are giving their services free and permission has been granted to perform copyright works, the charge may again be waived.

Musicals, operas, operettas and ballets can only be performed by permission of the copyright holder. Performers themselves are not protected except by the Performers' Protection Act which makes it an offence to record an artist without their written consent.

2. *The Mechanical Right.*   Copying music, by taping it from the radio, disc or your own concert, is also an infringement of the Copyright Act. The permission of the copyright holder must be sought, although it is possible to obtain a blanket licence from the Mechanical Copyright Protection Society (MCPS) for the recording of a public concert. Sound recordings and commercial records are themselves copyright, and copyright on them runs for 50 years after the date of recording. The Phonographic Performance Limited deals with this aspect.

3. *The Graphic Right.*   Copyright also exists in the finished publication, and runs for 25 years from the date of publication. This is a copyright in the printed image as issued by the publisher.

Index

Figures in **bold** indicate a main entry in the 'Composers', 'Works' or 'Terms' sections.

A Cappella **124**
Acis and Galatea (Handel) **82**, 166
Adagio for Strings (Barber) 40
African Sanctus (Fanshawe) **82**
Agnus Dei **124**, 154
Ah! Perfido (Beethoven) 128
Aida (Verdi) 141, 171
Albinoni, T. 167
Aleatoric Music **124**
Alexander Balus (Handel) **82**, 53
Alexander Nevsky (Prokofiev) **82**, 67
Alexander's Feast (Handel) **83**, 53, 143, 148
All in the April evening (Roberton) 69
Alleluia **124**
Alleluia (Thompson) 76
Alles was ihr tut (Buxtehude) 46
Alto **124**
Alto Rhapsody (Brahms) 29, 43, 166, 172
Amarus (Janàček) 56
American Flag, The (Dvořák) 37, 49
An dem Baum Daphne (Strauss) 74, 173
Anglican chant **125**
Anthem **125**
Antigone (Mendelssohn) 172
Antiphon **125**
Antony and Cleopatra (Barber) 40
Apostle's Creed 158
Apostles, The (Elgar) **83**, 50
Appalachia (Delius) **83**, 48
Apparebit repentina dies (Hindemith) 55, 168
Arabesk, An (Delius) 48
Aria **125**
Arianna a Naxos (Haydn) 128
Arioso **126**
Arne, T. 139, 168
Arnold, Malcolm 165, 169
Articulation 15
Ascribe unto the Lord (Wesley) 80, 169
At the round earth's imagin'd corners (Kelly) 166
Athalia (Handel) 53, 144
Atalanta in Calydon (Bantock) 39, 132
Atonement, The (Coleridge-Taylor) 47
Augenlicht, Das (Webern) 80
Ave Maria **126**, 164
Ave Maris Stella (Fricker) 51, 172
Ave Rex (Mathias) 168
Ave Verum, 164

Babel (Stravinsky) 74, 173
Babi Yar (Shostakovich) 72, 172
Babylon the Great is fallen (Goehr) 165

Bach, C. P. E. 36
Bach, J. C. 36
Bach, Johann Sebastian **39**, 21, 35, 36, 140, 166, 167, 168, 170, 173
Balbulus, Notker 149
Balfe, M. 171
Ballad of an unknown boy (Prokofiev) 67
Ballad of Heroes (Britten) 44
Ballad of Lady Barnard (Britten) 45, 169, 172
Ballad of White Horse, The (Gardner) 165
Banner of St George, The (Elgar) 50
Bantock, Granville **39**, 171, 172
Barber, Samuel **40**, 172
Barber shop **127**
Baritone **127**
Bartered Bride, The (Smetana) 73, 171
Bartók, Bela **40**, 166, 171, 172, 173
Bass 127
Batter my heart (Berkeley) 41
Bax, Arnold 40, 169, 172
Beatitudes, The (Franck) 51, 145
Beatitudes, The (Bliss) 43
Beatitudes, The (Rubbra) 171
Beatus Vir (Vivaldi) 31
Beethoven, Ludwig van **41**, 22, 37, 140, 166, 177
Bel Canto **127**
Bell Anthem (Purcell) 84
Belle dame sans merci, La (Hadley) 53
Bellini, Vincenzo 41
Bells, The (Rachmaninov) **84**, 68, 167
Belshazzar (Handel) **84**, 53
Belshazzar's Feast (Walton) **84**, 22, 26, 29, 79, 167
Benedicite **128**
Benedicite (Vaughan Williams) 78
Benedict, J. 171
Benedictus **127**, 154, 157
Bennett, Richard Rodney 165, 171, 173
Benvenuto Cellini (Berlioz) 171
Berkeley, Lennox **41**, 167, 168, 172
Berkeley, Michael 38, 165
Berlin Requiem (Weill) 80
Berloiz, Hector **42**, 166, 170, 171, 172, 173, 177
Bermudas, The (Hamilton) 165
Bernstein, Leonard **42**, 168, 169, 173
Bizet, Georges **43**, 171
Black Knight, The (Elgar) 50, 129
Blake, David 165
Blessed be the God and Father (Wesley) 80
Blest Pair of Sirens (Parry) **85**, 65, 167
Bliss, Arthur **43**, 166, 168, 171
Blind Girl of Castél-Cuillé (Coleridge-Taylor) 47

Blow, J. 167
Blue Bird, The (Stanford) 145
Boar's Head Carol 129
Boar's Head, The (Bax) 172
Bocca Chiusa 128
Bohemian Girl, The (Balfe) 171
Bon-bon Suite (Coleridge-Taylor) 47
Bononcini, G. 167, 170
Book with the Seven Seals (Schmidt) 39
Boris Godunov (Mussorgsky) 64, 68
Borodin, A. 171
Boughton, R. 172
Boy was Born, A (Britten) 44, 173
Boyce, W. 36
Brahms, Johannes 43, 20, 37, 166, 169, 171, 172
Breathing Exercises 14
Bridge, Frank 44, 172
Brilliant and the Dark, The (Williamson) 81, 171
Britten, Benjamin 44, 21, 166, 168, 169, 171, 172, 173
Brown, Christopher 38, 165
Bruch, M. 37
Bruckner, Anton 45, 35, 168, 172, 177
Burgon, Geoffrey 165
Bush, Geoffrey 165, 167
Busoni, F. 171, 172
Butt, Clara 124
Buxtehude 45, 167
BVM 127
Byrd, William 46

Cadenza 128
Caldara, A. 170
Calm Sea and prosperous voyage (Beethoven) 41
Calvary (Spohr) 73
Cannon, Philip 165
Canon 128
Cantata 128
Cantata Academica (Britten) 85, 44, 166
Cantata de la guerre (Milhaud) 62
Cantata for Christmas (Gardner) 170
Cantata from Proverbs (Milhaud) 171
Cantata Misericordia (Britten) 85, 22, 31, 44, 169
Cantata of St Crispin, A. (Hold) 169
Cantata pour louer le Seigneur (Milhaud) 62
Cantata Profana (Bartók) 85, 40, 166
Cantate de Croix de Charité (Milhaud) 173
Cantate de l'initiation (Milhaud) 62
Canterbury Pilgrims, The (Dyson) 50, 166
Canti di Liberazione (Dallapiccola) 86
Canti di Prigonia (Dallapiccola) 86, 168
Cantica (Chapple) 33, 165
Canticle 129
Canticle of Man, A (Rawsthrone) 68
Cantico Del Sole (Walton) 79
Canticum Canticorum (Penderecki) 66
Cantiones sacrae (Byrd) 46
Canticum Sacrum (Schütz) 72
Canticum Sacrum (Stravinsky) 86, 74
Cantilena 129
Cantique de Cantiques (Honegger) 55
Cantique de Jean Racine (Fauré) 51, 168, 169
Cantique du Rhône (Milhaud) 62
Cantus Firmus 129
Canzoni Corali (Pizzetti) 172
Caplet, A. 171
Caractacus (Elgar) 50, 166
Carissimi, Giacomo 46, 167
Carmen (Bizet) 43, 171
Carmen Vitale (Rawsthorne) 68

Carmina Burana (Orff) 86, 30, 64, 134, 167, 169, 173
Carol 129
Carols of Death (Schuman) 71
Carter, E. 171
Castrato 130
Catch 130
Catulli Carmina (Orff) 168, 169
Cavalli, P. 36
Cecilian Movement 130
Celestial Country, The (Ives) 56
Celtic Requiem (Tavener) 87, 75
Cenerentola, La (Rossini) 141
Ceremony of Carols, A (Britten) 44, 169, 171, 173
Chabrier, E. 171
Chamber Choir 21
Chandos Anthems (Handel) 87, 53, 125
Changes (Crosse) 38, 165
Chanson 131
Chanson à Boire (Poulenc) 172
Chant des Bretons, Le (Berlioz) 172
Chant des oiseaux, Le (Jannequin) 57
Chant Funèbre (Rossini) 172
Chapel Royal 131
Chapple, Brian 165
Charpentier, Marc-Antoine 46, 36, 144, 177
Cherubini, Luigi 46, 172
Chichester Psalms (Bernstein) 87, 42, 125, 168, 169
Child of Our Time, A (Tippett) 88, 22, 26, 73, 145
Child of the Universe, A (Josephs) 166
Childhood of Christ, The (Berlioz) 88, 42, 145, 170
Children's Crusade (Britten) 45, 173
Children's Songs (Lutoslawski) 171, 173
Choice of Hercules, The (Handel) 53
Choir Invisible, The (Joubert) 57
Choirs 131, 18, 21
Chor der Engel (Liszt) 59
Choral Fantasia (Beethoven) 89, 41, 166
Choral Fantasia (Holst) 167
Choral Flourish, A (Vaughan Williams) 78
Choral Symphonies 131
Choral Symphony (Beethoven) 89, 131, 166
Choral Symphony, A First (Holst) 55, 132
Chorale 132
Chorus 131
Christ on the Mount of Olives (Beethoven) 89, 37, 41, 124, 145
Christmas Cantata, A (Bush) 165, 167
Christmas Cantata, A (Honegger) 55, 170, 173
Christmas Day (Holst) 170
Christmas Oratorio (Bach) 90, 39, 170
Christmas Oratorio (See Christmas Story)
Christmas Oratorio (Schütz) 72, 144
Christmas Story (Schütz) 90, 72, 144, 170
Christopher Columbus (Milhaud) 62
Christus (Liszt) 90, 59
Cinq Rechants (Messiaen) 91, 62
Clemenza di Tito, La (Mozart) 130
Clocks and Clouds (Ligeti) 58
Coffee Cantata (Bach) 39
Cloud Messenger, The (Holst) 55
Coleridge-Taylor, Samuel 47, 166, 171
Come ye sons of art (Purcell) 91, 30, 31, 67, 167
Comoedia de Christi Resurrectione (Orff) 173
Compass 132
Concento di Voce (Orff) 172
Continuo 132
Contralto 133
Copland, Aaron 47, 172
Coplas (Tavener) 75

Coronach (Schubert) 171
Coronation Anthems **91**
Coronation Mass (Mozart) **92**
Coronation Ode (Elgar) **92,** 50
Counterpoint **133**
Countertenor **133**
Cowie, Edward 165
Cox, David 165
Creation Mass (Haydn) **93,** 54
Creation, The (Haydn) **92,** 21, 22, 29, 30, 144, 147, 151
Creed **133,** 153
Crociato in Egitto, Il (Meyerseer) 130
Croisade der Enfants, La (Pierné) 173
Crosse, Gordon 38, 165, 171, 173
Crown of the Year, The (Tippett) 77, 171
Crucifixion, The (Stainer) **93,** 146, 169, 170
Crucifixus **133,** 59
Crucifixus pro nobis (Leighton) 168
Cupid and Death (Locke and Gibbons) 139
Curwen, John 151
Czech Legion, The (Janáček) 57
Czech Song, The (Smetana) 73

Dallapiccola, Luigi 47, 168, 173
Damantion of Faust, The (Berlioz) **93,** 42, 166, 173
Damoiselle Elue, La (Debussy) **93,** 48, 171
Dance Clarion Air (Tippett) 77
Dancing Day (Rutter) 169, 174
Dante Symphony (Liszt) 59, 171
Daphne and Apollo (Head) 165
Daphnis and Chloe (Ravel) **94,** 68
Darke, Harold 165
Daughter of Jairus, The (Stainer) 145
David (Brown) 165
Davidde Penitente (Mozart) 63
Davies, H. Walford 172
Davies, P. Maxwell 47, 168, 171, 173
Deborah (Handel) 53
Debussy, Claude 48, 171
Delius, Frederick 48, 166
Déluge, Le (Saint-Saëns) 70, 145
De Profundis (Parry) 65
De Profundis (Schoenberg) 70
Descant **133**
Destruction of Sennacharib, The (Mussorgsky) 64
Deutsche Mass (Schubert) 71
Deutsche Motet (Strauss) 74
Deutsche Volkslieder (Brahms) 43
Deux cités, Les (Milhaud) 62
Diary of one who disappeared, The (Janáček) 57, 171
Dido and Aeneas (Purcell) 171
Dies Irae **133,** 155
Dirge for two veterans (Holst) 55, 168, 172
Dodgson, Stephen 165
Dona nobis pacem (Vaughan Williams) 29, 32, 44, 78, 179
Donizetti, Gaetano 48, 37, 167
Dove Descending, The (Stranvinsky) 74
Drayton, Paul 165
Dream of Adachigahara (Crosse) 173
Dream of Gerontius, The (Elgar) **94,** 27, 29, 30, 50, 124, 127, 151
Dreimal tausend Jahre (Schoenberg) 70
Dunstable, John 49, 142, 143
Dufay, Guillaume 48, 142
Dunhill, T. 172
Duruflé, Maurice 49, 168, 177
Dvořák. Antonin 49, 37, 166, 168, 170, 172, 178
Dyson, George 50, 166, 167

Easter Oratorio (Bach) **94,** 39, 170

Easter Oratorio (Schütz) 168, 170
Easter Sequence, An (Leighton) 173
Ecloga VIII (Pendercki) 172
Eden (Stanford) 73
Elegiac Ode (Stanford) 73
Elegy on the death of my daughter Olga (Janáček) 57
Elfenlied (Wolf) 81
Elgar, Edward 50, 166, 168, 169, 171, 172
Eli (Costa) 144
Elijah (Mendelssohn) **95,** 22, 37, 61, 124, 126, 127, 134, 144
Enchanted Summer (Bax) 40
Endymion's Dream (Coleridge-Taylor) 47
L'enfant prodigue (Debussy) 48
Enfants de Bethlehem, Les (Pierne) 173
English Eccentrics (Williamson) 81
Entflieht auf Leichten Kähnen (Wevern) 80
Entführung aus dem Serail, Die (Mozart) 127
Epithalamion (Bennett) 165
Epithalamion (Vaughan Williams) 78
The Epic of Gilgamesh (Martinů) 60
Equal Voices **134**
Erste Walpurgisnacht, Die (Mendelssohn) **94,** 61, 167
Esther (Handel) **95,** 53, 144
Eternal Gospel, The (Janáček) 57
Eton Choirbook **134**
Euridice (Peri) 130
Eve (Massenet) 145
Evening Watch, The (Holst) 55
Execution of Stepan Razin, The (Shostakovich) 72

Fairy Queen, The (Purcell) 139, 171
Faithfulness (Shostakovich) 72, 172
Falcon, The (Rutter) 166, 173
Fall of Babylon, The (Spohr) 37, 73
Falsetto **134**
Falstaff (Verdi) 78
Fantasia on Christmas Carols (Vaughan Williams) 170
Fauré, Gabriel 50, 21, 29, 30, 32, 168, 169, 171, 178
Faust (Gounod) 171
Faust (Spohr) 73
Faust Symphony, A (Liszt) 59, 172
Fauxbourdon **134**
Ferrier, Kathleen 124
Fest- und Gedenksprüche (Brahms) 43
Festgesang (Mendelssohn) 61
Festival Anthem, A (Berkeley) 168
Festivals **134**
Field Mass (Martinů) 172
Figure Humaine (Poulenc) 67
Finzi, Gerald 51, 167, 168, 169, 170, 172
Fire Worshippers, The (Bantock) 40
First of May (Shostakovich) 72
Five Ages of Man, The (Musgrave) 166
Five Carols (Davies) 171, 173
Five English Folk Songs (Vaughan Williams) 78
Five Flower Songs (Britten) 44
Five Prayers (Krenek) 171
Five Slovak Folk Songs (Bartók) 172
Five Tudor Portraits (Vaughan Williams) 167, 179
Flos Campi (Vaughan Williams) **95,** 78
Floss der Medusa, Das (Henze) 54
Flotow, F. von 171
Fly-by-Nights (Maconchy) 171, 173
Flying Dutchman, The (Wagner) 79
Folk Fantasy for Festivals (Harris) 54
Folk sons **135**
Folksong Symphony (Harris) 54
For God, King and Right (Bridge) 44

For St Cecilia (Finzi) 51
Forests, Song of the (Shostakovich) 72
Four Motets pour le Temps de Noël (Poulenc) 170
Four Motets pour un Temps de Pénitence (Poulenc) 170
Four Old Hungarian Folk Songs (Bartók) 172
Four Russian Folk Songs (Mussorgsky) 172
Four Sacred Pieces (Verdi) 112
Four Slovak Folk Songs (Bartók) 40, 169
Four songs from the British Isles (Tippett) 77
Franck, César 51
Free Song, A (Schuman) 71
Fricker, Peter Racine 51, 38
Friday Afternoons (Britten) 44
Friede auf Erden (Schoenberg) 70
From an unknown past (Rorem) 69
From Homer (Rimsky-Korsakov) 68
From the Bavarian Highlands (Elgar) 50, 169
Funeral Sentences (Purcell) 33

Gabrieli, Giovanni 51, 36
Gallia (Gounod) 52
Gardner, John 165, 169, 170
Garland for the Queen, A 96, 51, 56, 68
Geistliche Lied (Brahms) 43, 128
Geographical Fugue (Toch) 96
German, E. 171
German Requiem, A (Brahms) 96, 29, 37, 43, 127
Gesang der Geister über den Wassern (Schubert) 172
Gesang der Parzen (Brahms) 43
Gesualdo, Carlo 52
Gibbons, Orlando 52
Gibbs, Cecil Armstrong 172
Gilgamesh, Epic of (Martinů) 60
Glagolitic Mass (Janáček) 96, 56
Glee 135
Gloria 136, 153
Gloria (Vivaldi) 31, 32, 35, 36
Glories of our Blood and State, The (Parry) 65
Glorious Apollo (Webbe) 136
Glorreiche Augenblick Der (Beethoven) 41
Gluck, C. W. 171
God in the Cave, The (Rawsthorne) 68
God is gone up (Finzi) 51
God's Grandeur (Paynter) 168
Goehr, Alexander 165, 171
Goethe's Faust, Scenes From (Schumann) 71, 167, 179
Golden Cantata, The (Bliss) 43
Golden Legend, The (Sullivan) 33, 38, 75
Golden Vanity, The (Britten) 45, 173
Golgotha (Martin) 60
Gothic Symphony (Brian) 97, 132
Göttin in Putzimmer, Die (Strauss) 74
Gounod, Charles, 52, 170, 171, 172, 178
Gradualia (Byrd) 46
Graduals 148
Grainger, P. 172
Grande Messe des Morts (Berlioz) 97, 42
Graun, K. H. 170
Great Canon of St Andrew of Crete (Tavener) 75
Greater love (Ireland) 56
Grieg, Edvard 52, 172
Guerre, La (Jannequin) 57
Gurrelieder (Schoenberg) 97, 70

Hadley, Patrick 53, 171
Hail Bright Cecilia (Purcell) 167
Hail, smiling morn (Spofford) 136
Hamilton, Iain 165
Handel, George Frederic 53, 21, 36, 144, 166, 167

Hanson, Howard 38
Harmonie Mass (Haydn) 98, 54
Harmony 136
Harmony of Morning, The (Carter) 171
Harris, Roy 54
Harvey, Jonathan 165
Hasse, J. A. 167, 171
Hatton, J. 172
Haydn, Joseph 54, 21, 36, 167, 170
    Masses 174
Haydn, Michael 36
Head, Michael 165
Hear my prayer (Mendelssohn) 61
Heilig Mass (Haydn) 98
Heirs of the white mountain, The (Dvořák) 49
Helgoland (Bruckner) 172
Heloise and Abelard (Maconchy) 166
Henze, Hans Werner 54
Herald, The (Elgar) 172
Hercules (Handel) 53
Hiawatha's Wedding Feast (Coleridge-Taylor) 98, 47, 129, 166
Hierusalem (Dyson) 50, 167
Hill of the Graces (Berkeley) 41
Hills, The (Hadley) 53
Hills, The (Ireland) 56
Hindemith, Paul 54, 39, 168, 171, 172, 173
History of the Flood (Crosse) 173
Hoboken, Anthony van 174
Hoddinott, Alan 165, 169, 171
Hodie (Vaughan Williams) 98, 78, 170, 173
Holloway, Robin 165
Hold, Trevor 169
Holst, Gustav 55, 167, 168, 169, 170, 171, 172
Holy Mountain, The (Joubert) 57, 169
Homophony 136
Honegger, Arthur 55, 170, 173
Horovitz 168
Hosanna to the Son of David (Weelkes) 80
Hosanna to the Son of David (Gibbons) 52
Howells, Herbert 56, 38
Huit poèmes (Milhaud) 62
Hymn 136
Hymn of Jesus, The (Holst) 99, 55
Hymn of the Nations (Verdi) 78
Hymn of Zrinyi (Kodály) 58
Hymn to St Cecilia (Britten) 21, 44
Hymn to St Peter (Britten) 45
Hymn to the Virgin (Britten) 44
Hymne of Heavenly Beauty, An (Darke) 165
Hymns from the Rig Veda (Holst) 55, 169, 172
Hymnus Amoris (Nielsen) 173
Hymnus Paradisi (Howells) 99, 38, 56

I Sing of a Maiden (Hadley) 171
I Was Glad (Parry) 66
Idomeneo (Mozart) 130
In Ecclesiis (Gabrieli) 52
In Exitu Israel (Wesley) 80
In honour of the City of London (Dyson) 50
In honour of the City of London (Walton) 79, 167
In Place of Belief (Williamson) 81, 169
In terra pax (Finzi) 51, 167, 169, 170
In terra pax (Martin) 39, 60
In the beginning (Copland) 47
In Time of Pestilence (Rorem) 69
Infelice (Mendelssohn) 129
Insanae et vanae curae (Haydn) 54
Inscape (Rubbra) 167, 169

Insect World, The (Bennett) 173
Inter natos mulierum (Mozart) 167
Intimations of Immortality (Finzi) 51
Invocation to Music (Parry) 65
Ireland, John 56
Israel in Egypt (Handel) 99, 28, 53, 144
Italian Salad (Genée) 100
Ives, Charles 56

Jackson, W. 168
Jacob, Gordon 165, 172
Janáček, Leoš 56, 168, 169, 171, 172
Jannequin, Clément 57
Jehova quam multi sunt (Purcell) 67
Jephtha (Carissimi) 46, 101, 167
Jephtha (Handel) 100, 53, 54
Jerusalem (Parry) 101
Jessonda (Spohr) 73
Jesu meine Freude (Buxtehude) 46
Jesus and the traders (Kodály) 58
Joan of Arc at the stake (Honegger) 101, 55
Job (Parry) 66
John Clare Cantata, A (Arnold) 169
Jonah (Berkeley) 41
Jonah (Carissimi) 46
Jones, Daniel 165
Joseph (Macfarren) 145
Joseph and His brethren (Handel) 53
Josephs, Wilfred 38, 166
Joshua (Handel) 101, 53
Joshua (Mussorgsky) 64
Josquin des Pres 57
Joubert, John 57, 169
Jubelmesse (Weber) 80
Jubilate Deo 160
Judas Maccabaeus (Handel) 102, 53
Jundgement of Solomon, The (Carissimi) 46
Judgement of Solomon, The (Charpentier) 46
Judith (Charpentier) 46
Judith (Parry) 102, 66
Juditha Triumphanus (Vivaldi) 79
Jugendmesse (Haydn) 167
Julius Caesar (Handel) 130

Kabalevsky, D. 173
Kaddish Symphony (Bernstein) 42, 173
Kantor Halfar (Janáček) 57, 172
Kaspar Rucký (Janáček) 57
Kelly, Bryan 166, 168
Kenilworth (Sullivan) 75
Kent Yeoman's wooing song, A (Howells) 56
King Arthur (Purcell) 171
King Estmere (Holst) 55
King of the stars (Stravinsky) 74
King Olaf (Elgar) 50
King Saul (Parry) 66
King shall rehoice, The (Handel) 91
King Solomon's Prayer (Naylor) 166
Kingdom, The (Elgar) 102, 50
Klagendeied, Das (Mahler) 102, 60, 167
Kleine Geistlichekonzert (Schütz) 72
Kleine Orgelsolo Mass (Haydn) 167
Kodály, Zoltán 58, 106, 168, 171, 172, 173, 178
Kol nidre (Schoenberg) 70
Krenek, E. 171
Kubla Khan (Coleridge-Taylor) 47
Kullervo symphony (Sibelius) 72, 172
Kyrie 137, 153, 155
Kytice (Martinů) 60, 173

Lady and the Unicorn, The (Hoddinot) 169
Lalande, M. 36
L'allegro ed il Penseroso (Parry) 65
L'allegro, il Penseroso ed il Moderato (Handel) 103, 53, 166
Lamb, The (Tavener) 76
Lambert, Constant 58, 167
Lament for a Sparrow (Rawsthorne) 68, 169
Lament for Beowulf (Hanson) 38
Lamentations 137
Landjending (Grieg) 53, 172
Lark, Choruses from The (Bernstein) 43
Lassus, Orlandus 58, 171
Last Judgement, The (Spohr) 37, 73, 144
Lauda 137
Lauda per la Natività del Signore (Respighi) 103, 168, 170
Lauda Sion (Mendelssohn) 61
Laudate Pueri (Handel) 36
Laudes de St Antoine de Padoue (Poulenc) 66, 172
Laudes Organi (Kodály) 168
Lazarus (Schubert) 71, 145
Leaves of Life (Joubert) 58, 169
Legend of St Elizabeth, The (Liszt) 59
Legend of Smoke from potato fires (Martinů) 60
Leighton, Kenneth 166, 168, 173
Lélio (Berlioz) 103, 42
Let thy hand be strengthened (Handel) 91
L'homme armé 137
Libera me (Arne) 168
Liberated Queen, The (Sibelius) 72
Lie strewn the white flocks (Bliss) 43
Liebeslieder Waltzer (Brahms) 43, 169
Liebesmahl der Apostel, Das (Wagner) 79, 173
Lieder und Romanzen (Brahms) 171
Life Cycle (Mellers) 174
Ligeti, Gyorgy 58
Light Invisible, The (Leighton) 166
Light of Life, The (Elgar) 50
Light of the World, The (Sullivan) 75
Like as the hart (Howells) 56
Like two proud armies (Weelkes) 80
Lily of Killarney, The (Benedict) 171
Liszt, Franz 59, 168, 170, 171, 172
Litanies à la vierge noire (Poulenc) 66, 171
Litany 138
Litany (Mozart) 138, 167
Litany, A (Walton) 79
Litany to the Virgin Mary (Szymanowski) 75, 138, 171
Little Requiem for Father Malachy (Taverner) 75
Little Prayers (Rorem) 69
Liturgy 138
Liturgy of St John Christoston (Rachmaninov) 68
Liturgy of St John Chrysostom (Tavener) 75
Lloyd Webber, A. 166
Lo, the full final sacrifice (Finzi) 51, 168
Lobgesang (Mendelssohn) 104, 31
Lobet dem Herrn (Bach) 124
London Symphony, A (Vaughan Williams) 150
Long Day Closes, The (Sullivan) 173
Lord is my shepherd, The (Berkeley) 41
Lord is my Shepherd, The (Schubert) 171
Lord of Light (Cannon) 165
Lord's Prayer 162
Lotti, Antonio 59, 172
Love–Feast of the Apostles, The (Wagner) 145
Lovers, The (Barber) 40
Ludus Amoris (Harvey) 165
Lullay my lyking (Holst) 171
Lully, J.–B. 36
Lumina (Blake) 165

Lutoslawski, W. 171, 173
Lux aeterna (Ligeti) 58

Machaut, Guillaume de 59, 142
Maconchy, Elizabeth 166, 171, 173
Madrigal 138
Madrigal (Fauré) 51
Madrigal aux Muses (Roussel) 171
Magnificat 138, 161
Magnificat (Bach) 104, 39
Mahler, Gustav 59, 167, 171, 173
Mannerchor (Strauss) 172
Manon (Massenet) 61
Marienleider (Brahms) 43
Mars in a fury (Weelkes) 80
Marie-Magdalene (Massenet) 61
Martha (Flotow) 171
Martin, Frank 60, 39, 173
Martinů, Bohuslav 60, 171, 172, 173
Martyr of Antioch, The (Sullivan) 75
Martyrdom of St Sebastian, The (Debussy) 104, 48
Masque 139
Masque of Time, The (Tippett) 77
Mass 139, 153
Mass in B Minor (Bach) 104
Mass in Honour of St Sebastian (Villa Lobos) 173
Mass of Christ the King (Williamson) 105
Mass of Life, A (Delius) 105, 22, 48
Massenet, Jules 61, 172
Mater ora filium (Bax) 40
Mathias, William 38, 166, 168, 172, 173
Maunder, J. 170
Maw, N. 174
May Queen, The (Bennett) 129
McCabe, John 166
Méditation religeuse (Berlioz) 42
Mellers, Wilfred 166, 173, 174
Mendelssohn, Felix 61, 37, 167, 171, 172, 173
Merrie England (German) 171
Messa di voce 140
Messe basse (Fauré) 171
Messe de minuit (Charpentier) 31, 177
Messiaen, Olivier 61, 171
Messiah (Handel) 105, 35, 53, 124, 126, 144, 147
Metrical psalter 140
Metronome 140
Mezzo-soprano 141
Midsummer Night's Dream, A (Mendelssohn) 61, 171, 173
Mikeš of the Mountains (Martinů) 60
Milhaud, Darius 62, 171, 172, 173
Milner, Anthony 166
Miracles of Christmas (Rorem) 168
Misere 141
Missa 141
Missa Solemnis (Beethoven) 106, 41
Modes 141
Moeran, Ernest John 62, 172
Monteverdi, C. 62, 36, 171, 172, 173, 178
Morgenhymnus (Wolf) 81
Morley, T. 171, 172
Morning Heroes (Bliss) 43
Mors et vita (Gounod) 37, 52
Mort d'Ophelia, La (Berlioz) 171
Mortales (Mellers) 173
Motet 142
Mozart, Wolfgang Amadeus 62, 21, 36, 167, 171, 172, 178
Muses of Sicily, The (Henze) 54

Musgrave, Thea 166
Music Makers, The (Elgar) 106, 28, 29, 30, 50, 143, 166
Music Makers, The (Kodály) 106, 58
Music when soft voices die (Parry) 145
Musica Deo sacra et ecclesive angliconae (Tomkins) 77
Mussorgsky, Modest 63, 172
My beloved spake (Hadley) 53
My eyes for beauty pine (Howells) 56
My heart is inditing (Handel) 91

Naaman (Costa) 144
Naissance de Venus (Milhaud) 62
Nänie (Brahms) 107, 43
National Federation of Music Societies 34
Naylor, Bernard 166
Nebuchadnezzar (Dyson) 50
Nelson Mass (Haydn) 107, 26, 29, 32, 54
Neugeborne Kindelein, Das (Buxtehude) 167
New-born King, The (Jacob) 165
Nicolai, C. 37
Nicolas de Flue (Honegger) 173
Nielsen, Carl 64, 173
Nisi Dominus (Handel) 36
Noble Heart, The (Gardner) 165
Noces, Les (Stravinsky) 107, 74, 134, 167, 168, 169
Nocturne (Moeran) 62
Nocturnes (Debussy) 171
Nonsense Songs (Maw) 174
Now is the time of Christymas (Bax) 172
Nunc Dimittis 142
    Text 161
Nun's Priest's Tale, The (Jacob) 165

O care thou wilt despatch me (Weelkes) 80
O clap your hands (Gibbons) 52
O clap your hands (Vaughan Williams) 78
O how amiable (Vaughan Williams) 78
O Lorde, the Maker of Al Thing (Joubert) 57
O magnum mysterium (Davies) 47
O sacrum convivium (Messiaen) 61
O taste and See (Vaughan Williams) 78
O vos omnes (Vaughan Williams) 78
Obrecht, Jacob 64
Occasional Oratorio (Handel) 107, 53
Ockeghem, Johannes 64
October Revolution (Shostakovich) 72
Ode 143
Ode for St Cecilia's Day (Purcell) 107
Ode on the morning of Christ's Nativity (Rootham) 170
Ode on the Nativity (Parry) 170
Ode to Death (Holst) 55
Ode to Discord (Stanford) 73
Ode to Music (Williamson) 174
Ode to St Cecilia (Blow) 167
Ode to Wellington (Stanford) 73
Oedipus at Colonnus (Mendelssohn) 172
Oedipus Rex (Stravinsky) 108, 74, 171, 173
Of a rose I sing a song (Bax) 169
Of Beasts (Cox) 165
Offenbach, J. 171
Offertory
    Text 157
Office 143
O Wild West Wind (Elgar) 146
Old Hall manuscript 143
Old Hundredth 142
Oliver (Bart) 150
Olivet to Calvary (Maunder) 108, 170
Omar Khayyam (Bantock) 40

On Craig Dhu (Delius) 48
On Guard of Peace (Sullivan) 75
Opening of the Wells, The (Martinů) 60
Opus **143**
Or shall we die? (Berkeley) 38, 145, 165
Oratorio **144**
Oratorio de Noël (Saint-Saëns) 70
Ordinary **145**
Orff, Carl **64,** 167, 168, 169, 172, 173
Orfeo (Gluck) 130, 171
Orfeo (Monteverdi) 130, 171
Organ mass **145**
Organum **145**
Origin of fire, The (Sibelius) 72, 172
Orpheus behind the wire (Henze) 54
Orr, Robin 166
Otčenáš (Janáček) 57, 168, 169
Otello (Verdi) 126
Oxen, The (Britten) 171
Oxen, The (Rawsthorne) 68
Oxford Elegy, An (Vaughan Williams) 78

Pacem in terris (Milhaud) 62
Pageant of Human Life, A (Bantock) 39
Palestrina, Giovanni **65,** 21, 171, 172
Pange Lingua (Kodály) 168
Paradise and the Peri (Schumann) 71
Parry, Hubert **65,** 38, 167, 170, 171
Part-song **145**
Passion **146**
Passion, The (Poston) 172
Passion According to St Luke (Thompson) 76
Passion According to St Mark (Hamilton) 165
Passion According to St Mark (Telemann) 170
Passion According to St Matthew (Telemann) 170
Passion of Christ (Somervell) 146, 170
Passions (Schütz) 170
Pastorale (Bliss) 32, 166
Patterson, Paul 38, 166, 169
Paukenmesse (Haydn) **108**
Pavane (Fauré) **108**
Paynter 168
Peaceable Kingdom, The (Thompson) 76
Peasant cantata (Bach) 39, 166
Peasant Songs (Stravinsky) 171
Pearsall R.C. 172
Peer Gynt (Grieg) 53
Penderecki, Krysztof **66,** 38, 172, 173
Perfect Fool, The (Holst) 171
Pergolesi, Giovanni Battista **66,** 36, 167, 170, 171
Persephone (Stravinsky) **109,** 74, 173
Persichetti 171, 172
Petite Messe Solenelle (Rossini) **109,** 169
Petites Prières de St François d'Assise Poulenc) 172
Petites voix (Poulenc) 173
Pfitzner, H. 172
Phaudrig Crohoore (Stanford) 73
Phillips 171
Phyllida and Corydon (Moeran) 62
Pied Piper (Parry) 65
Pierné, H. 173
Piers Ploughman (Schumann) 166
Pilate (Martin) 60
Pizzetti, I. 172
Plainsong **146**
Planets, The (Holst) 55, 171
Plebs angelica (Tippett) 77
Poems on the homeland (Shostakovich) 72
Polish Requiem (Penderecki) 66

Polovtsian Dances (Borodin) 109
Polyphony **147**
Poston, E. 172
Poulenc, Francis **66,** 20, 170, 171, 172, 173, 178
Praetorius, M. 36
Prayers of Kierkegaard (Barber) 40
Preghiera (Rossini) 172
Prince Igor (Borodin) 171
Princess, The (Holst) 171
Pro Pace (Joubert) 142
Prodigal Son, The (Sullivan) 75, 144
Prokofiev, Serge 67, 173
Prometheus (Scriabin) **109**
Peometheus Unbound (Bantock) 40
Prometheus Unbound (Parry) 65
Promised Land, The (Saint-Saëns) 70
Proper **147**
Prophecy of Isaiah (Martinů) 61, 172
Psalmes, Songs and Sonnets (Byrd) 46
Psalms of David (Penderecki) 66
Psalmus Hungaricus (Kodály) **110,** 58, 173
Puccini, Giacomo **67**
Purcell, Henry **67,** 167, 171, 172

Quatrains valaisons (Milhaud) 62
Quilter, R. 171, 172
Quo Vadis (Dyson) 50

Rachmaninov, Sergei **68,** 167, 171
Raising of Lazarus, The (Joubert) 57
Rakastava (Sibelius) 72
Rake's Progress, The (Stravinsky) 147
Rameau, J. P. 36
Rape of Lucretia, The (Britten) 147
Rapresentatione de anima e di corpo, La (Cavalieri) 144
Rawsthorne, Alan **68,** 169
Rebecca (Franck) 51
Rebel Maid, The (Phillips) 171
Recitative 147
Recordare (Weill) 173
Redemption (Franck) 51, 110
Redemption (Gounod) 52, 110
Reger, Max **68,** 37, 172
Reincarnation (Barber) 40
Rejoice in the Lamb (Britten) 44, 168
Rejoice in the Lord alway (Purcell) 67, 84, 125
Requiem **147**
Requiem (Mozart) 63, **110**
Requiem (Verdi) **111**
Requiem canticles (Stravinsky) 74
Requiescat (Dallapiccola) 173
Respighi, O. 168, 170
Responses **148**
Return of Odysseus, The (Arnold) 165
The Revenge (Stanford) 73
Reveille, The (Elgar) 172
Revelations (Burgon) 165
Rheinberger, J. 37, 170
Rigoletto (Verdi) 127
Rikadla (Janáček) 57, 171
Rimsky-Korsakov, Nikolai **68,** 171, 172
Rinaldo (Brahms) 43, 172
Rio Grande (Lambert) **111,** 29, 58, 167
Ritorno di Tobia, Il (Haydn) 54
Roberton, Hugh **69,** 171, 172
Roi David, Le (Honegger) **111,** 55
Rollant et Oliver (Fricker) 51
Roman Spring (Milner) 166
Romance of the Dandelions, The (Martinů) 61

Romeo and Juliet (Berlioz) **112**, 42, 131, 166
Rootham, C. 170
Rorem, Ned **69**, 168
Rosamunde (Schubert) **112**
Rose for Lidice, A (Rawsthorne) 68
Rose of Sharon, The (Mackenzie) 145
Rose Pilgefahrt, Der (Schumann) 71
Rossini. Gioachino **69**, 169, 170, 172
Round **148**
Roussel, Albert **69**, 38, 171
Rubbra, Edmund **69**, 167, 171, 173
Ruth (Cowen) 145
Ruth (Franck) 51
Rutter, John 166, 168, 169, 173, 174

Sacred and Profane (Britten) 45
Sacred Service (Bloch) **113**
Sadko (Rimsky-Korsakov) 171
St Cecilia **148**
St Cecilia mass (Gounod) 33, 37, 52, 178
St Cecilia mass (Scarlatti) 167
St Francis (Milner) 166
St John Passion (Bach) **113**, 39, 170
St John's Night on the Bare Mountain (Mussorgsky) 64
St Ludmilla (Dvořák) 39, 49, 145
St Luke Passion (Penderecki) **113**, 66, 146, 173
St Martha and the Dragon (Tate) 166, 173
St Matthew Passion (Bach) **114**, 39, 170, 173
St Nicolai Mass (Haydn) 170
Saint Nicolas (Britten) **114**, 22, 29, 31, 44, 152, 170, 173
St Peter (Benedict) 144
St Peter (Jones) 165
St Paul (Mendelssohn) **114**, 39, 61, 127, 144
St Paul's Voyage to Melita (Dyson) 50
Saint-Saëns, Camille **70**, 167, 172
St Teilo (Mathias) 166, 173
Salve Regina (Haydn) 35, 54, 167
Salve Regina (Scarlatti) 167
Samson (Handel) **115**, 53, 144
Samson (Horovitz) 168
Sancta Civitas (Vaughan Williams) 78
Sanctus **148**
Sanctus and Benedictus
   Text 154, 157
Sara la baigneuse (Berlioz) 42
Saul (Handel) **115**, 53, 144
Scarlatti, Alessandro **70**, 36, 167
Scarlatti, D. 167
Scenes from Goethe's Faust (Schumann) 71
Schifflein, Das (Pfitzner) 172
Schmidt, F. 39
Schoenberg, Arnold **70**, 152, 172
Schola Cantorum **149**
Schubert, Franz **71**, 37, 168, 169, 170, 171, 172, 178
Schulwerk (Orff) 65
Schuman, William **71**
Schumann, Robert **71**, 167, 171, 172, 179
Schurmann, Gerard 166
Schütz, Heinrich **71**, 36, 144, 168, 170
Sea Drift (Delius) **116**, 48
Sea Pictures (Elgar) 50
Sea-surface of Clouds (Holloway) 165
Sea Wanderers (Bantock) 40
Sea Symphony, A (Vaughan Williams) **116**, 22, 29, 77, 167
Seasons, The (Haydn) **116**, 54, 144, 147, 167
Sécheresse (Poulenc) 66
Sechs geistliche Lieder (Wolf) 81
Sechs Lieder (Schumann) 172

See, see the shepherd's Queen (Tomkins) 77
Semele (Handel) **117**, 53, 166
Sept paroles (Gounod) 170
Sept réponds de ténèbres (Poulenc) 173
Sequence **149**
Serenade to Christmas (Tate) 166, 170
Serenade to Music (Vaughan Williams) **117**, 78
Sermon, a Narrative and a Prayer, A (Stravinsky) **117**, 74
Serse (Handel) 150
Service **149**
Sessions, Roger **72**
Set me as a seal (Walton) 79
Seven last words (Haydn) **117**, 54, 170
Seven last words (Schütz) 117, 144, 168
Seven Songs Home (Davies) 173
Seven songs of Bridges (Holst) 171
Shakespeare Sequence, A (Gardner) 169
Shepherd's Calendar, The (Maxwell Davies) **118**, 48, 173
Shield of Faith (Bliss) 43, 168
Shires Suite, The (Tippett) 77
Shostakovich, Dimitri **72**, 172, 173
Sibelius, Jean **72**, 172, 173
Sight-Reading 19
Signs in the Dark (Berkeley) 41, 167
Sigurd Jorsalfar (Grieg) 53
Silence and Music (Vaughan Williams) 78
Silver Swan, The (Gibbons) 52
Sinfonia Sacra (Rubbra) 70,
Sir Patrick Spens (Howells) 56
Slava (Rimsky-Korsakov) 68
Sleep (Nielsen) 64
Smetana, Bedrich **72**, 171, 172
Soir de neige, Un (Poulenc) 67
Soldats de Gedeon, Les (Saint-Saëns) 172
Soleil des eaux, Le (Boulez) **118**
Solomon (Handel) **118**, 53
Solstice of Light 47, 168
Somervell, A. 170
Song of Destiny (Brahms) **118**, 166
Song of Liberty (Bantock) 40
Song of Miriam (Schubert) 169
Song of Music (Hindemith) 171
Song of Oleg the Wise, The (Rimsky-Korsakov) 68, 172
Song of Peace (Persichetti) 172
Song of Ruth, The (Mellers) 166
Song of Songs, The (Bantock) 40
Song of the Athenians (Sibelius) 173
Song of the Forests (Shostakovich) 72, 172
Song of the Guerrillas (copland) 172
Song of the High Hills, The (Delius) 48
Songs of Ariel (Martin) 60
Songs of England (Thiman) 166
Songs of Farewell (Delius) **118**, 48, 166
Songs of Farewell (Parry) **118**, 29, 43, 66, 166
Songs of Hoy (Davies) 48, 173
Songs of Nature (Dvořák) 50
Songs of our times (Prokofiev) 67
Songs of Springtime (Moeran) 62
Songs of Sunset (Delius) 48
Songs of the Fleet (Stanford) 167
Songs of the Sea (Stanford) 73, 167
Songs to be sung of a summer night on the water (Delius) 48
Sons of Light, The (Vaughan Williams) 78
Soprano **149**
Sorotchinsky fair (Mussorgsky) 64
The Soul's Ransom (Parry) 66
Source, The (Tippett) 77
Spectre's Bride, The (Dvořák) 39, 49, 166
Spells (Bennett) 165

Spem in alium (Tallis) **119,** 75
Spirit of England, The (Elgar) **119,** 50
Splendour falls on castle walls, The (Delius) 48
Spohr, Louis **73,** 37
Spotless rose, A (Howells) 56
Spring (Rachmaninov) 68
Spring Cantata (Orr) 166
Spring Cantata (Persichetti) 171
Spring Symphony (Britten) **119,** 44, 166, 173
Springtime in Funen (Nielson) 64, 173
Stabat Mater **150,** 162
Stabat Mater (Rossini) **120**
Stainer, J. 169, 170
Ständchen (Schubert) 71
Stanford, Charles Villiers **73,** 38, 167, 170, 171, 172
Steffani, A. 168
Stern von Bethlehem, Der (Rheinberger) 37, 170
Strauss, Richard **74,** 172, 173
Stopwatch and an ordnance map, A (Barber) 40, 172
Stravinsky, Igor **74,** 21, 167, 168, 169, 171, 173
Street cries **150**
Stücke (Orff) 65
Stücke fur Männerchor (Schoenberg) 172
Sullivan, Arthur **74,** 38, 173
Summer is Icumen in **120**
Summer's Last will and testament (Lambert) 58
Sun shines over our mother land, The (Shostakovich) 72
Sunt lacrimae rerum (Orff) 172
Suppé, F. von 39
Surrexit Hodie (Kelly) 168
Survivor from Warsaw, A (Schoenberg) 70, 172
Susanna (Handel) 53
Symphonia Sacrae (Shütz) 72
Symphonie funèbre et triomphale (Berlioz) **120,** 42
Symphony for Voices (Harris) 54
Symphony for Voices (Williamson) 81, 132
Symphony of a Thousand (Mahler) **121,** 22, 60, 132
Symphony of Psalms (Stravinsky) **120,** 74
Svitezyanka (Rimsky-Korsakov) 68
Szenen aus Olav Trygvason (Grieg) 53
Szymanowski, Karol **75,** 171

Tadolini 120
Tag der Gerichts, Der (Telemann) 76
Tagezeiten, Die (Telemann) 76
Take him earth for Cherishing (Howells) 56
Tale of Old Japan, A (Coleridge-Taylor) 47
Tales of Hoffmann, The (Offenbach) 171
Tallis, Thomas **75,** 173
Tannhäuser (Wagner) 171
Tate, Phyllis 166, 170, 173
Tavener, John **75**
Taverner, John **76**
Tchaikovsky, Peter **76**
Te Deum **150**
    Text 159
Telemann, G. P. **76,** 36, 170
Templa quam dilecta (Drayton) 165
Temple Universal, Le (Berlioz) 172
Tempus destruendi—Tempus aedificandi (Dallapiccola) 17
Tenor **150**
Ten poems to words by Revolutionary poets (Shostakovich) 72
Terre Promise, La (Massenet) 61
Tessitura **151**
Thanksgiving for Victory (Vaughan Williams) 173
Theodora (Handel) 53
There is no rose (Joubert) 57

Theresa Mass (Haydn) **121**
These things shall be (Ireland) 56
They are seven (Prokofiev) 67
Thiman, Eric 166
This have I done for my true love (Holst) 55
This is Our Time (Schuman) 71
This is the record of John (Gibbons) 52
This Worldes Joie (Bax) 40
This Worldes Joie (Mathias) 166
Thompson, Randall **76**
Thou dist delight mine eyes (Finzi) 172
Three Shakespeare songs (Vaughan Williams) 78
Three Churubic Hymns (Tchaikovsky) 76
Three Slovak Folk Songs (Dvořák) 172
Three Village Scenes (Bartók) 40
Threepenny Opera, The (Weill) 80
Threni (Stravinsky) **121,** 74
Thou knowest Lord the secrets of our hearts (Purcell) 67
Thule, the period of Cosmography (Weelkes) 80
Time of Fire, A (Jackson) 168
Tippett, Michael **77,** 171
To the name above every other name (Bax) 40
Tod Jesu, Der (Graun) **121,** 146, 170
Tom Jones (German) 171
Tomkins, John **77**
Tonic Sol-fa **151**
Too much I once lamented (Tomkins) 77
Torches (Joubert) 57
Tosca (Puccini) 126
Tour de Babel, Le (Franck) 51
Toward the unknown region (Vaughan Williams) 77
Transfiguration de Notre Seigneur Jésus Christ, La (Messiaen) 62
Traviata, La (Verdi) 126
Treble **152**
Tree of Life, The (Hoddinott) 165
Trees so High, The (Hadley) 53
Trionfi (Orff) 64
Trionfo di Afrodite (Orff) 64
Triumphlied (Brahms) 43
Triumphs of Oriana, The **122,** 81, 80
Triumph of Time and Truth, The (Handel) 54
Trois Chansons de Charles d'Orléans (Debussy) 48
Trois petits liturgies (Messiaen) 61, 171
Trovatore, Il (Verdi) 141
Trumpets, The (Vintner) 166, 168
Turandot Suite (Busoni) 171
Turn of the Screw, The (Britten) 152
Tutti **152**
Twelve, The (Walton) 79
Twelve-tone music **152**
Two Ballads (Bliss) 171
Two Christmas Songs (Crosse) 171
Two Lullabies (Bennett) 171
Two satires (Schoenberg) 70

Ultimos Ritos (Tavener) 75
Unaufhörliche, Das (Hindemith) 55
Urbs beata (Joubert) 57
Utrenja (Penderecki) 66

Vanity of Vanities (Bantock) 39, 132
Vaughan Williams, Ralph **77,** 21, 167, 169, 170, 171, 173, 179
Veni Creator (Szymanowski) 75
Venus and Adonis (Blow) 139
Verdi, Giuseppe **78,** 22, 171
Verse anthem **152**
Vesperae solennes de confessore (Mozart) 178

Vespers **152**
Vespers (Monteverdi) 62, 173
Vexilla Regis (Ireland) 56
Via Crucis (Liszt) **122,** 59, 168, 170
Victoria, Thomás Luis de **78**
Vierge, La (Massenet) 61
Villa Lobos, H. 173
Village Scenes (Bartók) 171
Villanelle (Massenet) 172
Vin herbé, Le (Martin) 60
Vinter, Gilbert 166, 168
Vision of aeroplanes, A (Vaughan Williams) 78, 169
Vision of Judgement, The (Fricker) 51
Vision of St Augustine, The (Tippett) 77, 122
Vivaldi, Antonio **79,** 31, 36, 168, 170, 179
Voice **152**
Voice out of the whirlwind, The (Vaughan Williams) 78
Voices of Sleep (Patterson) 166
Voyage (McCabe) 166
Voyage of Maeldune, The (Stanford) 73

Wagner, Richard **79,** 171, 173
Walsinghame (Bax) 40
Walton, William **79,** 167
Wandrers Sturmlied (Strauss) 74
War Requiem (Britten) **122,** 44, 173
Warlock, P. 171, 173
Wash me thoroughly (Wesley) 80
Ways of Zion do mourn, The (Handel) 53
Weber, Carl Maria von **79**
Webern, Anton **80**
Weelkes, Thomas **80,** 172
Weeping babe, The (Tippett) 77

Weill, Kurt 80, 173
Welcome Ode (Britten) 45
Welcome to all the pleasures (Purcell) 67, 167
Werther (Massenet) 61
Wesley, Samuel **80**
Wesley, Samuel Sebastian **80,** 169
Westerlings (Davies) 47
Western Wind Mass (Taverner) 76
Whale, The (Taverner) **123,** 75
When David heard (Tomkins) 77
When David heard (Weelkes) 80
When lilacs last in the dooryard bloom'd (Hindemith) 55
When lilacs last in the dooryard bloom'd (Sessions) 72
Where does the uttered music go? (Walton) 79
White flowering days (Finzi) 51
Wilbye, John **81,** 172
Wilderness, The (Wesley) 80, 169
William Tell (Rossini) 69
Williamson, Malcolm **81,** 169, 172, 173, 174
Wills, Arthur 166
Windhover, The (Tippett) 77
Winter Bonfire (Prokofiev) 67, 173
Wir bauen eine Stadt (Hindemith) 173
Wolf, Hugo **81**
Wolf's Trail, The (Janáček) 57
Wondrous Night, The (Hoddinott) 171
Wood 173
World is charged, The (Bliss) 43, 168

Ye choirs of new Jerusalem (Stanford) 74

Zadok the Priest (Handel) **123,** 91
Zelenka, J. D. 36
Zwei Gesänge (Strauss) 74